SOCIAL ASTONISHMENTS

SOCIAL ASTONISHMENTS

DAVID CORT

THE MACMILLAN COMPANY, NEW YORK
COLLIER-MACMILLAN LTD., LONDON

© David Cort 1959, 1960, 1961, 1962, 1963

"Believing in Books," first published under the title "On Lying" is reprinted from the *Columbia University Forum* by permission of the publisher, © Columbia University 1961. "The End of Slavery" is reprinted from the *Columbia University Forum* by permission of the publisher, © Columbia University 1960. "Blood-bath for Black Africa" and "Survival Everywhere" (under the title "The Problem of Eternal Life") were first published in *The New Republic*.

The Macmillan Company, New York
Collier-Macmillan Canada, Ltd., Toronto, Ontario
DIVISIONS OF THE CROWELL-COLLIER PUBLISHING COMPANY

Library of Congress Catalog Card Number: 63-22800

First Printing

Printed in the United States of America

$\mathcal{A}$UTHOR'S NOTE

I LOVE *The Nation, Monocle, The New Republic, Perspective,* and the *Columbia Forum,* because they have granted permission to reprint these essays. Each of us (and perhaps such corporate entities as magazines) has the feeling that he is somehow a "social astonishment," or could be if the circumstances were just a little different. This forgivable vanity is nevertheless not harmless. These pages will show some of the ways in which we could be, or already are, too astonishing for our own good. The reader will know best, beyond the need of any crude signals, when to laugh and when to sob.

The proposition is that, as Christ said, mankind is awful, but the species is committed by its big brain to aspire to decency and honor and tolerance of other forms of life, and Christ asked men please not to feel superior to one another, saying that He would adjudicate.

He has not done so, and therefore books like this are written.

David Cort

Contents

ONE

SOCIAL CEMENTS

$\mathcal{H}$OW TO MAKE A NATION

$\mathcal{T}$HE WORLD is now full of bunches of people trying to look, act or at least sound like nations. A bunch of people surrounded by an imaginary line on the map is of course not automatically a nation. There is a need here for some sort of manual explaining how a mere bunch of people can be translated into a nation. Political scientists have neglected this subject, perhaps because all previous history had not prepared them for the current phenomenon of nationhood conferred, as if by a blackjack, on bunches of people who do not even know the name of their "nation."

This kindly operation is in fact a terrible satire on the ancient concept of the nation, and must make the people of well-established nations ask when, how and why they themselves became nations. The process was always long, bloody, hard and heroic. The new nations are born quickly, easily, unheroically, and then turn bloody, for their little tyrants all intend to remain forever as head-of-state.

The trick of converting a bunch of people into a nation is magically simple. The clue was given the other night in a radio program on which some new military elite in the Congo sang a number of their marching songs. Suddenly for the first time the Congolese sounded something like a nation, instead of tribal renegades, or a rabble.

The first step in making a nation out of a bunch of people

3

is therefore indicated. Somebody has to go out in the woods, round up a couple of boys, and teach them the words and music of a marching song. The particular words and music don't really matter.

The next step in making a nation is to teach them to march down the main street in step, singing the marching song.

The next step is to add a small band.

The bunch of people now constitutes a small parade. The people on the sidewalks or in the adjoining jungle naturally flock to watch and listen. The important thought they have is that they are not in the parade. They take steps to get in the next parade. The small parade graduates into a bigger parade, and that into a still bigger parade, and at last the parades mature as the Big Parade. And now the nation is well on the way to healthy coexistence in the community of nations.

The parades have developed their own parade marshals and officers, and created a popular demand for new parades whenever the new patriotism begins to flag. It becomes indispensable to have the paraders available on short notice. Barracks are therefore provided for the paraders. The name for this phase of the parade is the army.

A good many nations now represented in the United Nations have never gotten any further than this. Their leaders are satisfied that an army capable of parading is not only the minimum, but also the maximum, requirement of a nation. Somewhat reluctantly, they add a police force, to keep the streets clear for official parades, and prevent unofficial, subversive parades, described as riots.

But now an unhappy matter of bookkeeping arises, for though the army and police have to be paid, they are not productive and cannot pay for themselves.

One solution nowadays is taxes. Taxes make a bunch of people conscious of the nation's dignity and sovereignty, in the same way a man knows he is alive when he has a toothache. This throbbing pain leads to a further development of nationhood. Taxes also create a wholesome formation of capital. However, since the capital is in the hands of the nation's leaders, it is treated as expense account rather than capital.

In practice, relatively few nations rely on taxes. They are of course uncollectible in all the smart areas of the world: most of Africa, the Middle East, Southeast Asia, Latin America and Italy. These unfortunate areas therefore cannot as yet enjoy the glorious full bloom of nationhood. It may safely be stated that before the invention of the income tax there were no real nations anywhere.

One alternative to taxes is to lease the nation's mineral, vegetable or animal assets to foreign investors, as do most underdeveloped nations. These leases can of course be repudiated from time to time.

At the present time, a wonderful supplement to such income is to get subsidies from the United States or Soviet Russia, in payment for "taking sides in the cold war," whatever that means. One can even get such subsidies for not taking sides. Any sensible general can see that this arrangement is perfected by taking subsidies from both sides not to take sides; and such heads-of-state are greatly admired and envied. In the late 1940's Nationalist Chinese generals collected all the American weapons they could cadge and then sold their armies and weapons to the Communists at "the top dollar," which the Communists were delighted to pay. The cause of the nation, in this case Communist, was thus greatly abetted.

The oldest, though it is now regarded as the newest, way to pay the army and police is to announce that the nation owns everything in the nation. This obvious and antique solution, now supported by the works of Marx, Lenin and Stalin, was grasped by Genghis Khan who had not even heard the word "dialectics." Even without that word and without electronics, Genghis had a nation with faster communications than Soviet Russia can show today. (This was also true of the empire of the Incas before Pizarro.) The glory of this solution is that nobody ever gets funny about the nation after he finds out that he doesn't own anything any more. The jokes are over.

The next refinement for this sort of nation is to pull up by the roots everything the citizens had foolishly thought made them a nation: the whole network of family, social, commercial, cultural and industrial relationships. When there is nothing inside a nation except the nation, it can be described as All-Nation, as some men are described as All-Man and are usually wearing a black eye.

All the foregoing phases of the nation can be documented with actual cases, many from the current world scene. But it will be more useful to go back and take a longer look at the stage that started it all, the parade itself, in whose emotional and ideological reverberations must be found every magical and unexamined premise on which the subsequent nation is founded. In other words, we can discover something about political science and the state of the world by looking carefully at the parades we are already familiar with; and I would wish that the foregoing were only a trifling joke.

The essential ingredients of a parade are: (1) marchers; (2) bands playing recognizable tunes (a formidable exception will be noticed later); (3) bystanders; (4) banners and floats displaying slogans, traditional heroes or some familiar symbolism; (5) an unexamined and inexpressible set of premises; and (6) afterwards, a bar-and-grill to riot in.

These are also the ingredients of an embryonic nation. Nothing can stop a nation that has evolved that far.

The key factor, which is the electric charge between and among the marchers and the bystanders, is the undefined point, or message, of the parade. Anybody who does not respond somehow to this is an inhuman fraud. A parade is humanly exhilarating; one feels oneself in the presence of the winning, if not the overwhelming, side; dissent is inconceivable. It is only later that one admits that that was the winning side only that day on that avenue, and that the wonderful feelings grow fuzzy at the edges.

Do you remember the wartime parades of the armed forces? They do not need the massed drums, or bugles, or bagpipes. The great rectangular battalions of men, all dressed and accoutred alike, proceed in exact unison down the metropolitan avenue, but in complete, deadly silence, except for the feet hitting the pavement together and the small rustling and rattling of gear. The implied threat or boast or bluff or lamentation silently turns the Congolese marching songs into a child's squawling, and in iron silence.

But the message is that the parade has already won the war. Let us suppose that on that same day equally imposing parades are also taking place in Tokyo, London, Berlin, Rome and Moscow. All appear to be all-conquering to the bystanders and the marchers. All make the same overpowering, but necessarily, in some cases, fallacious claim. Modern battles are not won in parade formation; those days are gone. (Yes, many of the great battles of the past have been won by parades, but they didn't have to parade into even one lousy machine gun.)

The parades one is familiar with do not seem in the least embarrassed by historical fact. The Fourth of July parade makes a farce of the Revolution it is supposed to celebrate. The premise of the parade is that Washington won the war with firecrackers, and that the Revolution was a vulgar rabble's noisemaking, whereas the American Revolution was rather a quiet war conducted by country gentlemen primarily in the country.

Labor Day parades have a similar effect of demoralizing the significance of labor. Workers have meaning only at their jobs; when they march, they masquerade as an army. In claiming to be something it is not, and ought not to be, the labor movement thus takes on a sinister quality it ought not to want.

The Italian-Americans' Columbus Day parade flaunts the thought that Italians really ought to run America, because an Italian got here first (forgetting the Vikings), though Columbus' descendants are Spaniards. This parade also makes a kind of bomb-throwing connection between the American Revolution, Garibaldi and the Sicilian Mafia.

The Polish-American parades, based on Kosciusko, make a more modest claim but still imply, with some substance, that liberty was invented in Poland.

Chinese parades are interested only in China, The Middle Kingdom.

I have seen one charming Greek parade, where the ancient city states, the Delian Confederacy, and the Peloponnesian War, were confused with the nineteenth century rebellions against the Turks.

The American communities that at present refrain from parades are the Jews, the Negroes and the Germans. A sort of haughtiness can be read in these abstentions. Who do they think they are?

It is time to confess openly that this whole matter of parades is definitely ambivalent. I will not claim the protective coloration of irony in any of the foregoing, but I must admit that parades fascinate me, even as I recognize that they are kind of horrible.

The great annual parade in a number of American cities, and my favorite, is the Saint Patrick's Day parade. On that day the Irish nation is indubitably the first nation of the earth.

One remembers the facts of Irish history, beginning so wonderfully open, in the centuries before and after Saint Patrick, closing slowly during the Viking and Norman invasions, freezing into a death mask of religiosity, conceit and fratricide, and ending in the closed Ireland of today. The parade in New York follows this sequence, beginning with the open part: hordes of innocent Anglo-Saxons, Scandinavians, Italians, Poles, and Ne-groes, marching they know not why.

We see bands of high school boys and girls, usually with a bare-kneed drum majorette prancing in the chill breeze, child-ishly intent on her manipulation of the outsized baton which she does not quite dominate. Behind her, still more touching, come six smaller children, also pathetically red-skinned and heroic, wobbling the batons in a patent terror of failure. And then comes the formidable phalanx, to be sure, but it is com-posed of straggling schoolgirls garbed identically, to be sure, but not in any threatening array, and toward the rear ranks hopelessly out of step and gossiping back and forth. The variety of faces in these groups is of almost every race and type and character known to Man, and thus entirely American.

One year a Negro band came along subtly turning the tra-ditional tunes into jazz, and stepping with the thrilling smart-ness of true beat. I haven't seen this band again, perhaps it was too close to a separate, non-Irish nation, a premature Congo, to satisfy the Irish parade marshals.

One accepts long stretches of dullness, the ladies' auxiliaries, the sodalities, political organizations, the police and street-clean-ing departments. But at last, fairly late in the long day, the heart of the matter can be heard shrilling in the distance like infuriated elves, for here comes the first of the county bagpipe bands. All the rest was introduction and irrelevancy. The true belief, the very center, comes howling up the avenue. These men in their kilts and sporrans march with a self-centered seri-ousness, whether or not they are hired mercenaries from a New Jersey or Brooklyn bar-and-grill. The dress of the wild clans seems to possess them, and they stroll as if they were coming down out of a glen into the plain, putting dread into all the mean plainsmen. For the little tune the pipes are playing is overcome by the tuneless screaming of the escaping air. A continuous hurricane keens through this music, and the heavily beaten drums are necessary to remind us that the music has a beat.

The county units carry the embroidered and decorated banners not only of South Ireland but also of the six "lost" counties of the north, where long raged The O'Donnell and The O'Neill, "Head of the liberality and valor of the Irish," long after the southern clans had been reduced to beggary and banditry, when the long-haired O'Neills swaggered through London, on embassy.

This part of the parade celebrates the closed aspect of Irishry. It says that a thousand years ago (just as Ireland was being ravished by the Danes) the Irish got hold of something good though not exactly defined, and have never seen any occasion to change it. The old banners showing the forgotten, and probably idiotic, heroes are for this day the winners in a bar-and-grill politics that means nothing. For example, the great Parnell, so far as I remember, is not remembered in this parade.

The unarguable propositions of the parade, dimly apprehended, do not bear sane examination. They are all a half-remembered dream. And this dreaming may very well have a corrosive effect on what remains of the reality that inspires the dream. While the Saint Patrick's Day parades get bigger and more boastful, Ireland dwindles to 2,900,000 inhabitants from the 9,000,000 for all Ireland in the famine year of 1846. While the boast gets bigger, the fact gets smaller. Is there a connection? Why not? Great stories have always grown eloquent as they died. The glories of Venice were famous in the seventeenth century while it sank to its death; the last glories of the Ottoman Empire, of St. Petersburg and of Vienna are more easily remembered; and all had splendid parades. "Strike up the band!" may not be the signal that the great days have come, but that they are over. The silent battalions may instead be the ones to think about.

We need not confine ourselves to literal parades. Any group or person that is never, under any circumstances, self-critical, is a parade, and is at the moment glorious, and is probably doomed. The extreme Right and Left, assuming that these designations have any meaning, are obviously of this sort, but the liberal center is not without its parades. Mrs. Roosevelt seems to be a parade, for example, while her late husband never was, to the complete confusion of the Republicans. We have people who try constantly to be parades, like Herbert Hoover and Henry Luce, but nobody marches. Everybody has at least one friend who tries to be a parade.

There are of course natural and inevitable parades. The secret is that a parade requires no further thought and can be loved wholeheartedly; thought about its premises is not needed or wanted. And is it not generally a requirement of what one loves that one not be obliged to think about it, to analyze it, to doubt it? One must conclude that a proper parade is a truly lovable event. Or one can begin to wonder whether thoughtless love is quite as useful and respectable an emotion as one is often asked to believe. Or one can stop thinking.

One can try saying, on Saint Patrick's Day, in the hearing of Irishmen, that Parnell was a Protestant, essentially an Englishman, and half-American. I once did this, and was quickly in trouble, yet the whole statement can be documented. In such situations one must see that one is put in the position of being against love; one is messing up a parade. One should not mention that Saint Patrick was probably a Welshman who first saw Ireland as the victim of kidnappers. The color worn on Saint Patrick's Day is green, but the old Irish think that wearing green is bad luck.

Thus, even the Irish parade senses that something is wrong, that the great day's skirling of glory, which is really the "Irish cry" or keen or coronach, the weeping forepart of the revenge, may lead to the end of the shining road. The splendid, sorrowful, ominous hour, to the long, keening, thrilling wail of the massed bagpipes, must peter out in a dirty shambles in a nameless bar-and-grill.

On the larger stage, nations born of parades will do well to consider this obscure branch of political science.

1962

*P*EOPLE AND DOGS

*M*ORE DEMONSTRATED love is undoubtedly shown to the 26,000,000 dogs in the United States today than to any other single group, including babies and male singers. Since each dog has successful relationships with several people, it will be seen that the dog contributes the principal social cement holding America together.

Perhaps in gratitude, the Westminster Kennel Club's Dog Show takes place in New York next week, for the eighty-sixth time since 1877, and will probably be shown on a national TV network. *The New York Times* has called this "a fantastic event, in the emotion, the strain and the exaltation it generates." Something very big is evidently going on here. Since it breaks down into two elements, dogs and people, let us take the dogs first.

Why a dog-owner likes his or her dog is largely controlled by why the dog likes him or her, and this in turn goes back to the ancestry of the dog, which is scientifically described as "a tractable wolf." It is instructive that humankind should choose to love a creature that can bite through a bone but generally decides not to, if the bone walks on its hind legs. A good part of the American economy—for example, $500,000,000 a year for dog food—is devoted to persuading this tractable wolf that the upright bone is a friend, and not worth biting into.

The dog's sociability, adaptability and alliance with man are zoologically peculiar and are explained by its ancestry. This begins in Eocene times (40 million years ago) with the civet-like Miacis, a short-legged tree-dweller. From this came a line of bear-dogs, and also a short-legged dog, Cynodictis. From this latter, one descent led to the wild dogs of Africa, India and South America, another to the "father of the dog family," Tomarctus, in Miocene times, ancestor of the wolves, dogs, foxes and fennecs. Alone in the animal kingdom, the wolves and dogs depended on running down their game to exhaustion and seizing it. To do so, their legs grew longer, their cleverness sharpened and they learned to hunt cooperatively. Their genetic adaptability and their social life raised their intelligence to a certain plateau, surpassed, it is true, by their individualist cousin, the fox.*

The social instinct of the dog is expressed in its impulse to mark trees and posts along its path with urine, and to "read" such marks left by other dogs, wolves and foxes. Whatever humans may think of this practice as transferred to the modern city, it is still the communication system of the *Canidae*. In the wild, it tells a wolf whether the passerby was male or female, native or stranger, sick or well, happy or in trouble. In this way news is spread, and the community is alerted. This same desire to communicate, and to receive communications, appears vividly in the dog's relationship with its owner. People who talk to their dogs have smart dogs.

The vast variety of breeds among dogs would be impossible among cats or any other animal that is not, as the zoologists say, "plastic." All cats, with the partial exception of the long-legged cheetah, are physically alike except in size and marking.

Before man took over dogs (at least 50,000 years ago), dogs had already sorted themselves out into a number of plastic types. Primitive tribes still possess only one type of dog, but the first civilized states collected a number of types. (Exceptions: the Biblical Israelites and the Hindus, who both abominated the

* For more on this, see *The Origin of the Dog* by Edwin H. Colbert, a curator at the Museum of Natural History, New York. (Science Guide No. 102: published by the museum.)

dog.) The basic types can reasonably be catalogued in the same way as was done in ancient Rome.

Shepherd dogs. What is now called the wolf-dog type is seen in the various huskies, sheep dogs, collies, Pomeranians, schipperkes and corgis (3,000 years old), and probably the Chinese chows and the Norwegian elkhounds.

Scent hounds. The Greeks hunted with beagles, the Romans with bloodhounds. From the foxhound came the pointer, and from this the Dalmatian.

Greyhounds. The sight hounds in the Seluki and Afghan forms go back 5,000 years. (They are unrelated to the dachshund, elkhound and otter hound now grouped with them.)

Sporting dogs. This is essentially the spaniel type, from which have come the setter, Newfoundland (Alcibiades had a dog very like it), St. Bernard, retrievers, poodle and papillon.

War dogs. The mastiff type has produced the bulldog, boarhound, Great Dane, bull terrier, pug, boxer and probably the Pekingese.

The Romans had a sixth group, house dogs, which may have included almost anything, and apparently omitted the terrier, from which we have produced a great variety by combining it with hounds.

Dog genealogies are even less certain than human genealogies, so that the foregoing can only be a reasonable guess. But the groupings by which dogs will be judged at the Westminster Dog Show next week are based on an inscrutable fantasy with a tradition usually younger than the first dog show in Newcastle, England, in 1859. Until then there had been no modern concept of breeds, except as to function, and most of the present breeds were still unknown.

The official dog-show groups have frequently been ridiculed, but without any alternative theory of genealogy. The groups at the Westminster Show will be: (1) sporting (improperly lumping setters and spaniels with pointers); (2) hounds (improperly grouping sight and scent hounds, and putting the otter hound, elkhound and dachshund with the sight hounds); (3) working dogs (improperly including mastiff dogs with wolf dogs and throwing in some spaniel descendants); (4) terriers (whose long-legged miscegenations belong elsewhere); (5) toys (a justifiable *mélange* of small dogs); and (6) non-sporting (an outrageous evasion of responsibility in grouping descendants of the wolf dog, the pointer, the spaniel, the mastiff and the terrier).

This farce is not merely theoretical. Breeds competing in these groups are going in opposite directions. They are non-comparable. All that justifies the dog people in comparing them is that they are all still the magnificently plastic dog.

This plasticity is shown constantly in the appearance of "new" breeds and the extinction of old ones. The latter include the turnspit, Old English White Terrier, Old German Pinscher, mastin, finder, broken-haired terrier, etc. The new show has judges available to consider the merits of two fairly new Hungarian dogs, the Vizsla, a pointer, and the Komondorok, a big white shepherd; a Tibetan guard dog, the Kuvaszok; and a Belgian shepherd, the tervuren.

Just now over half of all American registrations are the poodle, beagle, chihuahua, dachshund and German shepherd; the remainder are divided among the 108 other breeds. Since 1900, the American favorite has progressively been the English setter, collie, Boston terrier, airedale, German shepherd, Boston terrier again, cocker spaniel (from 1936 to 1952), the beagle, and now the poodle. The cocker spaniel began to decline right after Nixon used one on TV to justify his political existence; at least he turned to the right breed for help.

The popular breeds in our city civilization are probably chosen for their "amusing" traits. Contrary to amateur sociology, very few people choose an unfamiliar breed, like a Rhodesian ridge-back, purely as a status symbol. A dog is bigger than a car. Nor is man foolish in inventing breeds, and in having favorites. A purebred puppy, as against a mongrel, will develop a predictable character, and the owner will have the kind of company he wanted.

Thus we come to the people at the dog show. Professional dog people love dogs the way generals and top sergeants love people. Show dogs are trained. A petted family dog does not do well in the ring. The winners are brainwashed automatons, stoic warriors from Sparta, theirs not to reason why; and, as personalities, they are at the bottom of the canine world.

This is no protest. These people sincerely believe that a show dog will feel at the top of the canine world by winning best in show at the Westminster. They know their dogs better than you or I do (I am still working on people). The animals are proud and must understand that this insane business, so far apart from their natural genius, is intensely sane to the humans. They realize that they must for the present forget their hereditary plasticity, and become rigidly nonplastic. If Tomarctus showed up at a dog show, with every breed in its loins, it would be chased out into the street. By being, it would destroy every antiplastic pretension of the Westminster Kennel Club.

For the "exaltation" noted by *The New York Times* at the Westminster Show is based on conflicts of pride and prejudice. The dog's allegiance to man has undoubtedly given mankind many of its most terrible infatuations. There is an amazing theory that man's first sense of property rights was born when he realized he "owned" a dog, because the dog felt "owned." Certainly the unearned love a dog gives a human cur gives him or her a feeling of power, which he then tries to transfer to his less perfect standing in the human world. The love of a dog, to revise the famous saying, is the last resort of scoundrels. The leadership idea is very strong among dog-lovers.

This is not to say that the Westminster Show exhibitors are scoundrels, but might say that they have partly given up on people. When one does this, one must look for a better, nonhuman style of character. And where should one find it but in the breed of dog one loves?

Dog people, it is often said, somehow resemble the dogs they are showing. If you think this is just an old joke, look at the people at the Westminster Show. The people were not born that way; functionally, they would be quite inadequate as dogs. The fact is that the various arbitrary breeds of dogs act on humans somewhat as Charles Dickens did: they are caricatures which become models for actual humans. An individual sees in the dog's comportment and attitude, or in Dickens' creation, exactly what he considers the ideal port to present to life.

When we look to the upper hierarchy of the dog-show world, we find a snarling, unapproachable tyranny that suggests the more disagreeable and unpopular breeds, such as the mastiff. Dog officials, unlike any others in America from the Supreme Court down to a baseball umpire, never explain the reasons for a decision. The American Kennel Club is more inscrutable than the Kremlin.

The club dictates to a weird industry of show officials, breeders, pet shops, veterinarians, cosmeticians, dog magazines and dog-food makers. Of America's living 26,000,000 dogs, about 450,000 new-born puppies are registered with the American Kennel Club every year; thus there are now about 4,000,000 living, registered, "pure-bred" dogs in the United States, in whose behalf there has been paid in about $8,000,000—$2 a head—for registration. This listing is compulsory for any dog shown at any of about 800 annual U.S. dog shows and over 1,000 informal "sanction matches." The number of animals actually competing in a given year is perhaps 70,000. Shows use a point system by which a dog can win five points in a single show and no more, even at the Westminster Show. With fifteen points, he or she is called a "Champion" and his name is always prefixed with a Ch. The title is worth about as much as being addressed "Hi, champ" on Broadway, or a little lower than a Kentucky colonel; but it indicates some expenditure on the owner's part. Once a dog has its Ch., it is withdrawn from point competition, or it could be a Ch. a hundred times over: a farcical position.

The cash interest in this illusion game is considerable. The Westminster Kennel Club farms out its show to the Foley Dog Show Organization of Philadelphia, which puts on about 100 shows a year. The Foleys use the same benches, tents and cages at all shows. Their trucks are constantly moving about the country. They boast that they have never canceled a contracted show; if they ever had, we might know whether they would have returned the exhibitors' $7 entry fees. In the midst of catastrophes, the show has gone on, and they have kept the money.

Other trucks are also in motion. These are driven by professional dog handlers, taking an average of twelve of other people's dogs, and as many as forty, to a single show. The cost to the owner is $25 for a one-day show; a bonus of at least $50 if the dog wins best of group, and of at least $100 if it wins best in show. The handler also charges $2 a day for the two weeks or two months he has kept the dog before the show.

Dog-show judges favored by the American Kennel Club also make an excellent full-time living. Most clubs pay their expenses.

The A.K.C. can outlaw anybody it chooses from all this gravy, without explanation and without recourse. Even the relatives of any such outlaw are barred from showing their dogs anywhere. The tone of the A.K.C. goes straight back to George III and Ivan the Terrible, if not further.

The majesty of the dog hierarchy was severely shaken by last year's Westminster Show, corrupted by the spotlight of network TV. Eleven stations had signed up, with two more coming on at 11:15 P.M. for the final best-in-show judging. But the show people, already rattled by being out in all the light, got word that "some" of the stations were cutting out for the eleven-o'clock news. From then on, the officials ignored all the announced and sacred schedules of judging. Brace-judging, timed to begin at 10:45, was over by 10:40, just as a brace of basset hounds arrived in good time to be judged. The best-in-show judging was over in seven minutes, to unprecedented boos and catcalls, by 10:58 P.M. Actually all thirteen stations were ready to come in at 11:15 for the final judging. The panic was quite unnecesary.

The breakdown of the old haughty morality, at the first invitation to the strip tease, ended something. The A.K.C. declared some mild penalties against its own people in the following days, but the glint of whorishness lingered in its eye. "Happily it's all over now," said an A.K.C. vice president, like a dowager with a giddy hangover. The test of that will come at next week's Westminster Show. Something *is* probably over, and something begun—but they may not be what the dog hierarchy think.

It must occur to one that a society's attitude toward the dog is highly indicative. The dog is even adaptable, as the horrors accepted by Pavlov's dogs prove, to a Communist society. The dog, in a way that not even Jonathan Swift would have dared, satirizes any society it finds itself in, by its simple love and acceptance. The plastic dog, asked to freeze into aristocratic non-plasticity at the Westminster Show, satirizes the reputable principle of aristocracy. The dog does not especially want to be aristocratic; the mongrel people on hand do. The dogs and the people make two different travesties on aristocracy, both unintentional. The dogs are wonderfully plastic, but not quite as plastic as humans.

1962

BELIEVING IN BOOKS

$\mathcal{M}$Y ATTITUDE toward the printed word at this time in my life would seem to someone else barbarian, carnivorous and selfish. I read primarily for trustworthy information, which I intend to put to immediate use. I do not read for happiness but for hunger. Later on, I will return to other ways of reading.

The telling sign of the man who reads for information must be his irritation on being lied to. And here one must point out an unexpected, even paradoxical, fact. One is not likely to discover a liar by beginning with skepticism. It is much better to begin with the attitude that one believes absolutely anything in print. Theoretically, such a reader should be the delight of practical jokers—at the beginning. But there is no other way to receive new information than with complete credulousness—at the beginning. The liar will always be discovered by the truly naïve reader, given the peculiar nature of the truth, as the liar continues.

Many lies are solid orthodoxy, and the individual must think for himself. When I read writers who say that the center of the earth is solid, or that all men are a single species,* or that

* To this a reader, a professor of zoology, protested: "There have been a few (fortunately only a few) people who said that there are several living species of man. . . . It is usually not difficult to think of a bad reason why some of these people talked this demonstrable untruth: They tried to uphold racism."

The answer, as published together with the protest:

"For a scientist to indict a scientific theory on the grounds of guilt by association with a political theory should be a scientific scandal, if it were not so orthodox.

21

the moon would be a good place for a rocket station, for example, I know that these people cannot possibly know what they are talking about; I begin to wonder why they are lying to me; and usually I can think of a good reason.

The truth, it should be emphasized, is never clearly labeled, and never given away for nothing. "This emotion inherited

"The key word here is 'species.' Ludlow Griscom wrote in *Modern Bird Study*, 'To sum up, then, we are still unable to give a final definition of a species, and there are no universally valid criteria, capable of experimental proof.' A species is not defined by the limits of successful interbreeding. Many species, and some genera, do successfully interbreed and thus procreate new successful species, as the golden-winged and blue-winged warblers now interbreed to create two new recognized species. The explanation is that it takes some time for a species to achieve 'reproductive isolation.' These species of birds, and the species of Man, have not had that much time.

"The 'scientific' proposition that all living men are members of a single species is actually based on the wholly unscientific faith, initiated by great nineteenth century Englishmen, that mankind is somehow superior to the laws of the animal kingdom. Obviously, very few living men are 'pure-blooded,' of any conceivable original species; the exceptions might be the pygmy negritos, the Andamanese, the Australian aborigines, etc. Most aboriginal species, if they were such, have vanished, and with them vanished thousands of years ago all grounds for the political 'racist' theory. But the crossbreeding of species presents science with a large number of interesting data on which its piety righteously slams the door.

"One sees communities and even families that breed very true to type. If the scientists could get a little scientific now and then, one would like to know whether these are subspecies, races or breeds. The very word, 'breed,' reminds us of Man's discovery that he can breed out quite a variety of dogs from the (is it three?) original species; and the dog is to modern man almost as sacred as himself.

"The subject of my piece was that life does actually go on its own way, quite independently of men's textbooks, and that the way to find out about it is to look at it, rather than to duck into the book. The crossbreeding between different species and genera is going on, no matter what the book says. To say that it can't be going on because Hitler could have made an argument out of it, has the effect of abolishing the whole scientific method and pretension.

"And is it so much worse to be able to say, correctly, that all the living races of Man are members of a single genus?" —D. C.

from childhood, the anger on discovering that one has been lied to, may be the last safeguard of democracy. It presupposes a world of honest men; it does not permanently accept a convention of deceit as honorable, amusing or even bearable": so it was once said, and one could add that if we do accept a convention of deceit, we will all go down together to extinction.

As a rewrite man, I have recently read a life of Jean Paul Getty, the miserable billionaire; a touching autobiography by Conrad Hilton, the hotel man (his secret seems to be praying and dreaming); some harrowing books on our water resources; and a genuinely witty book entitled *A & P: A Study in Price-Cost Behavior and Public Policy*, by M. A. Adelman.

All these books deserve careful reading, but let us stay with the A & P book, since it explores an enterprise we are all touched by. It is also the most truthful of the books cited above. The truth of it may derive not only from the character of Professor Adelman but from A & P's refusal to tell him anything; he used only the 50,000 pages of sworn testimony in the government's hearings and trials of A & P under the Robinson-Patman Act: a stupendous piece of free research.

The thoroughness, open-mindedness and modesty of this study impress one at once; the author knows he is hunting elusive game: what really happened? The reader is at once on his mettle. And he has that wonderful feeling of seeing how life is actually conducted, and of being entirely out of fashion. Such a feeling, such a book, will never make the doctrinaire happy.

The book, one would assume, has got to be against A & P, certainly a likely goat to tether for any tiger. But it is not. It only sees what it looks at, and it does not lie. What Adelman sees is the lunacy of Robinson-Patman. He concludes from the government's trials of A & P under Robinson-Patman that the law has become that a seller not only can, but must, charge a buyer for certain services the buyer performs himself, i.e., brokerage, transportation, warehousing, etc., and for the cost of financing these services. "To sum up the new doctrine," writes Adelman, "it asserts illegal restraint of competition to exist in any business firm which (1) can be set up as more than one accounting and profit-making unit, or (2) directly or indirectly sells anything to a competitor. We shall seek a long time, I fear, before finding a firm which is not breaking the law."

It is obvious, even to a layman, that the government is crazy; and it can be disastrous for governments to slide gracefully into lunacy. The happiness of getting to the heart of a difficult matter comes as one reads on: "There is a widespread impression that the Chain Store Investigation of the Federal Trade Commission disclosed much price discrimination in favor of large buyers. The Investigation established no such thing . . . It is perfectly clear that the FTC was investigating not price discrimination, in the economic sense, but price differentials . . . What is true of the FTC report is even more obvious in the Congressional hearings on the Robinson-Patman Act. (As for the floor debates, the less said the better.) . . . Doubtless some knew what they were doing; obviously most did not . . ." These are the lawyers who run our world, and they seem quite mad.

But it develops that businessmen are not much better. In the course of his history of A & P, Adelman shows that John Hartford for twelve years hammered at his division chiefs to "reduce the gross profit [percentage] to increase the volume . . ." But his chiefs simply couldn't bring themselves to do it. The two Hartfords had complete control and complete loyalty, but John couldn't get this one little thing done, until the company nearly foundered in 1936.

Hartford had an interesting theory on whether to "react to situations" or to "make the situation." The latter, even if one hasn't $100,000,000 in cash, would seem preferable. If a competitor cuts brand prices, the theory says to ignore that situation, but to "make" another situation by underselling him on meat and produce. This reminds one of military theory in World War II, especially on the Russian front. Both armies were busy "making situations" and trying to ignore the other's "situation." The army that was first obliged to react to the other's situation lost the battle.

A book like Adelman's can be recognized as following a very hot scent of reality; it also exhibits an intense love of that reality. I like to find this in a book.

I like to read backwards; that way, you take the author unawares, climb up his back, as it were, and frustrate his ingenious arrangements of the material. The first law in reading for information is to know whom you can trust; and often the honest man can be recognized by one sentence read out of context, the swindler by two. The richness, the truthful complication of the writer's mind can also best be discovered in this way. Anyone who can be dull and simple about this world is obviously not to be trusted, unless he is not writing about this world at all. The dullness, or richness, of a writer is almost necessarily in every sentence—and the sentence is still the basic unit of communication. It is a fair test of a writer, though not of his book, to open the book in the middle and read one sentence.

What makes this just is that the truth (we are not speaking of art) is never a fair arrangement; it is either a microcosm or a macrocosm; even the former leads out to the larger universe. And always, whenever we open another book, we hope to learn everything.

A writer who would object to being read backwards is probably a scoundrel. He must resent the reader's desperate need to know what is true and what is not. But the reader may be just as serious in reading as the writer was supposed to have been in writing—but perhaps was not, quite. This seriousness is characteristic of good rewrite men. They have to be supernaturally intuitive, unerring in spotting a "good source" and a bad one; all their antennae are waving until they have decided which is which, and the clue may be a very slight thing. If a writer gives a fact that hurts his case, it is well to listen closely to him. If the writing has that skilled gloss, that shellac of facts, that patina, one might as well throw the book out.

And I mean don't read another word. For the human mind is treacherous itself; it does not retroactively throw out all the material it had gathered before it realized it was all suspect. A year later one will hear oneself dispensing its misinformation with authority.

I am not even discusing the naked foolishness of believing anything absolutely, as college boys are required to believe the words of the textbook in order to pass the examination and collect their credits. Of course every teacher should begin his first lecture with the caution that nothing he can tell is necessarily and absolutely true. The reason he does not is that so much skepticism would be too much for the boys and girls to handle, and they would not bother to memorize suspect wisdom. The open mind is what one would like to encourage, but the mind firmly closed on that textbook, like an enraged clam, will pass the course.

My reading has not always been so barbarian, though now my main pleasure in Literature lies in knowing that the works of Marcel Proust exist. Once, though, I degenerated to reading four or five mysteries a week. I always intended to reread one to isolate just when, how and why the writer had misled or lied to me; but of course one never does. One learns something of the world from well-written mysteries, but one is also thrown off by a completely false accent to life. People haven't the energy, in life, to plot so much evil for one another; there are a thousand possible reactions, besides murder, to any injury; and so, the twanging nerves that mysteries string are not of much practical use in dealing with people. Their reading of mysteries did not help either Woodrow Wilson or Franklin D. Roosevelt. Both went abroad and were swindled by the foreigners; the mysteries should properly have whetted their suspicions to the finest possible edge. But suspicion is a thing very few people can entertain without letting the hypothesis turn, in their minds, into fact. Therefore, decent people are afraid to be suspicious; only scientists can walk around and around a hypothesis without even beginning to confuse it with truth.

In life, there is another objection to the mystery's solution by murder. To kill another human being is to be a little more intimate with him than self-respect permits. It is no accident that the killers are generally debased or deranged. The act of reading mysteries, for a normal human, is lifelike but not life. I gave it up when I realized that it was merely time-killing.

Entirely by chance two summers ago, I caught up, within two weeks, with some of the works of Beckett, Camus, Nathanael West, Bernard Malamud and some others. These seemed to me to have some of the quality of *A & P: A Study in Price-Cost Behavior and Public Policy;* they convinced me that at least they wanted to show how life is actually conducted. They rejected clichés and appearances and in this, if in nothing else, they cheered me.

Confronted with Beckett's peculiar vision, one laughs uncontrollably for about twenty pages, and then stops laughing for good. (This was much what I did with the A & P book.) Here I met for the first time the new hero, who reappears through most of this new fiction—usually speechless, psychically irresistible to the other characters, loaded with inexpressible message, somehow convincing the others that his message, if only he could get it out, is the master-word. This hero's acts are inscrutable, or senseless, but dimly limn some higher design which, as translated into the hero's life, is simply lunatic. Lesser writers make this character caricature; one had him a man who was literally dumb, hence endlessly receptive to confidences to which he could not respond, hence deeply worshiped by his followers. Such a story line is certainly inferior to that of the A & P book. The next hero might as well be a statue in the park, perhaps of Robinson or Patman.

Nathanael West, the best and the earliest of these novelists, was representatively disingenuous. I knew him. He used to address respectfully as "you writers" a number of journalists whom he gave passes to the swimming pool in the hotel he and his mother were slowly losing in the Depression. I accepted the respect but I have since seen from the publication dates of these amazing, revolutionary novels that he was already a "writer" himself when he extended this deference. The hotel swimming instructor, like someone in West's fiction, was clubfooted and immensely social; the hotel was going to pot (it was the Sutton in New York City); and West was imperturbable. His impeccably friendly mockery, coming from a gentleman who probably bought his clothes at Triplers instead of Brooks's and was sorry about it, his self-deprecation, his pleasure with the tough talk and bravura of the journalistic elite, were part of his style. His basic ideas seemed not greatly different from those that genteel ironists frequently develop for purely conversational purposes, or turn into limericks. But the colossal difference turns out to be that Pep West was in dead earnest. He stayed with the ideas. He knew they had some meaning beyond his convenience. He felt an obligation to get the ideas out in the open where nobody could miss the meaning, and this he did. And yet to meet him, one would suppose that Nathanael West would not be in dead earnest about anything. On his word that he was not a "writer," I had read almost nothing by him until 1959. He had convinced me in the Hotel Sutton that it would not be worth my while.

West's pose, and my credulity, may have a bearing on the new novelists. The current high-style fiction exploits a truth we are quite ready to accept, in part: that human communication is impossible. The conclusion: give up. Let jazz speak for you; let silence speak its bottomless eloquence; let liquor or drugs put two souls on one high-riding, delirious movie-land cloud. Here, we are to believe, will be true communication. To make fun of it would be, in one of my least favorite words, a supererogation.

Let us therefore conclude with a note on the nature of communication. The whole development of language has been influenced by the instinctive recognition that it is really impossible, and probably undesirable, to communicate fully. One proof of the fact is the unconquerable aversion of adjacent peoples to speaking one another's languages. Language is an agreement on certain crude symbols for what all the members of the group can agree on: certainly a very small fraction of the total individual thought of the group. Thus, we have dictionaries, and even English-French and French-German dictionaries.

But the language is always drastically limited by the fact that we do not agree, really, on very much, because we do not propose to confess very much about what is going on in our heads. And we cannot confess anything until we know the word for it. The area of confession and recognition is now and then enlarged by the poets, novelists and scientists. And this process of extension is always resisted by the Philistines and Yahoos.

The new novelists seem to have gone over to the Philistines. Words have failed; communication is impossible; the only honor lies in silence.

But are not their wordless heroes, losers all, only the former "strong, silent man" turned inside out? The latter was predictably the winner; the former is predictably the loser. But literature is not a score-card. It is more than a choice between memorizing the formula for victory or reading one's own obituary in advance. And this is part of the reason why *A & P: A Study in Price-Cost Behavior and Public Policy* is so interesting. Here nobody exactly wins or exactly loses; and whatever happens happens for the wrong reasons. Everybody is trying desperately to make sense, and is talking nonsense. And after the curtain has come down, one knows that the story writhes and meanders on.

But with the wordless heroes, one cannot remember their names or just what went wrong. They are martyrs to an incomprehensible religion. One would like to visit the graves, but there are no graves.

1961

$\mathcal{S}$EX HAPPINESS FOR
ABSOLUTELY EVERYBODY

$\mathcal{T}$HIS NORMAL young couple like each other. Each finds the other somehow miraculously unique. But instead of rushing to the church or leaping into bed, we are told, they now trudge hand in hand to a marriage counselor. The furious first flush is doomed; the awesome soap opera now begins.

More usually, one of the happy pair reads a marriage counselor book. The Kinsey Institute for Sex Research replies to a formal inquiry that its library holds 1,400 of these books. Clearly this is no longer a virgin field. As to which is the definitive work, the Kinsey Institute identifies as one of "the better marriage manuals now available" *A Marriage Manual* by Drs. Hannah and Abraham Stone (Simon & Schuster), at last accounts in its forty-fifth printing since first publication in 1935 and revision in 1951. It may be safely assumed that this book has had some impact on American bedroom life, unnoted by the benighted. (Incidentally, Simon & Schuster have made a specialty of these sex manuals, perhaps as a replacement for crossword puzzles. There is a significance in this editorial progression that just narrowly eludes me. They have a new one, *Man and Sex*, directed solely at men.)

A Marriage Manual, aimed at both partners, is the first such book that, in a long and happy life, I have had occasion to read. It is really too late for it to have any effect on me. Still, a sort of vicarious pity develops as one identifies with the blank-faced, engaged couple asking questions and getting answers for 270 pages, plus assigned outside reading of fifty-seven books, plus a bibliography of about 150 books. The voice patiently answering and explaining is so kind, so patently a champion of understanding and sympathy and friendly intimacy, that one almost forgets what life is really like. It is all on the level of a guided tour of the United Nations.

Nevertheless, anyone who reads this book and the fifty-seven others must become, in a theoretical sense, a professional. And sex is the great amateur art. The professional, male or female, is frowned on; he or she misses the whole point and spoils the show.

The professional will indeed find some interesting items in *A Marriage Manual,* or any of its kind. He can boast to his vis-à-vis that the male sperm travels an amazingly circuitous route before getting out into the big world. Or she may well be interested to hear that the female egg cell is in business for only about two days, but that one must add two or three days to this "dangerous" period, if that's the way one feels about it, because live sperm loitering in the vicinity may survive for that period.

Such biological exposition has its place and justification. But when we translate much of the book's sage counsel into real life, we find ourselves teetering on the edge of farce. It is soberly advised, for example, for the somewhat impotent groom, that "marriage should not be entered into unless the future wife is fully cognizant of the man's disability and is willing to accept him in spite of his condition." "My dear," says the fellow, "there's something you should know." Surely the words would stick in his throat. The self-assurance required to take such a gamble with his heart's desire is certainly not given to this man. The relationship, like most others, is a hand in a poker game; and is he to turn his nothing-cards face up at this point? As a human being, he is loaded with baseless hope; perhaps this time things will be different. And he has already phrased half a dozen alibis, anyway.

The phenomenon of such advice may easily have spawned the fiction school represented by Nathanael West and Samuel Beckett. Society with the kindly smile is out to destroy the hapless individual, without giving him a chance to ruin himself by himself. Even if the lady marries him and his disability vanishes, what does she say when she is angry at him for any inconsequential reason? As one imagines the epithets boiling out of her larynx, and the poor man's outraged countermeasures, one sees another marriage wrecked on too much good advice.

It might be wiser for that man to tell his girl that he has always been a grand stallion; he may even convince himself. Anyway, he can then blame any failure on the girl: a much better poker hand. The human solution has always been to keep the mouth shut on bad news, and take life's chances as they loom.

Other advice covers premarital examination of seminal fluid, in case the groom is short on sperm; blood examination for the Rh factor; premarital dilation of the hymen in virgins; "an understanding attitude, mutual sympathy, a conscious effort, and deliberate restraint" (fine words, indeed); plenty of "foreplay" (a word not in the dictionary); and the lady's ignoring of fictional descriptions of female raptures and restraint of the impulse to tell her husband how indifferent she is (good advice, this). The authors quote, but do not necessarily endorse, Balzac's belief that a man should not marry "before he has studied anatomy and has dissected at least one woman." Hasn't anybody advised women first to dissect at least one man?

I must admit to a suspicion that such books are largely aimed at drumming up trade for doctors and doing a PR job for the profession. A good deal of space is given to the rare condition of vaginal spasm (vaginismus), that is, a hysterical clenching that prevents consummation. Obviously, any couple in this difficulty are going to go to a doctor; why tell everybody about it? But, of course, it makes doctors feel needed, and superficially justifies the whole book.

The social and moral position of the book is that of a nice elderly couple—as the authors were—who want very sincerely to be broad-minded and up to date. It is a purely lovable attitude, but it leads to what I take to be the main propaganda point of the book, after the biology, adjustments, etc., have been cleared away. This is that every woman in the world is entitled to frequent orgasms, and that every husband is required by some new Mosaic law to help the good work along.

Theoretically true, actually abominable and disastrous. Should one lift one's eyes from the page and look at the real world instead, unawed by these two kindly doctors, one sees that for a large proportion of women, at this very moment in their lives, a shaking emotional convulsion in the home, perhaps accompanied by embarrassing outcries, would undercut the whole foundation of the woman's life. The house is full of children; the walls are thin; and, finally, she regards it as highly undesirable to give her husband so much psychological advantage over her. A mild, loving, fond pleasure is one thing; a pit of ecstasy is quite another. Should the husband begin any of the erotic maneuvers prescribed by Drs. Hannah and Abraham Stone, the wife would either laugh at him, or remonstrate.

This is not merely an opinion. The authors give several sets of statistics that roughly coincide on the fact that 60 percent of women reach what they call a sexual climax rarely or never. Probably most of the other 40 percent are childless or adulterous. But it is agreed, and probable, that the 60 percent truly love their husbands, and truly enjoy their embraces, and are likely to be faithful wives and good mothers. Why cannot men therefore agree that these ladies know what they are doing? Why cannot marriage counselors do so?

Making sexual rules for women strikes me as an egregious impudence. They are primarily affected by factors the man is unaware of. A few are as potent at the age of twenty as the best men. Some are absolutely frigid into the thirties, and then come alive, with mixed feelings. Some start slow, have a mild heyday, and firmly abandon sex in their forties. Most spend their lives kidding their husbands. A few waste away looking for a hero who will be worthy of them. But in each such group, temperamental differences produce wide variations. A woman can change completely to suit the society or situation she finds herself in. If the asexual role is indicated, she turns asexual. A man has no such chameleon ability, unless he is that abomination, a professional.

In short, I cannot imagine what the lady author of *A Marriage Manual* thought she was doing in trying to explain sex to women. Men are the only people sex is worth explaining to. They at least are trying to do something about it.

But are nice, kindly, uninspired doctors competent to do the explaining? Some predecessors of this book have been Ovid's poems, the *Kama Sutra*, and *The Perfumed Garden*, as the authors proudly point out. But how much more talent went into the earlier works! It is unfortunate that the greatest writers did not apply themselves to this subject, but perhaps they knew very little about it. Or perhaps they had the wit to see that the subject was too big for anybody.

To define the size, one would have to multiply at least three very large numbers. But in any generalized "manual" (an interesting word, in this connection), one can present only one pair of tubes, glands and organs, certain words such as companionship, intimacy and sympathy, the methods of contraception (this is called "Family Planning"), and a few possible moves and positions—described under the heading, "The Art of Marriage."

The art of marriage is quite different from this. Most men would agree that it consists of listening to a woman for several hours without getting tired, and inhibiting the appropriate rational comment on the propositions she enunciates, and other adjustments, all fairly difficult for young men, but fairly easy for older men.

The bedmanship is, in real life, secondary or tertiary, and this truth is what drives a real Don Juan into a helpless rage. Men who are sexual maestros, know it and can prove it, will discover, if they are only that, that they cannot keep a woman, even an inferior or equally passionate woman. But they can keep the woman just by hanging around the house, and maybe washing the dishes, and getting her friendly with his female relatives. Don Juan, even with $100,000,000, cannot beat the system, unless he is also Louis XIV. That is, he can beat it if he can endow her with unassailable superiority to other women, without marrying her. Nowadays this little feat is difficult to bring off; the Don Juan is soon reduced to rubble by the alimony laws.

It would be interesting to make a marriage manual out of knowledgeable men's and women's objections to this book. The result would at least show that any simple description of all the males and females in the world does not begin to describe any one pair, and is therefore massively irrelevant. Further, one watches the fine little vision of bliss that the couple had brought to the doctor's office growing fainter behind the dust storm of generalized information. More faintly, one can hear the dogged mutter: Oh, but we're not like that at all. And of course they are right.

The horror of a mass society, buying this book in its forty-fifth edition, is that it cannot respect anything so individual and precious; it does not know the appropriate language; or fears the right words would be meaningless to some fractions of the mass, misunderstood by others, and offensive to still others.

Such a book, as an organized presentation of an imperfectly sensed passionate reality, deserves to be reviewed as a novel, or long poem. In this sense, one long passionate look immediately reduces it to ash. Suddenly, it isn't there any more.

1961

DON'T CALL ME:

THE TELEPHONE

IN THOSE heart-warming advice articles on the full, rich life, what is lacking is the word *without*. A day or so without newspapers, cigarettes, television, cocktails, sleeping pills, automobiles, food or water might be interesting. Even a day without a bath.

But not, for God's sake, a day without a telephone.

Most Americans today would not feel they existed in the world if they did not have a telephone. There are now 75,000,000 telephones in the United States, over half the world total of 140,000,000. The disease has caught hold so rapidly that only thirty years ago there were only 20,000,000 phones in this country.

What is said over all these telephones? Contracts are no longer concluded over the telephone; too many people have reneged on them. International diplomacy is not conducted over the telephone. (Incidentally, the telephones of the President of the United States and his Cabinet are checked once a week for wire tapping.) Histories and memoirs rarely record old telephone conversations. A good deal of crude selling is done over the phone; some preliminary love-making; most of the rest is ephemeral gabble, by which two people assure each other that they at least still exist, and perhaps also assure themselves of the same unremarkable and undistinguished fact.

The peculiar charm of the telephone was discovered by an

early Aldous Huxley hero in *Antic Hay*, who realized that while he was helpless in business face to face, he did very well on the telephone. Children and ineffectual people generally have since discovered that all their personal weaknesses are hidden when they talk at one end of a two-mile wire. They can writhe and blush and flinch unseen. The telephone is the ideal medium for a hollow bluffer; it makes all salesmen nearly equal.

The gifted salesmen have learned this, and prefer the live visit, or the long lunch, or other face-to-face dealings. As artists, they like a "live audience." It is true that once a man has made his physical, live impression, he can use the telephone with effect. A man like William Zeckendorf would have to reduce the range of his operations without a battery of telephones. Such people use the telephone as a power tool. Sitting at a desk looking at five telephones is, to some personalities, a positive invitation to be Napoleon. In a small way, anybody with only one telephone feels some fraction of this Napoleonic power. He or she can at least bother anybody on the planet who has a listed telephone. If you have made a better mousetrap, the world will not beat a path to your door, it will simply force you to get an unlisted telephone. You will thus lose touch with the people you would want to listen to. By letting all the idiots into the act, modern communication ends by cutting off communication entirely.

The great talkers of the world are on college campuses, in theatrical groups, and in India and Catalonia; but these are all face-to-face talkers. One must look elsewhere for the great telephoners. The most telephonized city in the world, with 83 phones per 100 people, is, to everybody's delighted acceptance, Washington, D.C. Next comes another peculiar town, Las Vegas (66); and then an unnoticed peculiarity, Skokie, Ill. (63.9), a saloon town surrounded by prohibition country. Following come Stockholm, Sweden (60), New York City (57),

Zurich, Switzerland (50.6) and Toronto, Canada (50.3).

In looking at this list, one begins to wonder whether cold weather—apart, that is, from special conditions like those of Washington and Las Vegas—correlates with telephonitis. The telephonized countries, running from 39 per 100 people down to 13, are the United States, Canada, Iceland, Australia, Scandinavia, the United Kingdom and Finland. (I may have overlooked somebody.) Then there is a sharp drop to 8 for both West Germany and France, to 6 for Argentina, Czechoslovakia and South Africa, to 4.6 for both Israel and Japan, to 3.6 for Portugal, 2.8 for Cuba, and to a group just below 2 per 100 people that includes Russia, Brazil, Costa Rica, Mexico and Poland.

This last group in particular suggests that percentage of telephones may not be exactly the definitive way to rate nations, though American Telephone and Telegraph would consider any such statement clearly communistic and subversive.

As we get down toward the least telephonized nations, suggestive groupings arrange themselves. For example, at around .5 per 100 people are Bolivia, Ceylon, Dominican Republic, Egypt, Nicaragua, Philippines and Saudi Arabia. Further down, around .1, are Haiti, India, Pakistan and Thailand. And still further, at around .05, are Afghanistan, Burma, Cambodia, Ethiopia, Iraq and Vietnam. One cannot quite say that all this is just what one would expect. Who could guess that Nicaragua has more phones than Burma, or Finland more than West Germany?

Telephonitis is more than a matter of electrification and industrialization. The largest number of phone calls per capita occur in Canada, Iceland and the United States. Surely it cannot be claimed that these three peoples have the most to say, or the Vietnamese the least to say, to one another. Even if the hot countries were equally telephonized, I suspect they would use the phones less.

The idea of telephoning on a hot day is much less pleasant than on a cold day. It may be that telephoning requires a little adrenalin, which adds to one's discomfort in hot weather. Telephoning is an aggressive, as well as a social, act. The telephone gives modern life a steady thread of anxiety, a fear of all that nameless aggression headed one's way, signaled by the alarm.

The telephone disease can be easily read in the two major types of patient. Lonely or socially underdeveloped people, at the sound of the bell, leap with mingled joy and terror, fall across the room and clutch at the phone. Breathing deeply, they utter a refined, gracious "Hello!" for they are expecting a glorious invitation to a new life, or the end of the world. When the common reality announces itself, they turn prim and stiff, and soon hang up.

The other kind begins to feel fretful when the telephone rings, take their own good time about answering and vouchsafe a weary, harassed "Hello." However, these, if female, may then talk for an hour, for they are telephone artists, masters of the medium.

Other masters of the telephone communicate without completing a call. Some send a message to a forewarned associate by letting the phone ring once, hanging up, and then letting it ring in various series of codes before hanging up. Some call person-to-person long distance, asking to reverse the charges, and convey the message by the name they give the operator (the other person does not accept the call). Some women not only have unlisted phones, but will not answer unless the phone rings three times, stops and then rings again.

I have a better system. I have worked in a big city for over a decade without a home phone. I live near stores, pay phones and most of the friends I see regularly. In consequence, I lead a decent life, almost devoid of that background of telephone anxiety and power. Don't call me; I'll call you. Some people send me telegrams, the worst and most expensive form of communication in America. (Special delivery letters are often faster than telegrams in the same city; long distance, the telephone is about the same price.) I find that my *not* having a telephone strikes awe and envy into most people, a reversal that would mystify the Cambodians.

But I will agree that the telephone is bigger than I. New oceanic cables are about to be laid from Hawaii to Tokyo and from Canada to Australia (the latter the longest in the world, with 335 submerged amplifiers to keep the gabble going). Black Africa will soon be on the world-wide hookup by way of Ascension Island, if I do not overrate Nkrumah.

Just how big the telephone is comes clear in the annual operating revenues of American Telephone and Telegraph and its principal telephone subsidiaries. (A. T. & T. usually owns about 99.5 percent of its subsidiaries). This figure would be what the American citizen pays for the right to gabble. It is now about *$8 billion* a year. The net income is a billion and a quarter.

This is not quite the whole bill the American pays. Another 15 percent of American phones are owned by some 500 "independents." This use of the fine word, independent, in industry, means out in the cold, much like many of the new "independent" nations in the world today. A single independent like General Telephone may include over 500 small companies. A call put through any of these and using A. T. & T. lines accrues A. T. & T. charges. In general, A. T. & T. collects all the gravy.

The company got its grip on America in 1900 by buying up American Bell Telephone, and in 1960 had 1,754,000 stockholders as against only 729,000 employees. It wants those little stockholders and it does not want those little employees.

Its public posture is that of the best friend the American people have ever had. (Many people grow rhapsodic over its magnanimity in canceling overcharges.) It keeps the picture window clean with a public relations department that doesn't seem to do any work, but does a lot. (I know somebody there; but, believe me, I haven't called him.) One thing they couldn't do anything about was the popularity of a novel called *Butterfield 8*, which related the telephone to immorality and probably led to the invention of the word, call girl. By policy decisions mysterious to me, there is still a Butterfield 8 exchange in New York City. Maybe it's good publicity. Its retention suggests that A. T. & T. is terribly sophisticated, or feels that its public neither reads books nor even sees movies—or, perhaps, doesn't give a damn.

This last theory is undercut by the great cleverness of A. T. & T.'s public relations department in issuing news releases to newspaper financial sections where, they have realized, nobody dangerous would ever see them.

That is where an April, 1961, story landed, in *The New York Times*, telling of a $150,000,000 suit by a General Telephone and Electronics stockholder against A. T. & T. and subsidiaries on the grounds that these had "made it impossible to market" a telephone-answering device manufactured by a General subsidiary. The stockholder was suing personally because General "feared the power of A. T. & T." That word, power, ought to make any American citizen prick up his ears.

A similar back-page treatment was given by *The New York Times* to a March, 1961, story revealing a device by which long-distance telephone calls can be received free and even local callers on pay phones get their money back. The inventor was selling his device at $1,500 apiece to bookmakers; it completely eliminates the company's record of the call. The police, evidently alerted by the telephone company, had found it by raiding three bookmakers' houses in Westchester County outside New York City. *The Times* moved the story up forward a few pages when the inventor of the device was arrested on March 30 in Miami.

One can see why newspapers would be as agreeable toward A. T. & T. as mothers toward the milkman. Whether any added leverage is ever applied, I do not know. However, businessmen have told me of legitimate, solvent concerns put out of business by A. T. & T., simply by cutting off telephone service.

The Westchester episode did not mean that A. T. & T. is against bookmakers. It happily and knowingly countenances installations by bookmakers and bucket-shop operators. (Who else has fifteen phones in one room?) Its only objection in Westchester was that the telephone surcharges were not running up; this it is opposed to. So long as you pay for talking, A. T. & T. is the greatest advocate of talk since Socrates. It does not pay its dividends by distinguishing between criminal and noncriminal talk. Or obscene talk.

It is not a trivial matter that a lady with a listed telephone is open to any stranger's obscene call. A. T. & T. simply advises such people to call police on another phone. (Still more talk.) But A. T. & T. could easily produce a device by which a woman in that situation could silently alert the operator or the police. But A. T. & T., with its charter, which is perpetual, points out that it is not in the business of public morality or public policy, any more than—or a good deal less than—you are. An obscene phone call also pays A. T. & T. ten cents.

Wire tapping, the newest threat to privacy and liberty, cannot at present be detected by public or private police except by examining every inch of telephone wire, and some taps are made by an unnoticeable use of paint. The telephone company, however, could detect or prevent it. The March, 1961, *Coronet* says: "Much wire tapping is made possible through the failure of the telephone companies to set up adequate controls and their laxness in combating wire tapping they know about. . . . It is difficult to believe that with the vast experience phone company engineers have developed . . . they could not discover ways to make wire tapping difficult, if not impossible." Most A. T. & T. publicity is about its electronic research miracles; what is asked here is a small and easy miracle, but one only useful to society, not to A. T. & T. stockholders in particular.

The miracles A. T. & T. likes include a recent one by which one can turn one's stove on or off by a specially coded phone call. (But appliance manufacturers haven't cooperated.) This delightful invention, which could lead to completely unde-tectable arsons, is entirely against public policy. A. T. & T.'s attitude is that if the public misuses A. T. & T.'s benefactions, that is the public's problem, not A. T. & T.'s. This suggests a free-wheeling irresponsibility that is breathtaking and begins to be slightly hair-raising. (But it's another ten-cent call.)

Businessmen have also complained to me that subscribers' de-posits totaling at least $100,000,000 (surely a rock-bottom esti-mate) do not draw interest at any rate fixed by law. The in-come is free money, as happy as any panhandler's. Business telephone charges are also twice those of residential phones. Why? Isn't this anticapitalistic? It suggests, at least, that A. T. & T., while encouraging futile talk, penalizes useful talk.

The citizen has had one single defense against the abuses of the telephone. That was simply to forgive the telephone com-pany the necessity to list his or her phone in the telephone book. It was at first startling when the telephone company showed signs of rage at this apparently innocent form of self-defense. Finally, with the approval of the Public Service Com-mission, it levied a charge of fifty cents a month, $6 a year, on anyone so anti-social as *not* to require listing.

This charge for declining a service (as if the customer were a child refusing its spinach) would appear invasive, dictatorial and illegal. But the situation was that millions of salesmen, dance instructors, charity drum-beaters, bucket-shop operators, slanderers, perverts and obscenity addicts were not getting their calls through, and were also bothering the information operators

(4,100 in New York City alone). A. T. & T.'s frustration at not completing these calls was driving it frantic. In New York City, unlisted numbers totaled 320,000 in 1958, 400,000 in 1960. After the New York Telephone Company struck back with its $6 penalty, it announced that 25,000 recluse subscribers had agreed to come into the telephone books. I would believe this only on a certified audit. The New York company announced its residence phones in 1960 as 3,500,000. But anybody who can add and multiply can see that all listed phones in the 1961 New York directories come to under 3,000,000, including business phones. My guess at unlisted New York City telephones would be over 500,000 and heading for 1,000,000 in a few years. Some people may evade both tax and limelight by listing under an alias.

A. T. & T. is a symbol of both the virtues and vices of industrialization which demands nearly perfect coordination and communication of all the elements of a society. Monsters like A. T. & T. fatten on the genius of men long dead, or often unrewarded, and fall into the hands of arrogant clerks, who try to enlarge their power in the total enormous equation. The question, whether in Bolshevik Russia or here, is: who calls which signals? I am afraid that A. T. & T. is calling some signals nobody asked it to call, and ignoring others it should be calling. In that case, under our system, somebody taps it quietly on the shoulder.

1961

THE PRISON

A CHILD, after he has done wrong, been caught, and while he is being punished by prolonged disapproval (psychiatrically, a poor way to punish), has a long, sad, lonely and highly moral vigil. Theoretically his views on life in this period should be of great value, but in fact he is only re-collecting his ego, not probing into the moral law. His mood is rather beautiful in a minor key, but useful neither to him nor to society.

This childhood poetry is repeated and multiplied in all the prisons of all the nations, though with differences. In America, the state and federal correctional institutions immure at any one time about 200,000 people, mostly men. This is about .1 percent of the whole population—about one in every 250 men. Each costs the taxpayer about $1,800 a year, directly.

The prisons, it is said by everybody including the prisoners, are failures. The worst failure of prisons is that they do not yet contain the great mass of serious and competent criminals, so different from the present inmates. It takes forty years to catch up with a Frank Costello and separate him briefly from his manicurist and the Copacabana night club. The members of his organization rarely experience the long, sweet sorrow of prison life. The actual prisoner has not thought to the point about life; Costello has; and the convicted criminal should not flatter himself that he is in Costello's class merely because he is a criminal. The prisons are for the failures; perhaps that is why the prisons are failures.

Both are, however, very expensive failures, and so we must

be grateful for a recent authentic revelation of the nature of the actual man now in prison in America. This took the form of a privileged poll of 500 prisoners of the Atlanta, Ga., Penitentiary by the prisoners themselves. The results appear under the title "Project Prisoner" in a special issue of *The Atlantian*, the inmates' own magazine. Since Atlanta has 2,700 prisoners, the sample is not complete, but its percentages of types of criminals are roughly the same as for the total prison population.

It soon becomes apparent in the tabulations that the results are meaningless when they are measured as of the whole 500, as if all kinds of criminals were alike. For surely a man reveals his character even more clearly by the crime he elects to commit than by the wife he chooses out of all the women in the world. He could not, he would not, anyway he did not, commit other crimes; he chose one or more in a narrow range. And the Atlanta survey begins to turn on the lights only when it breaks down its results into crime groups.

Before we go into these fascinating but difficult particulars, the crude over-all averages established for the 500 inmates were: age, 35.9; current sentence, 8.5 years; schooling, to the seventh grade; years spent in prison, 8.2; number of arrests, 11; previous sentences served, 2; age at first arrest, 18; average I.Q., 103.

To pay them the compliment of judging them as potential equals: a dismal crew, already architects of dismal lives.

The totality grows more humanly recognizable when it is divided into temperamental crimes given as 25 percent car theft (apparently an average and undistinguished crime), 14 percent narcotics, nearly 14 percent forgery, nearly 10 percent armed robbery, 6 percent larceny and liquor crimes and 4.6 percent murder. Any other groups mentioned here were down around 2 percent.

I take it that when one of these groups gives a group answer that is conspicuously off the norm for all the groups, we have something worth noticing. Unless it can be explained away by racial or social factors or the peculiar operations of the law, it is a clue.

On the I.Q.s, the stupidest were the murderers at 88 I.Q., followed by the liquor violators. The murderers were also the oldest (in their forties), had the least schooling and were among the best churchgoers. They were joined by the youngest group, the kidnappers, in low I.Q.s, little schooling and good church records in prison.

The brightest were the larcenists (112.5 I.Q.), the Mann Act violators, the narcotics cases, the forgers and the armed robbers. But all these had a little less schooling than the fairly stupid morals cases. The best churchgoers as a group were the narcotics and morals cases.

On the test of marriage, another dimension is given to the crime groups. The largest percentage of single men lay among the young and unintelligent kidnappers and the more intelligent sex criminals. The highest score in maintaining marriages went to the intelligent armed robbers with 66 percent, followed by the narcotics cases. In numbers divorced, the only startling figure is for mail-fraud cases who are zero single, zero married and 100 percent divorced.

Even in a secret, inviolable poll like this, one must be awed by the question, "Do you plan to continue in crime?" But the answers seem to me even more awesome: Yes, 11.3 percent; Don't know (figure "probably"), 17 percent; No (figure "maybe"), 71.7 percent. Figure some jokers both ways: the re-adventurers into crime must come to at least 30 percent, probably nearer 50 percent. The highest Yes figures were for the kidnappers, morals cases and forgers; and a lot of kidnappers and burglars didn't know. That small but remarkable mail-fraud group was alone in voting 100 percent No. It should now be added that this group reached the senior year of high school. The contrasting interest in more crime by the kidnappers and murderers becomes less ominous when one notices that their average sentences run for 59 and 35 years; indeed, the very frivolity of their interest may have inspired it.

"Is this your last time in prison?" ought to bring answers corresponding inversely to those above. And so we get a happy chorus of 100 percent Yes from the morals cases who had already avowed a considerable intention of continuing in crime. The burglars at 80 percent Yes also seem never to learn. However, the mail-fraud cases also voted 100 percent Yes; and these I seem to believe, since this answer corresponds with their 100 percent No to the preceding question. The murderers and Mann Act violators thought it a weary 37 percent possible that they would be back in prison, with Don't know, and this answer has some logical relation to their criminal intentions.

By now we can guess how they will all react to the prison situation. As to whether prison supervision was an asset, only the mail-fraud cases and the armed robbers gave a majority Yes. A ringing No was returned by the Mann Act violators (75 percent) and the murderers (71 percent).

Rephrasing the question to "Are officials here to help you?" did not change the responses much. The larcenists, narcotics cases, mail-fraud cases and armed robbers are not unwilling to say Yes. The kidnappers, Mann Act violators and murderers overwhelmingly reject any such thought.

Well, let's try again: "Do you find it difficult to adjust to prison life?" Here the kidnappers and the sex criminals are in agreement on the difficulty, but the murderers this time are fairly calm about it, at only 37 percent. The burglars are calmest of all at 10 percent, and the mail-fraud and liquor cases not quite as calm at 25 percent.

When we nag again on what is the prisoner's present attitude, the "hopefuls" are fewest among the long-term murderers (12 percent) and kidnappers (16 percent). The latter, with the longer terms, are younger and thus slightly more hopeful. The highest percentage of "hopefuls" is to be found of course with those feckless idiots, the morals cases (66 percent). At the next sober, reasonable level come the mail frauds, narcotics and armed robbers, as we had nearly expected. Of course, the words "hopeful," "indifferent," "resigned," etc., mean very different things to different individuals in this situation.

A few incidental sidelights on the group pattern can be added. In the matter of escaping custody, the high score belonged to the burglars (80 percent) followed by the larcenists (57 percent); the least enterprising in this respect were the mail-fraud cases (zero) and the narcotics offenders (2.7 percent).

The older men naturally feel most strongly that first offenders should be segregated, and these are the liquor violators, murderers, mail-fraud and narcotics cases.

The general average of the inmates who had had trades ran around only 60 percent, but the morals cases were at 83 percent and the mail-fraud cases at 75 percent. It is saddening to notice that the often estimable armed robbers here drop to only 43 percent, and are also the lowest in learning a trade in prison (23 percent). Perhaps these people are playing a game with the authorities, invisible to me, or perhaps they would be genuinely ashamed of any trade other than armed robbery. A less unexpected sadness comes with the fact that the young kidnappers are only 16 percent in the matter of having had a trade before prison. But again it may be asked: when does a man consider that he has a "trade"? What are the criteria of a "trade" and of "having" it? Can the writer of these lines be said to "have" a "trade"?

One must have begun to descry in the foregoing bare statistics the cloudy emerging outlines of some half-seen types of people, self-revealed almost unconsciously. One may be skeptical, but I believe much of this revelation is valid, for a reason inherent in data generally. These data were not taken to prove our point, but to prove something else, almost the opposite; that is, that there is a single, generalized prisoner who is a pretty nice fellow. This inquiry thus approaches the research, as it were, by the back window.

The useful conclusion is that treatment of prisoners might profitably vary with the crime, throughout society's relations with them. Taken in that way, none of them is hopeless.

Every undifferentiated statement that can be made about criminals has, from this point of view, the ring of nonsense. For example, James V. Bennett, chief of the Federal Bureau of Prisons and one of this country's leading penologists, describes "the more than 100,000 defeated, embittered, twisted, queer, handicapped and seriously neurotic individuals who pass annually through the gates of our prisons." This statement has some status as poetry and accomplishes the chief purpose of most writing on the subject: to prove that the man's heart is in the right place. But, as we have seen, each of Mr. Bennett's adjectives may apply to a majority of one group and not to another. Or all the adjectives may be said to apply to nearly everybody alive.

It is unnatural to house masses of men within walls, as the 5,200 at San Quentin, the 4,600 at Ohio State (the penitentiary), the 4,650 at Joliet. The result will certainly appear noisome, but to beautify the joint will prove little, and even to admit the prisoners' wives on occasion, as some suggest and as the Latin Americans, Russians and some Asiatics do, would have very different effects on different groups of convicts. It would certainly not help the 100 percent divorced mail-fraud cases, or the unmarried morals cases, and might incite them to riot.

The 500 prisoners at Atlanta are equally unhelpful when they try to reveal themselves as a totality. Thus majorities in the Atlanta poll say they had a happy home life, an average family background, were unjustly sentenced, usually tell the truth, write their families, don't see enough of their families, do not especially miss family life or sex, and so on. Anybody from President Eisenhower to Frank Sinatra might have returned these answers; they may describe everybody or nobody.

The truth is that a given period of a society creates its special crimes, and summons out its special types of criminals. We no longer have the terrible crimes of lese majesty and religious heresy, for which people were torn apart and burned alive. Evasion of income tax and alimony payments have been rotated into place. The harsh kidnapping laws were passed against hardened, middle-aged criminals and have produced the young, stupid, unmarried, churchgoing type. Car theft, a crime encouraged by all Detroit's glamorous and seductive advertising, is too widely attractive to produce any single type, so far as I can see. It is also among the least severely punished crimes. But after an act has been made a crime, it takes a given sort of personality, experience and mood to commit it. And this person in a different kind or period of society could easily have lived a blameless life. It does no good to say that society is positively to blame for the criminal and the crime; society is what it must be.

Society's problem is first to catch the criminal, and then, what to do with him. In some societies the answer is to kill him at once, which ends the individual problem cheaply. The second answer is to support him for life in confinement, but this is dreadfully expensive. The third is to give him a graduated punishment by confinement and then, with a pious prayer, turn him loose. The fourth is to try to understand him and somehow undo in a few years the self-destructive patterns which are, how-ever, the criminal's most cherished private universe. This last is current doctrine, but not practice.

One might say that if all veteran convicts were redeemed and rehabilitated, the contribution to society in a positive sense would be so negligible as to be unnoticeable. A William Sydney Porter does sometimes land in prison, but it is a long time be-tween O. Henrys. Still, I noticed that some of the writing in the Atlanta Penitentiary survey was quite creditable, definitely above average high school level.

But I think it is more important to look at the free boys from fifteen through seventeen now on the streets, among whom the hardened criminals will be chosen almost by accident or lot. If we can get those boys past a year or so without a first crime, and then a commitment to crime and a pride in crime, they will be real men at twenty-one. The human material here is so salvage-able, so valuable, so close to salvation, that the hearts of the officials dealing with juvenile delinquents must be perpetually breaking.

The first crime is the important one. Many respectable people have illegal fantasies, but they are not necessarily damaging to the character so long as they remain that. The fatal step of carrying the reckless fantasy over into a real act must present the new criminal with a wholly revised picture of himself, which he rather admires and can never lose entirely. When he is caught, this picture is socially confirmed. And society is in for fifty years of trouble, damage and expense.

The focus of society's attention should be on this first crime, long before the Atlanta prisoners are polled. Here should be in charge the most capable people we can find. A modest sug-gestion is that part of the answer at that moment is much less public attention, or none at all—that is, no newspaper attention. Newspaper editorializing on juvenile delinquency is to be complimented on its success at frightening old ladies, infuriating men and exhilarating the young, but otherwise it is the most useless conceivable exercise of the journalist's art.

1959

*T*HE PRIVATE LEFT EYE

A FOOLPROOF SUBJECT today for social scientists (a category that includes practically everybody) is that American society is going to pieces, the young are out of control even by themselves, the adults are irresponsible, and the individual is lost and obsolete. The numerous explanations (slums, slum clearance, the automobile, TV, the income tax, John Dewey, Kinsey, Marx, etc.) and proffered solutions will not be reviewed here. Instead, attention will be called to the odd cause-effect correlation (which is which?) between historic times of social dissolution and times of large professional police forces. This is an obvious, perhaps meaningless, fact which can be examined in complete confidence that it is a fact.

It is insufficiently remembered, or realized, that young democracies typically have no public police whatever. Public order is then everybody's business, but especially that of the family, the paterfamilias, the community or a special class. The right of the people themselves to keep order was recognized in the Second Amendment to the United States Constitution: guaranteeing the right of the citizen to keep and bear arms.

We hear verifiable stories of our fathers and grandfathers laying down the law in their communities and, because we think of their society as having been pretty much the same as ours, we are embarrassed for such bumptious exhibitions. But our society has added something to theirs: a police force. And subtracted something: we are a generation which most particularly loathes being conspicuous in public and whose first instinct is to disavow a public crisis, crime or disaster. The public crisis was

a challenge to our fathers; now it is a challenge only to the
official police. The private citizen is no longer any kind of a
policeman on his society; he has abdicated most of the public
part of his social talents.

Sensing these atrophied talents in himself, he therefore has
a romantic interest in the fictional private detective. He is much
less sympathetic toward the public police, perhaps half-sensing
that their creation was what cut him down to his present size.

The dates are important. The silent films' Keystone Kops
were a not very travestied version of the early city police, always running in a pack the wrong way. New York City's force
had its first effective overhauling in the 1890's. The first real
state police (excluding frontier rangers) was the Pennsylvania
State Constabulary in 1905. The Federal Bureau of Investigation is dated 1908. New York's state police followed in 1917.
These dates mark the beginning, or the recognition, of a new
world. In the 1920's there were still upper-class "cop-haters."
The private citizens who had formerly run the society did not
generally cultivate the new police.

The nations that most bitterly resisted public police were
Great Britain and the United States, the strongholds of personal freedom and the individual hoodlum. Sir Robert Peel's
introduction of a regular London police in 1829 led to riots.
The resentment must have been grounded in the citizen's intuition that he was losing his own police authority. Not so on
the Continent. Before World War I, the "best" police in Europe and probably the world were in Russia (including the
dread Third Section of the secret police), in Germany (three
policemen to each thousand of population), France (three), and
Austria (two). The histories of these countries may be respectfully noted. The least-policed nation in Europe was Switzerland.

A self-policing society may have its failures, especially in times
of general distress. In America, the crime waves of the prepolice
era have been part romanticized, part forgotten. The public

arm consisted only of constables, marshals and sheriffs, usually elected, and well aware that gunmen also have votes. The private arm was the posse or lynch mob which, besides being a mob, was a temporary confederation of people who had other things to do.

When things got too bad, it became the custom to call in the private police, at first the Pinkertons, founded in 1850. This remarkable outfit had as its trademark a wide-open eye (oddly and significantly, a left eye, or eye sinister) which has gone into the language as "private eye." Viewed as a midpoint between the citizen police and the public police, the private police throw a strange, oblique light on the great transition.

All sorts of odd people were feeling their oats, and the Pinkertons moved in on them, as one can see in *The Pinkerton Story*, and a large bibliography. Most of the great criminals from Jesse James up, down and sideways, were Pinkerton cases. The Pinkertons were the first to put a guard on a President (Lincoln). The subsequent period saw whole counties, such as Jackson County, Indiana, in 1863, ruled by gangs, who robbed banks and trains, issued counterfeit money and welcomed travelers into a hotel to be strangled in their beds. The Pinkertons found and arrested the leaders but lost them to well-organized vigilantes, who hanged them. Strictly private enterprise, at all three ends. And which of the three is one to admire the most? The public authorities were later powerless against the Mafia, or Camorra, or Black Hand, and the Molly Maguires of the Pennsylvania coalfields. The Pinkertons very ingeniously insinuated their men into these closed and suspicious organizations, and destroyed them. In the famous Homestead strike, the Pinkertons moved in frontally (a fatal change of style), surrendered to the mob and were murdered by the mob. Since then, the Pinkertons have turned their back on antilabor work.

The bad name of the private detective may go back to William J. Burns, once described as "the most famous detective we have ever had in this country." In 1911 he said: "[They] did not trust me any more than they trusted other private detectives. And I didn't blame them. Private detectives, as a class, are the worst lot of blackmailing scoundrels that live outside of prison." In thus beatifying himself by opposites, he did his profession no service. One of his big jobs was closing in on the McNamara dynamiters of the Iron-Workers Union, which had a truly awesome taste for red massacre.

In England, a parallel breakdown of the gentry's police function was evident as early as 1800. Gangs roved the streets of London, mugging everybody they met. In that time of the Napoleonic Wars, it was estimated that one man in every six lived by crime. Victims bargained with thieves to buy back their property. Murder was an ordinary hazard by day or night. A single London constable might have to protect five square miles, and this in a time of general disorder. The outlaw in man was loose again, and the aristocrats evidently cringed back from it. Even after the formation of Peel's police, the "bobbies" did not dare enter alone into some streets in Westminster. Already in London the criminal defiance of the orderly society had ceased to be an obligatory challenge to the citizen.

It is surely of some interest that the invention of communism practically coincided with the invention of the public police. Both were responses to the industrial society coming into being. Both agreed roughly on one thing: order must derive from the Center. Whether or not this is true, it seems to be the solution of all modern nations of whatever ideology.

But man remains the same, and continues to prefer the atavistic solution of the private police, viz., the Scarlet Pimpernel, Sherlock Holmes, the Pinkerton Molly Maguire or the FBI agent in the Communist cell. Thus modern man finds himself in a society that does not fit his traditional daydream about himself. This is less true in Fascist and Communist states where the citizen is encouraged to police his neighbor's political heresies. A similar attempt is now and then made in America by the so-called "anti-Communist" subversives, thus refreshing their sense of importance and social talent.

Generally the citizens in a free society have abdicated all police function. There remain the private and public police.

The American police forces are much smaller than is realized: only 316,000 in 1957, or less than two to every thousand of population. The total breaks down into municipalities 215,000, townships 15,000, counties 37,000, state 28,000. (All figures could undoubtedly be cut in half, if it were not for the automobile.) The total is completed by federal police, primarily the FBI, which operates very much like the old Pinkertons and in fact inherited the Pinkerton files on criminals.

The private police are perhaps twice the numerical strength of the public police. New York State, for example, has 671 licensed agencies. One national agency, Pinkerton's, has 13,000 employees; Burns has 11,000. Including many hotel, department store and ball-park guards, detectives who do not work out of any agency, and part-time workers, the country's total must come to over 500,000.

The jobs of the public police are pretty much in the open, having been assigned by legislatures and elected officials. The private police is assigned its jobs by a client, who does not want publicity, unless he is getting divorce evidence. Hence the agency does not want publicity. The "private eye" learns quickly that he cannot be a public mouth, or he will soon be out of business.

This secretiveness, so understandable and suspect to the private citizen, invites a longer look at the "private eye," for there is always the possibility that he may operate outside society and outside the law. Pinkerton's has official rules against bargaining with malefactors or accepting rewards, but most small agencies would not dare claim so much costly, and perhaps crippling, integrity. The stories of the late Dashiell Hammett, who had been a Pinkerton man, present "private eyes" whose characters and problems are said by experts to have a good deal of verisimilitude, or at least to be reasonably possible. Not only these stories, but the true stories of Pinkerton and Burns in the great days show that the detective and the criminal tend to understand each other and sometimes even love each other. This is perhaps an inevitable and human, but certainly disturbing, relationship. It would tend to separate the detective emotionally from his normal, noncriminal fellow citizens. It must be a perilous, if useful, gift to "think like a criminal."

It follows that if the detective is on both sides of the fence, there is no fence, and the criminal is virtually inside society.

The impossibility, or undesirability, of a detective's revealing his attitudes and knowledges to an outsider may compound his professional reticence, and make him feel like an Eleusinian priest. As exploited in Hammett's stories, the private detective may also have the terrible liability that he simply "knows too much." Of course, everybody in one way or another "knows too much," if about nobody else, at least about himself. But the private detective is suspect in the eyes of some very tough people, including the public police. And this may be why the big agencies generally hire retired public police.

But all private detectives soon master the arts of mystification. A writer in the *Manchester Guardian Weekly* said of the British variety, "Secrecy not only covers individual cases but also the general purpose of the agencies. . . . Telephone numbers are unlisted. . . . [Some agencies] deal with foreign powers, but which powers and their requirements 'we couldn't possibly say.' . . . One detective has four telephones on his desk: one is marked 'Arson,' the second 'Missing Persons,' the third 'Divorce' and the fourth, which is red, 'Secret.' " The protection of foreign personages of high standing was suggested as, in England, the most profitable line of work for "private eyes."

There is some degree of horseplay in this British report, as there is in England generally. But it is still true that an affectation of invisibility, a literally divine asset if it were possible, must somewhere merge into farce, and that this pose or ambition will naturally obsess the private detective in all his waking life, and so make him more or less farcical. But remember that he has inherited all the self-dramatization that the private citizen formerly had and has lost, and is inhibited from confessing it. He is loaded with a sense of importance and of social talent. His neurosis is exactly the opposite of that of the déclassé private citizen. It may be noted that private detectives do not talk much; they only look at you. This was formerly the technique of the private citizens who ruled the community by their presence. An old man who once threw an armed assassin off his porch, without words, naturally had some authority in the community. The word got around. This became local law, more powerful than written and legislated law. But not today. For today bravos from anywhere would come up the porch every morning to test the old man afresh. The first-comer would kill the old man, having no awe of him. The lesson the modern world has learned is not to present a challenge to anybody or anything, in the sensible recognition that a challenge increases the trouble, its absence minimizes the trouble.

A defect of the public police is that the very uniform is a challenge. It says that the man in it has no interest in the community except to find its faults. Such challenges are very invigorating to the young. Certainly society or government or the police themselves would do well to remove this challenge.

For the enemy of the people is not the police; it is the system of laws (excluding the Constitution) composed by lawyers, who also monopolize all our legislatures and constantly give the police freshly insane jobs to do. An elderly lecher killed the host of a children's party and critically wounded the hostess, and was disarmed by their sixteen-year-old son, at great risk. Another son cried out, "Dad is dead!" whereupon the first used the murderer's gun to kill him. And he was indicted by a Connecticut grand jury for manslaughter, when he should have been given a medal for doing his duty as a private citizen, not to speak of his status as a son and a human being. In such cases the lawyers' laws seem expressly designed to demoralize our society, to destroy the last vestiges of survival instinct in our people, to dissolve the last social cements that can save us, and, I must suppose, to make more work for lawyers.

The elaborated lunacy of our laws paralyzes the public police as well as the people and creates the private police, and in such a case anyone can see the deadly social process dramatized. Mankind is stripped of his last right even to have an emotion, and the lawyers flap down around the carcass to scavenge. In the bird kingdom this is a vulture.

The most familiar example of the appeal to the private police is from the marriage partner who suspects his or her mate of adultery. Since marriage is a credit system, the inquiry is merely a form of credit investigation in visceral terms, and may influence considerable transfers of wealth. Certainly the public police, under our laws, could not care less about such matters.

Nor will the public police do anything to help large corporations prevent injury to their expensive installations, though it is certainly public policy to keep the plant going. But the firm in turn does not much care about the public policy of trapping and punishing the criminals, since this might injure its public relations. All firms dealing with the public are at constant war with a criminal fringe, but emphatically do not want to make this a public holy war; instead, they want to pretend it does not exist. And so the firm hires a private police.

An example of the private police is the credit rating firm of Dun and Bradstreet, which has five detective agency licenses in New York State alone. The credit information it sells must indeed be obtained by a "private eye." In the old village, everybody knew everything about everybody; in the metropolis where the proved scoundrel can disappear, it is useful to have an agency that can and will discover that he has always been a scoundrel, if anybody really needs to know. And one does sometimes need to know.

Transfer into real life the popular magazine plot of a family man threatened with the torture and murder of his whole family. There is very little he can do in advance; he cannot even find out from the public police whether the man has a criminal record. (Try it; I once did.) A "private eye," however, can immediately get this information, and act on it.

In many situations, a citizen may rightfully need to know something he cannot find out himself about another citizen. If the other's life has been a mess, only hidden by the anonymity of the city, it is not unjust that he acknowledge the fact. This is the investigative function of the private police; and it will and must go on forever, under any kind of society.

Agency people like to play down their investigative work, and emphasize their harmless guard and patrol duties, the specialty of the large agencies. But the smaller agencies admit that two-thirds of their work is investigative, and only one-third guard and patrol.

In the modern world, the word "tail," meaning to follow unnoticeably, is all but obsolete. Pinkerton and Burns could follow their subjects for months without ever being detected. But the automobile has ended the golden age of surveillance. Now it takes two or three cars equipped with short-wave radio to follow one suspect in a car, signaling to the cars on the parallel roads when the suspect makes a turn. Few clients can afford this, with two men in each car. One alternative today is the patient watch or "stake-out," with relays of men.

This has been superseded in some cases by the electronic watch. The parabolic microphone can eavesdrop on a conversation a block away; the resonator radio transmitter, planted under a desk or bed, will broadcast private confidences for a mile; the new tape recorders can be carried in a pocket; telephones can be tapped in increasingly sophisticated ways (but could be blocked by the telephone company, if it gave a damn about public policy).

There would be no point in describing the transitional legal status of such devices. They are undoubtedly on their way to being outlawed by various legislatures and will be used more and more, at the calculated risk. The FBI now says that it is tapping ninety telephones on an average day. Some private agencies have done a great deal better than that. Labor leaders and business executives have tapped the wires of their associates. But anybody who does this is confessing something much more revealing than most of what he will discover: that he does not trust anybody. This can be a very damaging confession, and will never be forgotten.

This confession in particular is one that the public police should never permit themselves to make, although too often individual police officers do so. "Everybody is a potential criminal," says the police officer who, by association and susceptibility, is himself a criminal; but the whole subject of the criminal potential of any human being is far beyond the mental powers of any policemen capable of saying that. A man who says it is labeling himself evil.

If the history of modern police has been too brief, we can look at Ancient Rome. Under regal and republican Rome there was no police; the clans and the paterfamilias enforced the morals. The first public police were invented by the empire: the city cohorts, a branch of the army. In A.D. 6, Augustus created the night police, the *cohortes vigillum*. Furthermore, one cohort of the praetorian guards, in plain clothes, guarded the Emperor's house on the Palatine. With these innovations, the individual Roman was irrevocably diminished in his police power.

Without going into the Romans' views on punishment (they were too intelligent to have prisons, whatever one may think of the alternatives), it soon became clear that this police was against the people, but more against some people than against other people.

The danger in the evolution from the citizen police to the private police to the public police, as described above, lies in the loss to the society of the enormous police energy in the citizen's wish and need to keep order, and his superior effectiveness in enforcing a local code of behavior. If one does something one knows is wrong and sees the disapproval of all the people one has always known, effective law enforcement is in progress. This must be vastly more corrective than being grabbed and beaten by strangers in uniform, tried by other strangers and led neatly into a prison for an indefinite term in intimate association with the selectively worst strangers in the whole society.

It is entirely imaginable, however, that our abominable prisons are filled with the men once best qualified to fight crime and police their communities, but now entirely lost to us, because we have forgotten our history.

1962

*T*HE UNIVERSE AND
BUCKMINSTER FULLER

*B*UCKMINSTER FULLER personally has some of the characteristics of the universe: he is multiphased, concentrated, magnanimous and unforgiving toward error, consistent, contradictory, extravagant, saving, optimistic, undoctrinaire, patient, and indomitable.

These qualities are embodied in an old-fashioned, square-rigged gentleman, scrupulously courteous, rigidly honorable. Fuller has the manner of an early American naval officer and seems always to be facing into the wind. He has a deep love for boats, especially sailboats. He cites the invention of the sea-holding ship as one of man's greatest steps toward mastery of the unknown. The prehistoric shipyard, he points out, was the first real assembly line.

All that has been printed about Fuller—and it is a monumental file—actually reflects a small fraction of his total work and thought. But this does not matter, since anything Fuller produces—such as the celebrated tensile domes—is true to his general principles. These relate to literally everything in the universe, and he is actively involved with everything. He long ago set himself a lifework that demands inhuman energy and continuous, brain-breaking labor.

Fuller's most familiar concern is with industrialization. He accepts industrialization not only technically, using all its advantages, but also morally and philosophically. In Fuller's opinion it should be written "universalization." Modern industry uses some of the techniques of the universe in mass production, but it often resents and perverts them. Fuller preaches an almost religious adherence to the laws of the universe. His domes, for example, are faithful to the true tensions on the surface of a sphere. They do not really rest on the ground like a rock; they exist in space in tension like a tree.

In the present period, a peculiarity of Fuller's is that he is impossible to find at any given moment. He is in almost constant transit all over the United States and the world. Theoretically, he has a New York City telephone, and a base at Southern Illinois University, and other bases at his various enterprises, or at his daughter's in California, or his sister's in Maine. But most days of the year he is nowhere near any of these, and nobody is exactly sure just where he is. He is as unpredictable as the universe, but operates by equally predictable laws, if you know the laws. When Fuller goes somewhere, it is usually an indication that something is happening there, not in a political, push-pull sense, but in a universal sense of synchronization of energies. Lately he has been in England, Greece, India, and Japan.

It is not very revealing to say that Buckminster Fuller is the product of five generations of Harvard men and the grandnephew of Margaret Fuller (the Gertrude Stein to Emerson and Thoreau), but it is not meaningless. Fuller seems to have selected from his Boston traditions the idealism and independence, and to have scuttled the Brahmanism.

It is astonishing how many irreconcilable worlds Fuller simultaneously occupies: big business, Bohemia, the universities, the arts, the engineers, Madison Avenue, the editors, government, the armed forces, yachtsmen, society, and mathematicians, as well as his own special world. "Fuller is in the world; he has to be dealt with face to face," it has been said. This is peculiarly true in that he generally avoids writing letters or telephoning. When he talks, he wants to do it person-to-person, preferably without aid of electronics.

This may be why he has published so few formal books. His classic is still *Nine Chains to the Moon* (Lippincott, 1938). Material for twenty other books exist in intermediate form. A valuable introduction to Fuller is given in Robert W. Marks's *The Dymaxion World of Buckminster Fuller* (Reinhold, 1960), which includes 160 pages of photographs and drawings.

Buckminster Fuller can write for himself, but usually in a specialized language. Robert Marks's work comes, therefore, as a translation of Fuller into at least the English of the schools. As such, putting part of the Fuller mathematics and philosophy out in the open where they can be scholastically seen, assayed and handled, it may very possibly, even probably, open a revolution in thought. Fuller is not a philosopher in the mere sense of playing with semantics, but in the rare sense of struggling with the observed facts of life, or what he calls "the universe." It is always moving to watch one man engaged in this gigantic and loving fight, alone, overmatched and unblinking. And here, in this book, released from the bondage of the Fuller private dialectic, anyone can see the epic combat.

In the first chapter, when I found Dr. Marks translating the Fuller concepts—"valving," "regenerative," "synergy," "macro-micro-oscillocosm," "event constellations," etc.—it became evident that at last out of these concepts a visible explosion was taking place on the printed page. The experience of seeing them take shape in an assimilable idiom is much like seeing a genie rise out of a bottle on the beach and look around for the problem to be solved.

Since the book is itself a review of Fuller's work, a "review" would require quoting it in full; condensation of Dr. Marks's condensation is beyond my ability. He traces Fuller's point of view to Occam and Descartes: specifically, to "Occam's Razor," that assumptions must never be multiplied beyond absolute necessity (which ended a lot of medieval nonsense), and to Descartes' interest in "the totality of possible events." To operate between this classic negative and this positive requires both high discipline and high adventure. The combination is rare, and when it occurs, something is likely to happen.

The dymaxion house, car, bathroom, map, geometry, etc., presently happened, but in social terms nothing much happened, for about twenty-five years. In this fascinating period, Fuller's failure to cash in seemed to Henry Luce of *Life* and some dowagers to represent simply "failure," in the sense that the playwright, Arthur Miller, writes that "a failure in society and in business has no right to live." Fuller and his universe evidently did not know what Luce and Miller were talking about. For in fact Fuller was producing prototypes of things of vast potential use to "society and business," things that worked, were efficient and cheaply made. Society wasn't interested, *at that moment*, but the apathy did not dismay, or slow down Fuller, or even interest him in the irony that the "failure" was American society's. Dr. Marks's later chapters implicitly describe the painful satire on the American business world corresponding to Fuller's "failure." Actually the joke gets better all the time, but Fuller would not appreciate it; he is not at all interested in such ironies.

In the existing world, Fuller's position is necessarily confusing. The philosopher designation would be acceptable and harmless, except that he has been on the payrolls of big corporations like Armour, Phelps-Dodge and Time, Inc., and not invisible. Like Socrates, Fuller has known "everybody," he goes out in society, he is an old-school gentleman, he used to go to night clubs, he answers anybody's question at length and gladly suffers fools; he is physically powerful, able and gentle. One cannot escape the comparison to Socrates, himself a great gentleman, and a very patient one. But Fuller also has a staff of lawyers who carefully defend his innumerable patents, he constantly lectures at all the leading universities, and a kindly cynicism that is quite unnatural to him has lifted him out of the category of "mad inventor," a designation that never fitted the actual man.

Fuller is in the world; he has to be dealt with face to face. He may walk into a great corporation's board meeting; he may walk out of a Maine surf; he may be seen sculling a stalled motorboat in the Thousand Islands; or talking in the quadrangle of a South African University; or lecturing in Rangoon or Tokyo; or making a gentle point to Prime Minister Nehru; or clambering over one of his structures at any one of twoscore American universities. Whoever you are, he will try to meet you on your own terms and translate them to those of the universe, again like Socrates. All very well. But what kind of creature is this? To the big businessmen, as well as the little philosophers, it is obviously a monster. However, the former at least have at last embraced the monster, because he is necessary and profitable. Some corporations would be in trouble without the once-lunatic ideas of Fuller.

The philosophers might begin with the geometry on page thirty-nine. In this, which would interest Euclid, we begin by close-packing around one sphere as many same-size spheres as possible, and continue to layer on subsequent shells of same-size spheres. The first layer has 12 spheres, the second 42, the third 92, the last figure being the number of atomic elements. Oddly, these three numbers combined produce 146, the number of neutrons in uranium, the 92nd element. Add another basic 92, and you have 238, the number of nucleons in uranium, whose atomic weight is 238. In this relation of numbers, some insight is opened into the relationships of the atomic world and the structuring of the universe. From his packed spheres, Fuller derives formulas and a geometry of structuring in terms of lines of force. Mathematicians and engineers seem to be able to follow this with joy and understanding.

In a sense more practical than mystical, the Fuller mathematics hypothesizes a human society of increasing plenty and happiness, without politics, the reverse of the Socialist forecast. It is here that I must dissent, noting that Fuller, by no coincidence, is temperamentally optimistic and magnanimous. A beautiful future rams straight into the nature of man, which will probably remain selfish, hardhearted, shortsighted and thoroughly political, as will human society. Most people are more adept at expressing their meanness than their love, and actually happier in doing so. The Fuller universe offers us a better world, and can prove that it is there for the taking. But there remains the human perverseness that used to be called Original Sin. My resistance to the Fuller optimism can be ascribed to my share of the ancient disease.

The achievement described in this book is protean; but in fact it is only about a third of the whole Fuller body of investigation and speculation. Some of the rest can be found in Fuller's own *Nine Chains to the Moon* (Lippincott, 1938), in my *The Big Picture* (chapters on Universe, Earth, Current Events) and in the March, 1960, *Architectural Design*. But what is needed is publication of Fuller's tape-recorded lectures in five seminars. His lectures, if he is not allowed to edit them in his celebrated "feed-back" style, are quite comprehensible and wonderfully honest and exciting.

The worldly-naïve strain running through Fuller is that of a Faust who would try to convert Mephistopheles; he has repeatedly turned away when the devil would not play on his terms. A great magnate once told him that the way to get rich was to make things complicated; Fuller smilingly went on trying to make them simple. Henry Luce once told him he was a fool to tell everybody everything he knew; Fuller smilingly went on trying to tell it all, knowing that he was really telling it to himself and correcting it as he went along; while Luce, like the rest of us, hugged his own barren and shriveling secrets. Fuller proves in at least this one career that magnanimity, optimism and love of one's fellow man (plus enormous brains and hard work) pay off, as against greed, fear and suspicion (even with brains and hard work). The ordinary man has not even begun to understand how completely and effectively Fuller is on his side. This revelation evidently must come slowly, though it has already come to the young people in the colleges.

The communication with the whole people, which Fuller wants, may not really be compromised by his current status as the darling of the businessmen, a role he accepts only to be socially useful. These people need him, they will forgive him every dread heresy, for they cannot break his patents, hard as they may try, and they have tried. But whenever Fuller is confronted by anybody else's interpretation of his work, he betrays a politely concealed trace of unhappiness. The useful conclusion is, simply, again: "Fuller is in the world; he has to be dealt with face to face," not at second hand.

This may also be the reason why he has had only local successes with the professors, who can deal with a book but not with a living man. Professor Marks's book partly bridges this gap, and has already made the Fuller system assimilable by the faculties, in relating them to Occam's Razor and Descartes. The curious fact is that one can learn more about Fuller as man and thinker by reading a good life of Socrates. Still, he is not Socrates; he is Fuller.

Fuller takes the modern knowledge, not given to Socrates, that the universe is entirely composed of energy, and adds the accumulation of remembered human experience both before and since Socrates began thinking. This total, not money, he considers our true wealth. The energy is finite and cannot be decreased; the experience is constantly on the increase; the sum of true wealth is therefore potentially limitless. Having thus defined man's actual situation, excluding the crude estimates of politics, Fuller offers human society a "design science" that is comprehensive, as of the past, and anticipatory, as of the future.

This sounds reasonable and useful to a layman, but unfortunately industrialists, politicians, and professors were not told of any such science at their mother's knee, nor can they now find it in most current college catalogues. Nevertheless, American industry and government have found in the last decade that they have had to accept Fuller's structures as an indispensable part of the American establishment. Fuller's acceptance varies from nation to nation, university to university, but in general his definition of what he means by "universe" has not found orthodox acceptance by American academicians. And Fuller obviously does not want it, if it is to be given on a misunderstanding of what he means.

Fuller's revolution, a shocking one, is against the whole encrusted mass of traditional scholastic nonsense, revised from time to time but always without looking at the whole observable reality, *sans* nonsense. All that Fuller asks can be stated as: "Look at it. Use it. Forget about me."

The systems of the traditionalists don't work. The systems of Fuller and the universe do work. In the end, the controversy will come down to that.

The heresies of clean, precise thinking end up as faith, hope and charity. They dismiss all politics as after-the-fact temporizing, from Karl Marx to our own founding fathers. Since I like the founding fathers, why does this not dismay me? Fuller points to the great destiny for mankind, and I say that I know more about mankind than he does. Who is he to tell me that these creatures will ever be decent? And the wonderful hope is that I may be wrong, and Fuller right.

1961

TWO

SOCIAL
ASTONISHMENTS

*D*IAMOND NECKLACE,
THE AFFAIR OF THE

*T*HE QUALITY of a fine diamond is that it is (relatively) small, concentrated, intense, hard, impassive, beautiful and immune from change, age and decay. Diamonds reside at the very secret center of some human souls, the one thing in life worth saving in a disaster. Once even a queen, as will be shown, coveted certain diamonds in a way that in a wolf would be called ravening.

Those days have gone. The reason we can hardly believe in them began with the Diamantina mines in Brazil and was completed at the opening in 1871 of the bottomless blue-ground pits of Kimberley and De Beers. Whenever as much as that is added to the world, something else is taken away. What is lost, for example, is any capacity to understand what diamonds meant to Marie Antoinette. For one more adjective must always be added to describe a particular diamond's strange power. That word is rare.

There was once a reputable theory that diamonds were one of the causes of the French Revolution in which Marie lost her head. In histories before 1900 one can still find this theory indexed under "Diamond Necklace, The Affair of the." As the baskets of diamonds were trundled out of the Kimberley pit, everyone had to stop believing that diamonds had ever had the power to begin a revolution. About that time historians decided that everything was caused by economics. Should they ever rediscover that it is people who make all the trouble, they may also rediscover the fateful Diamond Necklace.

I should like to retell the story, for the diamonds' sake and also to investigate that dangerous branch of human deportment described as Farce, which can be more powerful than diamonds.

Farce in real life is much the same as farce on the stage. A perfectly acceptable human feeling or attitude is enlarged, exaggerated and "pressurized" until it is swollen and ridiculous. As this happens, unsuspected flaws in the conventional morality become absurdly, or insanely, obvious. The action is heartless; the characters are frivolous; the cunning clowns triumph over people of consequence.

Marie Antoinette was in fact a victim of Farce motivated by diamonds, though she later proved her personal courage at her imprisonment and death. When she bore a daughter to the huge, dull, young King in 1778, he gratefully offered to buy her the famous necklace, first assembled for Madame DuBarry by the Paris jewelers, Boehmer and Bassenge. The price of 1,600,000 livres might represent today about the same number of dollars. She should have taken it, but she was trying to be a good French wife and patriot just then, and she asked that the money go instead for a man-of-war to help the American colonists in their fight against England.

She had changed her mind by 1781 when she bore the King the first Dauphin, who died too soon for the Revolution. She had seen and touched those great diamonds some of which had probably come from the new Diamantina mines in Brazil. But this time, alas, the King refused her.

She took it well but the court was not deceived. "Everyone" knew that the necklace was for the Queen; it could be no other's. Marie was thus qualified for the farce on two counts: her real power over the government of France and her weakness for the diamond necklace. The diamond necklace waited.

But the farce hero was still lacking, the idiot who would dare to offer the necklace to the Queen.

A hush falls on the clip-joint of Farce. The outer door creaks. The expected customer is announced. He enters.

There is consternation. This is impossible. The man who seats himself can buy the necklace and needs the Queen, but he is not to be played with. There has been a mistake. This is a grandee known in every court in Europe, the familiar of every prince and also of every knavery and vice. He is far too powerful, clever and rich to take a role in Farce. As he casts a languid, seeing and knowledgeable eye over the scene, the bystanders recoil.

It is not only a Rohan, it is the most subtle and ambitious of the Rohans. This family had been a Huguenot house allied to the Guémenées, only slightly less illustrious than the Montmorencys, with the precedence and rank of foreign princes at the court of France: a consideration now much more obsolete than diamonds. This Rohan had a virtually hereditary right to the archbishopric of Strasbourg, a very rich see which made the holder a prince of the Holy Roman Empire, an eminence no longer coveted by anybody.

This last had been the choice of Louis René Edouard, Prince de Rohan-Guémenée of the Soubise branch. A product of the worst elements of the Bourbon court, he could scarcely be called a churchman at all. He preferred a life of gaiety and politics. Still he had been named grand almoner, cardinal (on the Polish king's nomination) and archbishop and abbot several times over. He had the blood of kings of Brittany, marshals of France, beheaded traitors, and he had an income equal to more than two million dollars a year. He was that abomination of ordinary men, the almost invulnerable man. He had only one liability. The Queen of France hated him.

As ambassador in Vienna until 1774, he had somewhat over-tried his invulnerability by joining the anti-Austrian party against Marie Antoinette. Carrying carefree cynicism a little further, he had made bold to carry to the Austrian Empress scandalous gossip about her daughter, Marie. He also made fun of the Empress in a court where there were no confidences. He seems to have had a vice of talking and writing much too much, but doubtless very amusingly.

Any part of this might have been fatal for another man, but the prince could almost afford to do as he liked. He had the friendship of kings, his position in the church, and his blood relatives who were stationed in key positions all through the court of France. The governess of the children of France and the Queen's closest friend was Madame de Guémenée until her husband, the prince's cousin, went bankrupt in 1782. The Queen could do nothing against the prince.

Her revenge was touchingly impotent. She indulged in the luxury of hating him.

This was not at all satisfactory to the Prince de Rohan-Guémenée. Despite his past offenses and the desperate problems of the office, he wanted to be named prime minister of France. He put it to himself that he would win back the Queen's favor.

All that was needed to that end was a miracle. And the prince did not consider that a miracle, at the court of France, was particularly outside his proved powers.

And so the prince too was qualified for Farce both by his power and by his weaknesses. If the Queen and the Prince were each more conscious of the power than of the weakness in her-self-himself, who will cast the first stone? In both the Queen and the prince the structure of feudal society had quietly collapsed; both were essentially incompetent and dishonest at their real jobs. But to bring them together in Farce, the genius of the farceur was still required.

The necessary farceur turned up in the person of a lady on

the fringes of the court, descendant of a royal bastard, who called herself Jeanne de St. Remy de Valois and had an adventurer for a husband. The prince, turning fifty, entered on a dalliance and, between dalliances, still talking, confided to Jeanne his hopes of the Queen. But, Jeanne told him, she and the Queen were very close indeed.

The prince had tried much more exalted embassies to the Queen and they had all ignominiously failed. He looked at this little nobody and must have thought, "What I need is a promoter. The others were too polite. This one is just vulgar enough to do it."

The aristocrat's perpetual faith in the promoter is of the essence of Farce. When the Russian Tsarina listened to Rasputin, when the German generals listened to Hitler, when the late Senator Taft listened to Senator McCarthy, we can always hear the same disingenuous thought turning over, "Ah! A man with the common touch. This is what we've needed, a promoter." The great promoters do not disguise their vulgarity; they make a parade of it.

But a promoter, like the genie in the bottle, may get out of hand, precisely because that is just what he plans to do.

The thing moved a step at a time. Jeanne was of course more influential with the Queen than all the others combined. She told the prince that the Queen had at least listened. She told him that the Queen had smiled. She told him that the Queen had looked pensive. She told him that the Queen would accept a contribution to one of her charities, through Jeanne. The prince pressed the money into Jeanne's hands, much more than was indicated.

The gap between the prince's opinion of his power and his real power was being closed by the farceur, at a fair price.

A little later, Jeanne gave the prince a letter which warmly thanked him for the contribution, and a correspondence budded between the prince and somebody who signed the name of the

Queen of France. (At the subsequent trial this turned out to be a forger named Reteaux de Villette.) The prince cautiously enkindled his end of the correspondence with all the protocol passion of which he was then one of the acknowledged masters in Europe. The bud seemed to open a little way, it faltered and then it was blooming.

It seemed to the prince that the writer of the letters was in love with him, not entirely to his surprise. Probably he too felt something in return, a humble and enlarging glory and ambition for which there is unfortunately no other word but love. He had always known that he had charm but this late, improbable dividend of his charm, just when he had feared it had left him, which would make him prime minister of France and confound his foes, must have seemed to him a confirmation that his entire approach to life had been mystically correct. The confirmation ran along the whole surface of his skin, for it must be remembered that his whole life had been couched in the warm bath of flattery. He was thus very gullible to this sort of reassurance.

Charm certainly has an important place in human affairs. But to depend on charm alone, as the prince had done, to accomplish anything useful is to become the puppet of anyone who will say only, "You are charming." Had he been power-less, or had he added charm to a real power leverage, the charm might have been of some use, but here he and his real power were standing solely on charm, which was a trap door. One can hardly imagine the incredulous, half-terrified hilarity of Jeanne and her friends as they read the prince's coquettish advances toward the Queen and composed, between tears, the Queen's shy and tender and wholly improbable responses.

To such a correspondence there had to be a climax. What else but a guilty but decorous meeting between the Queen and the prince? This was arranged by Jeanne who had had plenty of

time to think about it and who was, after all, completely con-
versant with the imaginary relationship, down to the last comma.
In Farce, the scene was absolutely compulsory.

And so, at whatever risk, Jeanne had to stage it. The prince
was told to present himself in a grove in the gardens of Versailles one night. A veiled lady was there. (At the trial it was
brought out that the lady was one with the odd name of Marie
Lejay who had been renamed by Jeanne, the director, Baronne
Gay d'Oliva. She is said to have resembled Marie Antoinette
in her figure and carriage.) As she floated through the shadows,
the prince approached and fell on his knees, offering her a rose
suffused with his hope and vanity. A voice said through the
veil, "The past will be forgiven."

The prince must have asked for another rendezvous but would
of course have been tenderly rebuked by the Queen's writers.
He could still contribute to "the Queen's charities," and did
so. Coincidentally, Jeanne bought a house and entertained on
a grander scale. It does not seem to have occurred to the prince
that his lavish subsidies to "the Queen's charities" might be
subsidizing Jeanne. Her solvency seemed to him, as to everybody, merely a proof of her intimacy with the Queen, of which
she spoke frequently. This gabble was believed, not only by the
prince, not only by the people of France later on, but in an
immediate practical sense by the jewelers who still had the
necklace. For the great diamonds of the necklace had been
patiently awaiting their cue in the farce. The jewelers, Boehmer
and Bassenge, asked Jeanne to draw the Queen's attention again
to the necklace, for they knew how much she wanted it.

As the climax swindle took almost visible shape before her,
Jeanne fell back in fright. This farceur seems to have acted
naïvely but the structure of the farce now rose before her, all
but complete, apparently awesome and frightening. The others
must have pleaded until the first paralysis left her. At last

Jeanne told the jewelers that the Queen would take the necklace but would deal through a very high personage, the Prince de Rohan-Guémenée.

Much has been made of the fact that the jewelers wrote the Queen of the transaction, and that she burned their letter. On such evidence, she has been accused of having sponsored the swindle of the prince. But it is far easier to suppose that her desire for the necklace and her hatred of the prince, aroused in a single letter, would have compelled her to throw the letter in the fire in thoughtless and imperious rage and frustration. She was in fact pregnant with the second Dauphin, and not in the mood for such games.

The farce wound on without her. The prince collected the necklace at the jewelers, promising to pay in installments. They were naturally transported by his haughty, semi-ecclesiastical manners, for such luxury tradesmen as jewelers keep to the last their respect for a dying but solvent aristocracy. The prince showed the forged authorization of the Queen's. But how unnecessary! Such a grandee could have anything he asked for: and how marvelous that he was now back in favor with the Court.

His carriage took him to Jeanne's house, which he had of course paid for. There he delivered the famous necklace of diamonds to a man he thought he recognized as a valet to the Queen. When the astonishing crystal beads had dropped out of the prince's hand, they were never again seen in France.

The joke may seem to have been thus completed but it was now about to be translated into real life, where everybody is always in deadly earnest. In this case everybody included the people of France and also the jewelers, Boehmer and Bassenge.

Immediately, the latter wanted to be paid. The prince, despite his 2,500,000-livre income, was not anxious to pay. He gave Jeanne some notes, which she nervously presented to the jewelers, but these were not satisfactory. The jewelers now went directly to Marie Antoinette.

What happened then is covered by a modern expression, "The wheels came off." Marie Antoinette told them (1) yes, she had wanted the necklace, (2) she had not ordered it, (3) she had not received it. This last was soon confirmed, for the stones were already being peddled in London by Jeanne's husband.

The Queen went through the whole gamut of ugly emotions, and settled on fury. To have been thought to love a man one hated might annoy the most phlegmatic of women. The Queen, not at all phlegmatic, chose to show her rage in a really theatrical way.

She waited until the prince was in his cardinal's robes in the palace chapel preparing to celebrate the rites of Assumption Day, August 15, 1785, and the whole court was gathered. There she had the Prince de Rohan-Guémenée arrested and removed to the Bastille. A good scene, but very dangerous.

The only sort of crime the prince could be charged with was of having entertained some truly impertinent misconceptions about the Queen. But in that day such thoughts still amounted to high treason, punishable by disemboweling, drawing and quartering. On the way to his cell, the prince succeeded in destroying the Queen's supposed letters, thus protecting himself against even that charge. The royal police were evidently lax. But in an affair at this level, where the influence of all the characters is prodigious, bribery and official connivance can be assumed at every stage. For the masks of Farce are off, and everybody is now in earnest.

The prince accepted as his judges the *parlement* of Paris. The people of Paris, and of France, were instantly on his side and against the Queen—the arrest scene had backfired. The devices of Farce had openly divided the key figures of feudal society. Whichever won, the integument of feudal society would be cracked wide open, and both parties would seem perhaps corrupt, but worse, ridiculous. The people saw that all the others had been acting in Farce and were forgivable; only Marie Antoinette had acted in real life; and the people would not forgive her her fury. The others were puppets; she was the victim. This was certainly not the result intended by the prince, Jeanne or the jewelers. But it was the result. For no farceur in history, whether Buckingham or Rasputin or Hitler or Mc-Carthy, has ever foreseen the result of his farce in real life.

The trial resulted in the acquittal of the prince, to the delight of Paris. Jeanne's husband, who had stayed in London, was condemned to a life sentence in the galleys *in absentia*, the ideal condition for a sentence to the galleys. Jeanne was sentenced to be whipped, branded and imprisoned for life. She received the first two parts of the sentence. But she soon escaped from prison —whether by the influence of the Queen or the prince—and wrote her memoirs abroad, ungratefully charging that the Queen had been a party to her swindle from the beginning.

The damage had already been done. The farce had given the mob the catchword, in this case "Collier de la Reine" or "Queen's Necklace"; in other historic cases other words: "Tyrant!" "Papist!" "Privilege of Parliament!" "Justice!" "L'Incorruptible!" "Jacobin!" "Sansculotte!" "Hors de loi!" "Vive l'Empereur!" "Teapot Dome!" "Remember the Maine!" "Jew!" "Communist!"

Had the royal couple had the respect of either the people or the aristocracy, the Court's desperate financial situation and later France's economic condition could have been solved in one of a dozen ways. Today high school students could tell you how to do it. The fatal disease was in the hearts of people, not in the economic system.

Within three years the mob stormed the Bastille with the cry, "Collier de la Reine." Within seven years the guillotine knife dropped on that lovely neck on which the "Necklace of the

Queen" had never been destined to fall. In the minds of the people, the necklace had come permanently to rest around the Queen's neck, as if to mark the very line at which the knife must strike, not caring that it had all been only Farce.

The story of the necklace should teach us to treat Farce with as much respect as a dynamite train. Once launched, the Farce of the Diamond Necklace could not be turned back. Its inevitability must make any serious person shake in his boots, for it suggests that a farceur of genius can destroy the most imposing structures of dignity. And today a medium for Farce that did not exist in the eighteenth century is provided by the daily newspaper.

One may be given further pause by the fact that most social convulsions are immediately preceded by a period when stage farce is fashionable. When Farce becomes too familiar in real life, the playwrights transpose a little of it to the stage in a last desperate effort to expose the hypocrisy and save the state. Sometimes, perhaps thanks to the playwrights, the crisis is safely passed; sometimes it is too late.

Stage farce was giving its warning as far back as Aristophanes' plays in Athens, which were followed by the Peloponnesian War and the ruin of Athens. In more recent times Don Quixote was followed by the Thirty Years' War and the ruin of Spain; the second Buckingham's farce, The Rehearsal, ushered in the final troubles of the Stuart dynasty; and Sheridan's theater in the London of 1775 opened a forty-year period of almost unbroken military disaster. Stage farce prospered in France in the latter eighteenth century, followed by the Revolution; again before 1870, followed by the collapse of Napoleon III; and everywhere in Europe around 1910, followed by the First World War. Stage farce had a frantic and mordant gaiety, especially in Germany, during the 1920's, followed by a worldwide Depression, Hitler and the Second World War.

Until quite recently farce has meant to most people merely

bedroom farce, which exposes the hypocrisies and unrealities inherent in the condition of marriage, yet has notably failed either to destroy or correct the institution of marriage. Farce, it is comforting to know, can sometimes pick a victim too large for it. But a more ominous sort of farce has lately erupted.

1958

$\mathcal{H}$EROD'S CHRISTMAS

$\mathcal{A}$ REAL BUT not unpleasant personal issue for every American every early December is whether to send out Christmas cards, what card to choose, and whom to send it to. Nuances of religious tact arise in the transmission of a given card, pietistic, devout, witty, sacrilegious, abstract, or merely jolly, among Catholics, Protestants and Jews, not to speak of the other faiths. A Catholic receiving a Holy Manger card from a known atheist may feel he is being patronized; a Jew receiving the same card from a Catholic may feel he is being bullied. And so on, in endless detail.

A great many people (five of my correspondents this last Christmas) have since 1949 lit on the gracious solution of sending out the U.N. International Children's Emergency Fund (UNICEF) cards. In this way they not only honor Christ's birth, but also help save the lives of some 56,000,000 of His favorite people, children, at the season when the Christ Child was being hunted down by the mercenaries of Herod Antipas. UNICEF may be the only effective indubitable proof that there is a hope for mankind "on earth as it is in Heaven."

And so the UNICEF Christmas cards, naturally, raise new Herods who send out to murder the little ones, all that can be found, in case the One should escape and give His name to the day of Christmas. These latter-day tetrarchs are the Daughters of the American Revolution, 1025 Commonwealth Avenue, N.W., Washington, D.C.; Lawrence Timbers, American Legion, 317 First West, Seattle 99, Washington; Carl McIntire, a former Presbyterian minister, 756 Haddon Ave., Collingswood, New Jersey; Billy James Hargis, P.O. Box 977, Tulsa 2, Oklahoma; and Mrs. May Gaskill, officer of a local chapter of the D.A.R. in Barnegat, New Jersey.

"Then Herod, when he saw that he was mocked of the wise men, was exceeding wroth, and sent forth, and slew all the children that were in Bethlehem, and in all the coasts thereof, from two years old and under." In slaughter, a large generosity is indispensable. And so, according to the same Gospel according to Saint Matthew, "In those days came John the Baptist, preaching in the wilderness of Judaea. And Saying, Repent ye, for the kingdom of heaven is at hand."

The ancient words must surely come home to the Daughters of the American Revolution, Timbers, McIntire, Hargis, Gaskill and the others, perhaps in their dreams, as they send forth to slay all the children from two years and under, and surely they must sweat a little in their sleep, even as Herod, and no more sweetly.

Before we review the operations of these modern Herods, let us first see what UNICEF does in the world, and how.

UNICEF now feeds and cares for about 56,000,000 children and some mothers who are not members of the D.A.R. It has treated 31,000,000 victims of yaws (a charming tropical skin disease whose symptoms are similar to those of syphilis); 11,000,000 for trachoma and conjunctivitis; a million lepers; vaccinated 134,000,000 with BCG, a deterrent against tuberculosis; and eliminated endemic malaria in large areas by the use of insecticides. It supports 6,500 main health centers and 12,300 village centers, and is constantly trying to expand its services to the children of the world. It is doing something about more children's pain than the ordinary human being can bear to think about.

To get UNICEF aid, a nation must ask for it, match every dollar with two of its own, and admit UNICEF personnel to supervise it. Possibly for the last reason, the USSR has never asked for aid, or received it, though it contributes 2,000,000 rubles annually.

UNICEF's first job was to salvage the children of war-torn Europe, whether Communist, Fascist or whatever. Aid to Communist nations ended in 1950, except for Yugoslavia. Later Poland asked for aid, and accepted UNICEF supervision of it. After the Hungarian uprising against Russia, help was rushed to Hungarian children, without regard to their politics.

The United States contribution to UNICEF is subject to the condition now that it not exceed 46 percent of all governments' contributions (in 1953 the proportion was 68 percent). In addition, the United States contributes supplies of surplus dried milk. In 1960, ninety-eight governments made voluntary contributions, usually their own currency. Even the Communist nations seem ashamed not to contribute, and nine of them do. As an American, one can only wish that the American contribution were greater, not less, for this is precisely what America is supposed to stand for.

Like all U.N. agencies, UNICEF necessarily includes nationals from Communist states: three out of thirty on its executive board, and four out of the 556 members of its staff. American staff members are screened by the FBI. The Executive Director has always been an American: Maurice Pate.

In 1961, the United States allocation of $10,000,000 was not due until the other nations' matching funds were in hand; meanwhile the United States, as a bookkeeping transaction, lent the U.N. some of the funds earmarked for UNICEF. However, on the due date in late December, the United States presented UNICEF with its check for $10,000,000.

Now enter Herod.

The attack on UNICEF began in October against the churches' program of turning children's "Trick or Treat" Halloween rounds to the useful purpose of UNICEF collections.

The attack on the UNICEF Christmas cards burgeoned around December 1. How the word spread I do not know, but the original lie factories were those named above: the D.A.R., Timbers, McIntire, Hargis and Gaskill.

The commonest lie was that UNICEF is a tool of communism, irreligious and 80 percent subsidized by the United States. This figure is achieved by including an evaluation of the dried milk at the rate of the U.S. Government's price support of dried milk within the United States. The UNICEF milk is surplus, or valueless. Perhaps the D.A.R. would rather see it used as fertilizer instead of fed to hungry babies.

"Of total contributions to UNICEF, the United States contributes nearly 80 percent" (Hargis). "These cards have nothing to do with Christmas, God or Christ. They are . . . part of the drive to destroy Christmas as a distinctly religious occasion. . . . Americans, and especially children, are being conditioned to accept peaceful coexistence, which is a strategy of the Communists just now to lead us into surrender or defeat" (McIntire). This man wants to change Christmas into a warmongering festival.

"Shall we awaken some day to find that Dec. 25 is being celebrated as a 'One World Peace Festival' instead of a Holy Day of the Christian Church? Christians, be alert! . . . The cries of the children of the world rend our hearts. Let us respond in the Christian American way and save them from being forever in bondage to the charity of the welfare state" (D.A.R., "Report to America").

As if this were not bloodcurdling enough, a New Jersey D.A.R. chairman, Mrs. May N. Gaskill, conceived that the UNICEF Christmas cards were a "Communist-inspired plan to destroy all religious beliefs." Mrs. Gaskill's mailman was presently staggering under bags of UNICEF Christmas cards, at least 400 of them sent her by adoring University of California students.

Hargis of Oklahoma got really fundamental in revealing that the U.N. is the creation of "careful Kremlin planning," detected by his keen eye in a sentence in *The Daily Worker* of Jan. 6, 1936: "The real issue is collective security before it is too late." He then follows the Kremlin trail to Dumbarton Oaks and Yalta. As one who reported those times, I must tell Mr. Hargis, "The jokes end right here."

The horrid tidings of the Herods went on the air from Bob Siegrist of WLS Chicago, Martha Roundtree of WOR New York, and McIntire on some New Jersey stations. It was picked up by various columnists.

But some underground communications system was at work. All across the country local newspapers received a letter from a reader, usually a lady, who parroted the corrupted "facts" processed by Timbers, Hargis, Gaskill, McIntire, *et al.* UNICEF has a map showing the incidence of the aboveground explosions.

Certain thoughts and even sentence structures reappeared endlessly all over the country. "The Soviet Union does not permit UNICEF to operate within her borders." (It receives no aid, but sells the cards.) "Communist countries receive twenty-five times more than they contribute." (Crazy!) "Eighty-seven cents of every dollar collected goes to run UNICEF." (The administration figure is about seven cents on the dollar.) "It renders no service to children or to mothers or citizens of any country." (What? What?) "The greetings printed on the UNICEF cards contain the greetings printed in the Russian language." (Some cards use all five of the official U.N. languages, including Russian; others use four languages; others are blank.)

The bedlam gets still better: a reader writes in the Monterey *Peninsula Herald:* "All the money collected this year for UNICEF went to help make up Russia's deficit in the U.N."; another in the Denver *Post:* "From the beginning, the U.N. has ignored God"; others in the Baton Rouge *Advocate:* "Three-quarters of U.S. contributions went to Communist or Communist-dominated countries"; in the *Daily Hampshire Gazette:* "UNICEF money goes to Communist countries and is handed over to the officials, not to the children, and then disappears completely." The *National Review* and Lee Mortimer in the *New York Mirror:* "UNICEF contributions buy guns to shoot Katangese." This last has a beautiful, stark, clean villainy, but the *National Review* retracted the next week.

Wild, untrammeled, feckless lying like this makes for dull correcting. UNICEF patiently wrote every paper pointing out the facts. Decent citizens protested as best they knew how. The Detroit *Free Press* gave space to an especially heavy Donnybrook, instigated by a D.A.R. lady. One woman wrote in the Phoenix *Republic:* "The best way to give vent to my feelings in the matter is to buy just as many UNICEF cards as my budget can possibly stand, and then buy some more."

A similar thought seems to have occurred to Jacqueline Kennedy, who announced publicly that she had bought 100 UNICEF cards. Pope John also made his annual contribution to UNICEF of $1,000, accompanied by a warm message.

The U.S. sales of the cards in 1961 set a new record at 10,000,000 cards and an income of $1,250,000. This was matched by sales in the rest of the world.

The untidy affair gives us some depressing information about the isolationist Right in America. In the first place, it shows itself hard-hearted to the point of inhumanity, including its womenfolk. Secondly, it is stupid. And thirdly, since many of the fictions cited above could not possibly have been innocent, it is dishonest. In view of this diabolism, one is tempted to advise the Right to give up its foolish search for a program that is intelligent, honest and godly, and instead simply embrace four-square the platform of the Black Mass. The Devil is waiting.

Perhaps the most disgusting sentiment I read was this: "The D.A.R. contributes much of its time and money for the benefit of children, in . . . stressing love of God and country." The D.A.R. is in favor of children, if pious and patriotic, even if dead. The kindly voice speaks, and one turns to see that it issues from a monster.

1962

THE END OF SLAVERY?

THE WORLD, they say, paraphrasing Lincoln's more lo-
calized prediction, "cannot endure half-slave and half-free."
Since freedom has remained for most of human history a rare
and dearly bought prize, defended man by man and generation by generation, this lovely proposition, glibly parroted by
our own statesmen and publicists, may herald either utopia or
another long night. It is especially ripe for cross-examination at
the present moment.

Given the great flexibility of the words "free" and "slave"
and also "endure," we can take the proposition as simply
sloganeering to the end of giving "freedom," in any definition,
to a people before Moscow gives them Communist masters.
The West's idea of freedom is negative, on the assumption that
the freed people will then invent their own positives. If they
cannot think of any successful positives, Moscow is loaded with
them and will magnanimously replace one slavery with another.
The West is more demure.

The "freeing" of Black Africa (the part of Africa south
of the Sahara) in this context seems to me an absent-minded
enormity that cannot now be reversed. The status of "slave"
has been abolished, but in a world still full of masters. The
West has reversed 500 years of Western history, while Russia
gladly accepts custodianship of the old tradition. Black Africa
is thrown like a broken toy on the scrap heap for anybody to
pick up. One gets the impression that it has been judged worthless by the masters of the West. And the people of the West
must have begun to wonder what exactly their governments

think they are doing. Most baffled of all must be the Belgian ladies who were gang-raped in an oddly friendly way by Congolese soldiers who were asking the ladies' officer husbands not to desert the Congo. A sympathetic defense of the rapists was actually heard on an American radio discussion program, though late at night.

Lunacies of this sort have to have a historic explanation. In this case it is that the United States is the paramount power in the free world, and gives the signals, knowingly or unknowingly. Since 1917 the United States has had a blinkered commitment to the magic phrase "self-determination of peoples," while avoiding any commitments to them, once self-determined. Of about 100 million people self-determined after World War I, a little over 3 million actually voted to be so in plebiscites; riots proved a more effective means to that end. Is it very radical to say that this American policy invited the rise of Hitler and World War II, and might easily do as much for World War III? The "freedom" given the Poles, Czechs, Yugoslavs, Finns, Lithuanians, Latvians, Estonians, Transylvanians, etc., was that of a child thrown into deep water by a father who walks away quickly. The inevitable "rescue" of these waifs was begun by Hitler and finished, with some failures, by Stalin. The "rescue" of China and Southeast Asia was begun by the United States, and has had much the same finish.

This American blueprint for freedom is not new. A century earlier, the United States had guaranteed a similar irresponsible freedom to the Latin American regimes, whose rescuers since then have been largely indigenous, in conformity with the guarantee. The specific fragmentations into sovereign states had very little point except for Portuguese Brazil and, of course, most island republics; for example, so little was known or cared about the Incan Empire that it was split half a dozen ways; the Mayans ended up in both Mexico and Guatemala; large empty areas are still in meaningless dispute. These creations could as easily have been united as fragmented still further, as Panama was detached from Colombia. Several have Indian majorities nearly as "submerged" as anybody in Africa. Several, as in Haiti and Cuba currently, are ripe for class and race wars.

Events in Asia and Africa strikingly repeat this old history, under the same remote, disinterested, faintly troubled blessing and best wishes of the American Republic.

Further, the United States now blesses the birth of new sovereignties which slam their doors on the rest of the free world and at a time when migration is again on the increase; that is, we seem to disapprove of any more migration and development. Most Americans will deny that their own pioneers won a victory for (Communist word) "colonialism," or "imperialism." They were instead champions of exactly that eternal and blessed hope of man, migration and development. But the indigenes, we now seem to say, own the property, even if they cannot use it or defend it. This sort of property has been regarded by the chancelleries for a long time as a "vacuum," invariably open to trouble.

The current policy is supported, of course, by a literature. For example, in the *Saturday Review* recently one could read about South Africa, which has 10,000,000 Negroes and about 3,500,000 whites, 60 percent of the latter unfortunately Afrikaaners, Hitler's former friends. The article said: "The cosmos does not permit proud, coarse, nasty little sadists forever to torture, encage and starve helpless men, women and children. A mountainous debt of rage is accumulated, and it gets paid off in an explosion which wipes the tormentors off the face of the earth. . . . When will the blood bath come?" The author, a white man, further elaborated the call to blood in his book, *The Death of Africa*. One must be as dismayed as if a Negro had counseled the massacre of troublesome Negroes. Have we so soon forgotten that this solution was Hitler's for the Jews; and that these solutions must be paid for?

"Black Africa for the blacks," is the slogan here. One remembers "Germany for the Aryans," "America for White Protestants," "Palestine for Arabs," "India for Hindus," all accompanied by more or less bloodshed, rape and rapine. Not even the groggiest liberal can dare to abhor the principle in one case, and adore it in another. If Black Africa must be exclusively for blacks, all national doors may properly slam shut. But the world is not going in that direction. Africa cannot be an exception; it cannot turn into a human zoo, a feral preserve for the law of the jungle.

Black African society is much more primitive than were those of the Aztecs and Incas when the conquistadors arrived. The Congo tribes differ materially in talents. The tribes around Leopoldville are considered by many observers a degenerate race. The Luba-Lunda group of Katanga had a well-defined empire. The most advanced are generally plains-dwellers showing some Arab influence. The tribes to the northeast were overrunning the country when the Belgians arrived to stop them. A Western-style politician, even though black, soon appears to all these people not very different from the former white rulers. In Nigeria, the conflict is still more outlandish, for a medieval society with turreted castles flourishes in the north. In Uganda are the Bantu aristocrats, the Hima, who want their own kingdom back. And then there are Africa's great killers, the Zulu, who depopulated a million square miles with their splendid invention, the *assegai*, and would march, on command, over a cliff.

America has one great asset in helping Black Africa: talented and dedicated American Negroes. Rafer Johnson, our remarkable Olympic athlete, has already offered himself to the U.S. State Department. America is in fact the one country that has this asset to so high a degree; Russia doesn't have it at all. I suggest, then, in passing, that our schools badly need courses in African languages, especially Swahili.

The problem of the empty areas, in the current excitements, can be put into further perspective with two more easily checked facts.

The first is that the great powers of the moment hold a more imposing overbalance of brute might than any former great power has held in all history. The Communist world or the free world, either one, can slap down any difficulty in its own neighborhood by showing only the least of its weapons. Neither can be bluffed by the other, as we have seen in Hungary and Tibet. A scheme for inciting the two great power blocs to cancel out their overwhelming powers in conflict might seem very attractive to a playboy head of a small, new-made, painfully impotent state. To suppose that this thought has not occurred to some of the new heads-of-state would be to underrate the human mind.

The second fact is purely demographic and has to do with the frequently heard statement that the "colored races" dominate world population. The word "colored" means nothing; anything that doesn't live under a rock is colored; and even race means little or nothing to the Moslems and Latin Americans. However, world population in 1950 divided as follows: Caucasoids 58 percent, Mongoloids 33 percent, Negroids 9 percent. Crossbreeds confuse the race picture but do not much affect the Negroid percentage. Another difficulty is the Chinese figure, now inflated sometimes to 700,000,000. It was 460,000,000 in 1948; 640,000,000 by United Nations estimate in 1957; and 580,000,000 by a Rand McNally estimate in 1959; all such estimates seem to me dreamy masterpieces of a propaganda ministry. If the ministry doesn't soon get it up to a billion, the staff will all be executed. Remember *Lebensraum*.

The Negroid race deserves a better share of this world than

that 9 percent, but it probably cannot handle Black Africa un-aided. No solution will be offered here by me. The elements in the various situations must first express themselves. African farce and tragedy will provide material for novels for the next ten years. The city mobs will riot and the tribal centers of power will test their strengths. The most ominous of the tribes—and their silence has been remarkable—are those related to the Moslem world to the north. The real African movements are hidden; they are obscured, rather than revealed, by silly riots.

The trouble is that the slaves have not been freed; they have only been turned loose to find new masters.

1960

ℬLOODBATH FOR
BLACK AFRICA

𝒩OW LET US look at the book, *The Death of Africa*. One would wish that a million Americans would read Peter Ritner's brilliant and rapid (other adjectives will be given later), almost-up-to-the-minute story of Africa's peoples, politicians, assets and liabilities. Why they will not is that the book inevitably resolves into another "Hundred Neediest Cases," for which Ritner is asking from the United States six to eight billions of dollars, for an open-ended period.

The book is only about Black Africa: from the southern edge of the Sahara south. Freedom, absolute or within the British Commonwealth or French Community, has already come or will presently come to Tanganyika (population: 8,500,000 blacks), French Black Africa (25,000,000), Nigeria (34,000,-000), Ghana (5,000,000) federated with French Guinea, Belgian Congo (13,000,000), Somalia (1,500,000) and of course Ethiopia (15,000,000). To say that these more-than-100-million Negroes have any real hope of freedom is something Ritner would like to say but cannot quite get out. Indeed, he is inclined to suggest that the land, economy and traditions dictate some form of communalism, i.e., no private ownership of land. For the people themselves have largely ruined the land, as by overgrazing the plateau and deforesting the jungle —mistakes not yet made in the similar area of Brazil. Ghana's ebullient new dictator, Kwame Nkrumah, The Lion of West

Africa, was smart enough to inherit a treasury of $500 million derived from the British-developed crop of cocoa, now unfortunately blighted. Because his money is liquid, he is richer than America's only billionaire, J. Paul Getty, but Ritner thinks he needs more from the United States.

Ritner would prefer as investors, however, the gambling American swashbucklers of a past age, who would, of course, be met by the new Negro swashbucklers of Africa. Even as he asks that the memory of Cecil Rhodes be kicked out of Africa, he urges that Africa's future depends on new, but nonexistent and unlikely-to-emerge Rhodeses, with fresh money.

Still, there are prosperous areas of Black Africa and these invariably contain a measurable proportion of whites. Southern Rhodesia has 2,600,000 blacks, 200,000 whites; Northern Rhodesia has 2,200,000 blacks, 75,000 whites; Nyasaland 2,700,000 blacks, 9,000 whites; Kenya 6,000,000 blacks, 60,000 whites. Finally, South Africa has about 10,000,000 blacks and 3,500,000 whites, divided about 60-40 between Afrikaaners and the English-speaking.

The keystone of Ritner's "solution" for Africa is to get the West to abet and foment the browbeating, emigration and/or massacre of these white minorities in Africa. The "racial bloodbath," he says again and again, is coming. He speaks of the "absolute inevitability, of this 'atrocious catastrophe.'" His own quotation marks must only mean that this "supposed catastrophe" is no catastrophe at all, but a necessary relief and richly deserved. But before this happens, Ritner is willing to lead U.N. expeditionary forces into Southwest Africa, Angola and Mozambique, to take these areas away from South Africa and Portugal; and he is also to be busy shipping into South Africa "secret organizational and material support to the 'democratic'" (again, those grinning quotation marks) "revolutionaries inside the country—exercising the most painstaking care (but this will be a tricky matter) to discourage the Africans from rising until they can really defend themselves against the machine guns and pursuit planes of the Afrikaaner."

Ritner is 33 years old; or somewhat older than Tom Sawyer. I am older than Tom Sawyer and I cannot joke about the massacre of nearly 4,000,000 white men, women and children, who are just now caught in a rule of "red-necks," much like those of the American South. The Afrikaaners too are poor compared to the English-speaking population, who actually own the country. Perhaps the Boer War has to be fought all over again; perhaps it was unwise to give the Boers the political benefit of their numerical majority among whites. When democracy becomes the rule of the mob, it becomes a disaster, and has become so in South Africa. Ritner's solution is to bring in a bigger mob.

Only toward the end of Mr. Ritner's book does his buoyant, glib, smug, doctrinaire bloodlust step into the open, naked and unembarrassed. Until the last three chapters, he is reasonable, persuasive and fascinating, but by then, evidently in the assurance that he has painstakingly made a case, the keening begins: "Kill! Kill! Kill!" (The response to this of *The New York Times* reviewer was a prim "Some of his forecasts and suggestions are extreme.")

Robespierre was after all a Frenchman; Ritner is no African and had spent only three months there when he wrote this book. Perhaps he has already turned to other problems, having solved this one.

Ritner writes as if the 125,000,000 Negroes of Black Africa were about to turn into the terror of the world. This in a period when the relative power of the great powers is more stupendous than ever before in history. Africa is not being given its freedom out of fright but, I suspect, out of indifference and euphoria in the capitals of the West. The U.S. has world power and doesn't want to use it. And so it is encouraging the former systems of world government to dissolve into new sovereignties whose only connection with the world is a seat in the United Nations Assembly. Since this is also the period when any nation that has acquired one atomic bomb can start a world conflagration, this new bedlam may end in disaster.

Ritner sounds like Hitler and the late Senator McCarthy and all history's mountebanks who speak with this same bouncing, authoritative, merciless, over-the-shoulder incisiveness, ending the confusions, putting our mind at rest, and bringing on the whirlwind.

1960

REPORT ON THE JUGGERNAUT

*G*RANTED, it was an astounding achievement to get 70 million motor vehicles rolling on some 4 million miles of hard-surfaced roads—to man, fuel, service, park and garage them. If any foreigner cannot believe in the phenomenon, he can witness it any day: nearly 2 billion vehicle-miles per day, requiring 3 million barrels of petroleum per day, killing over a hundred people a day, injuring over 12,000 people a day in 33,000 accidents, and steadily growing, like an insane cancerous growth, to some horrid inevitability. On Sundays there are more moving parts on the roads than there are on Mondays in all the factories. The American people daily apply the greatest massed horsepower seen in all history, to get from here to there and back.

The fact that far more economical transport is available was perfectly obvious, but unfashionable, four years ago. There was no visible reaction to the statement then: "Because a single bus or train takes between twenty and 1,000 cars off the roads, we must certainly allocate subsidies to buses and, in particular, railroads. . . . If the railroads were equipped to carry 20,000,000 passengers a day, the huge subsidies for highways could be cut down to size" ("Our Strangling Highways," *The Nation*, April 28, 1956). The next year the thought was repeated: "One train can carry a thousand [motorists] to work. This fact is currently invisible to the American public, and will remain invisible until the day it becomes plainly and horribly visible. The automobile as now used is an extravagance that no ecology can afford; nor can this one" ("Knight in Two-Ton Armor," *The Nation*, April 13, 1957).

Such simple survival ideas tend to float impotently, like a germ in the Arctic.

But not forever. The courage has at last come to official agencies to resort to real solutions of the traffic problem. The New Jersey Legislature has passed a bill giving a $6,000,000 subsidy to nine commuter railroads. Los Angeles is considering rapid-transit lines, and "urgently requested" the state to build future freeways with space for rapid-transit rails. San Francisco will probably vote this November on a bond issue for a comprehensive rail-transport system. Philadelphia has already begun paying subsidies on a small scale to commuter railroads, and is considering further overhaul of its transit system. Chicago was the first major city to run transit lines down the green interspace of expressways. Connecticut's Public Utilities Commission has recommended that the four states served by the N.Y., N.H. and H. give it subsidies.

This all looks very anti-Detroit and un-American, but is in fact the counsel of last-ditch desperation. *The Wall Street Journal* recently gave some telling quotes: "The automobile has not merely taken over the street; it has dissolved the living tissue of the city. Its appetite for space is absolutely insatiable; moving and parked, it devours urban land, leaving the buildings as mere islands . . . in a sea of dangerous and ugly traffic" (Columbia professor of architecture). "Highways have gotten completely out of hand" (Director, American Society of Planning Officials). The highway boom is "a murder plot against our urban areas" (planning consultant). "It's almost axiomatic that you can't build enough highways to solve the commuting problem" (Stanford University traffic analyst).

Such doom-crying might also have gone unheard had not the roof finally caved in. This event came to the mayors of the great American cities in the apparently innocuous form of the 1960 U.S. census. Here was the catastrophic news that a number of their cities had actually lost population since the census of 1950—an unprecedented blow not only to the politician's self-love, but also to the city's share of state taxes. In such roundabout ways does crisis finally bring itself to the attention of politicians. Patriotism is never enough.

The immediate problem is to keep cars out of the cities' downtown business and shopping sections, now approaching the impassibility of an Amazon jungle. One way being considered is to slap tolls on the approach highways (as if car costs were not already high enough to convince any sensible car-owner). These monies can be given the commuter railroads. Another is to keep all vehicles out of the downtown area. Fifty cities, according to *The Wall Street Journal*, already have such plans. For human beings—that is, pedestrians—these "malls" will seem like a paradise regained.

If the tide has turned, it has picked the ironical moment when the federal government's $41 billion highway-building program is at full flood in the opposite direction, aiming to pour yet greater and less assimilable congestions of automobiles into the cities.

The federal government has affected a complete impotence to control the automobile, while at the same time financing five Congressional investigations in five years into its killing and ruinous ways. It still flatly refuses to assist commuter railroads in any way.

Yet even this dinosaur has at last been moved to a preliminary eye-blink: the first House of Representatives vote on whether to ask the automobile industry to produce safer cars. The cars affected were only those to be bought by the federal government, perhaps 10,000 a year: a very small tear in a

dinosaur's eye, and yet a sign of life. Detroit vigorously opposed even this blink, on the grounds of cost to the govern-
ment(!)—the highway budget is a $41 billion subsidy to De-
troit, supplying the tracks for Detroit's wheels—and that the
bill would constitute a subsidy to the safety-device manufac-
turers(!). On this Alice in Wonderland level, there was lively
debate. Exasperated by the nonsense, one Congressman asked
for the history-making roll call. The first open vote on safe
automobiles showed 265 for, 125 against, 45 not voting, in
August of 1959 (H.R. 1341).

The federal government's awed deference toward Detroit is
not necessary or any longer fashionable. Even the New York
Republican Club has issued its own research on automobile
safety as a matter of public policy. It says, "The new requests
[for safety changes in cars] are also unique in that a larger
number have been opposed by auto manufacturers. . . . Differences in what policies are desired are plainest between the 'medical and consumer' groups and the 'automobile and highway
promotion' groups. . . . The automobile and highway groups
. . . state that there is little need for design-safety legislation."

"It is charged," says the Republican report carefully, "that
speed and power are available considerably above driving abilities of drivers, beyond their possible need, and above what
public roads can handle"—all, it may be added, in violation of
public policy and private survival interests.

No male driver and few female drivers will permit their
driving abilities to be deprecated in this way. Nearly every
American is convinced he or she is a "good driver," meaning a
superior helmsman, gas-pedal-pusher and braker, and coordina-
tor of the three functions. But driving on a public road is a
social act; the test of a "good driver" must be social: does he
maim or kill, or cause others to do so? The skilled drivers are
generally those who do the maiming or killing, or skillfully

start the chain of events that forces someone else into an accident. Such a "good driver" may get out of the jam, leaving the wreckage behind, but his skills can be admired criminally.

The vote in Congress, 265 to 125, probably included exactly 125 of this kind of "good driver." The vote did not divide by party, but may have divided by age groups, for this seems to be a visceral matter, well below the neck.

It has been brought out that the worst place in America to walk is New York City—yielding over 450 pedestrian corpses and 13,000 cripples a year. It is also said officially that, at present rates, "every person now living in New York State faces the statistical prospect of becoming an accident victim at least once during his lifetime." This inevitability does not apply to any other misadventure imaginable, except only death itself.

In this area of the "good driver," the crusade has hardly begun. The "good driver" naturally tries to get into situations that challenge his skills, such as hitting a traffic light at 40 m.p.h. just as it turns green; his high score is relative to the other drivers, and takes no cognizance of the fact that a spastic, a rheumatic, or a mother with baby carriage happens to be standing right in his brilliant track.

If the preceding car goes through a turning-red light, he is honor bound to follow close and fast. It is therefore no fault of his if the crossing pedestrians are only halfway across the avenue when the lights turn against them, and have to hope that the oncoming cars do not number any more "good drivers." We can all describe a hundred situations in daily life where the bravura of the "good driver" endangers a dozen lives, where the flashing burst of speed, the dexterous left turn, the broken-field zigzag, the nifty grazing of a pedestrian, the bluffing engine-racing just before the light turns, spare one driver a few seconds' delay, and another human being forty or fifty years of this painful life.

Stated in these terms, the proposition could be built up to the point of equipping all pedestrians with machine guns, as a counterforce. If this were done, say, one day a year, varying the day for each avenue, without notice to drivers, the just would unfortunately die with the unjust, but we would soon have very few "good drivers" left on the roads. I know a number of old ladies who would set up shop on a good corner and lay down an indiscriminate barrage, with considerable justification, remembering past concussions, fractured pelvises and mid-traffic hysterias invited by truck drivers smilingly gambling their moving ten tons against the lady's trembling 110 pounds.

Everybody behind a wheel is potentially guilty; but the guiltiest, in my observation, are newspaper trucks, laundry trucks and government vehicles of all kinds; in general, the lower the function, the more dangerous is the driver. If he despises himself, his work, or people, he may be a killer. Some racial antagonisms also seem to be actively sublimated in driving.

A simple and bloodless way to get the dangerous drivers off the roads was suggested here ("The Ribicoff Remedy," *The Nation*, Jan. 24, 1959): to ask all the people to report reckless drivers to a central office and to investigate anybody who drew too many complaints. This too simple idea fell into a dead silence until, to my delight, it was revived in the July *Harper's*, but reserving the right of complaint to specially appointed motorists. I would suggest that a driver in the thick of traffic is in no position to copy down a license number; I prefer using all the people. But either way, the experiment is worth a trial.

Somebody else is intensely interested in dangerous drivers: the Association of Casualty and Surety Companies, whose members are not especially keen on paying the bills out of the insurance premiums. The cost of accidents this year will be $7 billion. The association, says its general manager, "maintains a round-the-clock vigilance to protect the insurance dollar against the raids of ambulance chasers, professional claim hikers and organized fraud practitioners. . . . The association's index system, a clearinghouse for personal injury claim information, [clears] over 2,000,000 claims per year. Nearly 15,000,000 personal injury claim records, now contained in the current files of those bureaus, lace facts together as methodically, precisely and quietly as a spider spinning a web."

So the angel of mercy that follows the slaughter and bloodletting turns out to be, not Florence Nightingale, but a spider! Lawyers who deal with insurance company claim adjusters tell me that this is an accurate self-portrait. Victims who never think of collecting anything for their injuries are far more common than those "professional claim hikers," a designation that might cover everybody who asks for anything at all. In fact, the insurance companies pocket billions from the undemanding stoicism of a large part of the population, and would dearly like to encourage such stoicism. They hate jury trials, where the stoicism ends and the jury tends to turn into a lynch mob. And actually they like that figure of only 2,000,000 claims "cleared" (not necessarily paid) in a situation where 4,500,000 people are injured annually by automobiles.

Somebody else who ought to be interested is the people. Yet most of them are willing to let things go on as they are, and to take their chances.

This peculiar, almost suicidal attitude can properly be blamed on the failure of the mass media to tell the people what the actual situation is. The mass media's delicacy in the matter is understandable, for to ask them to perform their normal patriotic function would require them to insult the reader and, worse yet, the advertisers. In such a dilemma, patriotism is not enough.

1960

*O*UR EPHEMERAL

CIVILIZATION

*E*VERYBODY KNOWS that much of the furniture of our civilization is designed to have a very brief life. Monumental as the sum appears at any moment, incredibly more momentous than the sum of any other civilization in history, the parts are individually ephemeral. Thus, the factories and skyscrapers, the automobiles and trucks, the roads themselves, the housing developments, the household appliances, the enormous factory machines and the kitchen pots, the plastic screwdrivers and the paper towels, all foreshadow their obsolescence or collapse and replacement. (All except churches and college campuses, perhaps.)

It will be proposed here, however, that we are even just a little more ephemeral than we are quite prepared to be.

For if there is one thing we are sure of, it is that we are leaving a full and permanent record of all our doings, experiments and conclusions. Many a library contains nearly 5,000,000 bound books, as well as masses of manuscripts, maps, photographs, art reproductions, microfilm, etc., beautifully indexed and ordered to exhibit to a researcher a thousand years from now every detail of our transient splendor and magnitude. Harvard's library, for example, has more than 5,000,000 volumes. Comparable mountains of paper are accumulating all across America. If a great writer, artist or scientist is ignored today, we can imagine that no great harm is done posterity, since he will be found intact in all the libraries. The high mortality of records—of the work of a Sappho, Menander, Aristophanes, Leonardo or Haydn—cannot, one thinks, happen here.

But wait a minute. A recent analysis of modern paper shows that the whole record of the past fifty years will have turned to indecipherable powder and tatters by A.D. 2000. The carefully ordered mountains of books and pictures will by then be useless moraines of sawdust. In the present way, our civilization's slide into oblivion will be more rapid and complete than that of the first *jongleurs*.

The details of the approaching library disaster can be found in the April 24, 1959, *Science:* "Permanence in Book Papers," by W. J. Barrow and Reavis C. Sproull, both paper experts. Books, once the chief end of paper production, are now a 2 percent factor as against newspapers, magazines, shopping bags, containers, towels, toilet tissue, wrapping paper, etc., which have a brief function. For years, paper technologists have hardly thought about permanence and have hardly ever seen a sheet of paper a hundred to a thousand years old. Ancient papers are only museum curios to the modern paper trade.

Certainly in 1906 the Library of Congress made every effort to produce a really lasting book when it published Thomas Jefferson's records of the Virginia Company of London on all-rag paper. Yet by 1928 the first volumes were falling apart, possibly "because of an excessive use of aluminum sulfate and rosin in the sizing." The bad air in cities, with its burden of sulfur dioxide, is often blamed for such deterioration. But according to Barrow and Sproull, this is a very minor factor and affects only the outer edge of the paper, if anything.

The ancient writing materials, papyrus, vellum and parchment, were very durable; and so were the early papers, introduced into Europe after the twelfth century. These were mildly alkaline or very slightly acid. Their durability is ascribed to the presence of calcium and magnesium compounds "introduced either during the bleaching of the rag with extract of wood ashes or through washing the rag with water containing bi-carbonates of these elements."

The first bad news for paper came when carbon inks were replaced by iron-gall inks which eat through the paper. Later additives in making paper were generally acid and destructive: first, potassium aluminum sulfate in the sizing in the seven-teenth century; now alum-rosin sizing. These acid details are hardly worth repeating here; librarians can find them in the Barrow-Sproull report. Whether acid paper is cheaper, easier and more profitable to make, the authors do not say. They care-fully describe the tests they made on all sorts of modern book papers, with the M.I.T. folder-endurance tester and the Elmen-dorf tear-resistance tester. All that need be repeated here is that they found conclusive evidence that virtually no book pub-lished after 1900, and not many just before that date, will be legible in, at the most, fifty years. To quote them:

It has been found that modern books—even those written with a seri-ous or scholarly purpose ("nonfiction") and published ("to last!") in hard bindings—are deteriorating rapidly, and many of those issued twenty-five to fifty years ago are now almost unusable. The paper of an average American publication of the first decade of this century retains only 4 per cent of the folding endurance of a typical new book paper of today. . . . This typical new book paper itself shows low initial strength (for ex-ample, folding endurance on the order of only 20 per cent of book papers already 200 to 500 years old) as well as indications that it is subject to rapid deterioration.

On this evidence, the enormous printed wordage of the last two generations is less significant for posterity than the ripple pattern on an ocean beach. It is true that some haphazard and fractional reprinting, as in paperbacks, will give some works another brief gasp of life. Much recent science is already partially obsolete, and new textbooks will always follow one another, heel and toe. Somewhat as the *jongleurs'* works had a garbled word-of-mouth life, our writers will have a fragmentary survival in quotation. It would indeed be shaking to suppose that by about the year 2000 everyone who has used the printed word in this period, would be, in the literal sense of the word obsolete, "completely used up."

But not so fast. The authors of "Permanence in Book Papers" tell us at last that something can be saved, perhaps all. The way to redemption is to take apart the hundreds of millions of bound books in the libraries of record, soak the sheets overnight in a solution of calcium and magnesium bicarbonate (the formula is given), then rebind. A semi-skilled worker can do the bathing part at the rate of about 2,500 ordinary pages a day; the rest of the process is periodically necessary routine in any library.

The librarians will probably balk at this arduous and expensive imperative for some time. They can be allowed another ten years' delay for most books, though about then it will be too late for a good many of their modern treasures.

This matter of the ephemeral books must hold for us a much wider, or classic, significance than that of a fortuitous, and corrigible, error in the modern manufacture of book papers.

"Ephemeralization" is in fact a key word in the industrialized ideal held up by writers on industrial civilization, including me. It has been said, quite properly, that the tools and fixtures should be increasingly lighter, more efficient, more easily replaced, more economical of materials, and that society should never be absolutely committed to the tools and fixtures of even the recent past.

We will pass over the irony that, as in the libraries, we are more ephemeral than we had known or intended.

But at its most reasonable, the doctrine of ephemeralization overlooks some possibilities. One is the possibility that some stage of past performance may have been much more efficient than the present stage; and that the only way of return is by means of the old, obsolete (but lost) models. Another is that to some degree society is always committed, more deeply than it knows, to the tools and fixtures it is using. A third is that mankind's true wealth can always be defined as a kind of capital, which cannot afford to be ephemeral. Under this heading come the total acreage of useful topsoil, the water table, the wild flora and fauna, the insect life, the mineral resources as related to annual consumption, the total of good, solid shelter, and of course the good condition of the knowledge of the past in the libraries of record. Respect for these assets and the desire to keep them healthy constitute a kind of cultural and ecological capitalism, which must often regard as abominable the works of both communism and financial capitalism.

This thought can be finished without using the words "entropic" or "anti-entropic."

For on the bay of Naples, a beautiful example of the non-ephemeral is at this moment coming to light after 1,900 years, under the direction of Amedeo Maiuri, Director of the National Museum of Naples.

Herculaneum, a town of only 6,000 people, comparable to many American suburbs today, was overwhelmed by a muddy landslide from erupting Vesuvius on August 24, A.D. 79. Thus we can now see the arrangements of people who had planned, not primarily for permanence, but for continuous use and enjoyment and pride. Herculaneum, in contrast to our American suburbs, had a beautiful theater, a splendid palaestra or gymnasium, a highly decorated basilica, two public baths, a regular city plan with fountains at the intersections, an abundant water supply and the famous Villa of Herculaneum full of sculptures and a library of papyri made to endure. The upper class of this provincial town had large, beautiful and permanent mansions with a view of the sea. The large middle class lived in comfortable homes with newly painted dining rooms, well-watered, shaded gardens, and mosaic floors. (The apartment houses of the second century had not yet made an appearance.)

People who have seen the part of the town already exposed express a desire to move right in, and find an anticipatory sense of happiness there. A genuine love of the community, the opposite of the cold concrete hearts of such city-planners as Robert Moses, has left a spiritual patina on the marble, bronze, mosaic and stucco of the dead city; and this cannot be ephemeral.

Compare old Herculaneum to American towns with many times the wealth and three or four times the population: Culver City, Calif., Highland Park, Ill., Morristown, N.J. and Port Chester, N.Y., all well above the average American town in local pride. Where are the baths, the fountains, the gymnasia, the fine libraries, the palaces and the tiny gardens? The American theaters, of course, would be for movies—and would be now half-empty. Even the once abundant water supply has run short for many American towns of this size. In every department, at every social level, the American towns are shamed by Herculaneum. Even at plumbing and sewage disposal, Herculaneum bests them.

Other, less admirable features of imperial Roman civilization are not here our subject. But the kind of sound, thoughtful, non-ephemeral building seen at Herculaneum must have deepened the awe which the Roman world impressed on the barbarian. This world did endure for another 400 years, and its legend remained Europe's ideal until the nineteenth century, when at last the title of Holy Roman Emperor was abandoned, in 1806.

One would like a little of that durability for the legend of one's own civilization.

And let it be emphasized that Herculaneum knew the difference between permanence, an unnatural and impossible condition, and the nonephemeral. Only sixteen years before, it had been reminded of its impermanence by a disastrous earthquake. The citizens were still rebuilding when Vesuvius buried them in a permanence of 2,000 years.

1959

THE TRAGIC
ENTERTAINER

*T*HE SEARCH for the tragic hero goes on. The martyr is still brought into the Colosseum, composed, twitching, crawling or dragged in feet first; but his identity has changed.

This was seen when several lively murder trials were swept quite off the front pages by the hurt feelings of an entertainer who five nights a week is in the living rooms of between five and ten million families who have TV sets. The tragedy was that his audience had not been permitted to hear him tell a joke. His network's Standards and Practices Committee had cut it out of the taped program. The next night Jack Paar said his last words from the center of the arena and walked out on the show. Forever? Hardly; he returned this week, the joke apparently forgotten.

It will be agreed that this affair plunges tragedy to a new low of triviality, nearly as ignominious as that of Arthur Godfrey's firing of a mediocre singer for a want of humility.

But the newspapers gave it headlines day after day and tons of wordage. Every nuance was investigated; it seemed to be of critical importance that the reader get exactly right the shadings of the newspaper's opinions on Paar's soul, public and private manners, taste, home life; and of course most readers already felt toward Paar more friendly intimacy than they felt toward most of their relatives. This made it as important as if their little girl had been snubbed at Sunday school.

Still, one can see why Jack Paar was immediately enraged. There is nothing more infuriating than to tell a joke in good faith, obviously trying to please, and then to find a lot of pompous jerks, suddenly swathed in the moral law, bearing down with their rules of good taste flapping. No joke can stand up. Even the very great jokes can get you into trouble. And you will never get out of trouble by explaining the joke.

Since this is so important, I will say that the tragic joke was one based on another I heard twenty-five years ago. A husband had told his wife that his club had given him a silver cup for the best account of the happiest moments in his life, and that these were the times he had spent in church with her. She later tells a member of the club that she simply cannot understand her husband's story, since he had been there only three times: once before they were married, another time when he had fallen asleep, and a third (which I have forgotten). Of course he had won the prize for giving his happiest hours as those in bed with her.

Paar's joke, as everyone in the United States now knows, took a similar misunderstanding, this time Wayside Chapel for the English initials W.C., meaning bathroom. Nearly any special disposition concerning chapel services would be funny if misunderstood as of a W.C. The formula is a classic.

Good taste is another of the subjects on which everybody has to be an expert. Not only the columnists, but the man-and-woman-on-the-street, expertised: "questionable," "poor judgment," "indelicate," "inept," "improper," "blue," etc., etc. Paar thought the Hearst press was leading the pack, and this meant Dorothy Kilgallen, Lee Mortimer and the TV reviewer, Jack O'Brian, but not Walter Winchell. Certainly the Hearst papers suddenly sounded wonderfully pure. Their views on religious good taste are certainly of moment; however, they run a regular comic cartoon about a foolish little monk and, if one wants to play this game, many people regard that as in distinctly shady religious taste. A monk's vows are very serious. Furthermore, Hearst anticommunism seems to me as feeble as it is frantic, in that it relies almost exclusively on Roman Catholic doctrine, surely not the capital objection to communism among about 150,000,000 Americans. There are, at least for me, better reasons for hating communism.

Kilgallen had guessed wrong and gone West to cover a murder trial when the Paar tragedy broke in New York. She stormed back to announce that all the other reporters were idiots, only she being cute enough to see that "The whole routine was as elaborately choreographed as an Agnes De Mille ballet; Paar felt the need of a great surge of audience sympathy to distract from the criticism he'd been getting, and NBC realized the stunt would cause front-page headlines from coast to coast. . . ." This merely indicates the fury she was in at having missed the fun, at seeing anybody else get publicity, and at not being first with the answer. In the Colosseum, her scoop would be that the martyr gave the lions ptomaine.

Morality, somebody has said, is a subject that lends itself to exaggeration—and that is what makes tragedy. The easiest, safest and most comfortable thing any human being does is to disapprove of another. Seeing this fatal genius in mankind, Christ asked men please to concentrate on their own trespasses.

If we try a little de-exaggeration, Paar's joke looks all right, especially at midnight. Furthermore, some of the steam leaks out of the recent TV quiz scandals where the tragic hero was Charles Van Doren. For an obscure citizen to accept the answers from the examiner before the examination, in order to play an assigned role, is scarcely wicked at all and would be only laughable if there were no prizes. There is wickedness here of course, but it lies with the examiner, and with the sponsor who requires that the answers be given out and the mockery continued. The citizen has no power and no responsibility; he can only watch the nonsense with his jaw dropping. But the tragedy settled on Charles Van Doren because he was the one in all the living rooms whom the people liked and trusted.

In the case of both Jack Paar and Charles Van Doren, we see the abuse by the venal bureaucracy, the invisible ones, of the naïve, boyish, innocent individual, each time on charges of an imperfect innocence. And this is in line with sacrificial practice in all cultures and all times.

To look ahead to the new era of tragic heroes—the TV hero meets the first requirement of tragedy: he is conspicuous; and the second: he is committed to a role, his "public personality"; and the third: he has enemies (executives, writers, critics, the competition and anybody who doesn't tune him in); and the fourth: he is essentially alone, while conducting his great work like a lumberjack walking a log in a whirlpool.

The shape of the new tragedy comes clearer when we see further that he is a comedian, or semicomedian. Dean Martin and Jerry Lewis break up their act; Sid Caesar and Imogene Coca break up their act; Milton Berle and Jackie Gleason go off the air; Henry Morgan is in and out of hot water; and all their hearts, we are to believe, are breaking.

If you think a comedian is not fit for tragic heroism, just look at comedians. They are especially highstrung. From being continually the life of the party, they are naturally hated by their friends. They look for jealousy, and always find it. They were, in the majority, very poor boys, and many had drunken mothers: witness, by their own stories, W. C. Fields and Jackie Gleason. Their acting triumphs over life are manic, and hence not easy to systematize for regular profit. They are show-offs, but not pretty: witness no names here. The differences in talent are disastrously obvious; and they can never be reduced. They live in a perpetual madhouse, and they must seek out their enemies nightly, at Lindy's Restaurant in New York. They are in every real sense out of the world, and yet they must keep contact with the real world, which it is their chore to amuse.

To be a comedian at all, one must have a strong streak of the antisocial, derived from a miserable childhood (you should hate at least one parent), other neuroses, an early grasp of human absurdity, a lunatic mischief, or a cold, unsympathetic intellect. The comedian must early learn to mask these unpleasant qualities behind a disarming smile, dead pan or look of idiocy.

It is by no means irrelevant that the above also describes, with some understatement, the comic writer, who is the Iago to the entertainer's Othello. The comic idiom, by the mysterious nature of laughter, is at once extremely contemporary and based on very ancient formulas. A new comedy is merely a new accent for the old jokes. Only geniuses (and don't wait up for one) make new jokes. This means that comedians, and comic writers, can only survive by thievery and must fight viciously for the false copyright that the little superimposed accent gives the stolen goods. The comic writer is both a thief and a "fence," or receiver of stolen goods. The TV writer, and not only the gag-writer, despises the performer, the true tragic hero, as was brought out on a recent Susskind forum of comic writers. Since the good serious writers are frustrated from doing their best by TV, they have evolved into perfect cynicism and mischief. It is a commonplace in this business to write material that will make the performer look ridiculous. And why not, when the executives, sponsors and performer are all too stupid to spot it? TV writers as a closed group would reward much closer attention than they have so far had.

As of comedians, a distinction must be made between the current crop, our tragic heroes, and the old guard, who rarely got into any trouble—Groucho Marx, Bing Crosby, Bob Hope, Danny Thomas, Jack Benny, George Burns and the late Bobby Clark; and we can surely forget Fatty Arbuckle, Frank Tinney, etc.

The difference appears in a sad, ghosted book about Keenan Wynn's life (*Ed Wynn's Son*, Doubleday, $3.95), for Keenan has been, though is not currently, a first-rate and delightful comedian. Keenan was certainly not a poor boy, but he had troubles none the less. Ed Wynn married a daughter of Frank Keenan, the grandee Shakespearean actor, and thus became a brother-in-law of Colonel Frank A. Sloan of a socialite New York family. It was a tough milieu for the roughhouse Jewish comedian, but he didn't back down. Keenan Wynn was a beautiful, fair-haired child who nearly died of mastoids. The ladies of the house did some secret drinking. And then there was the godlike figure of Frank Keenan, a benevolent nineteenth- or even eighteenth-century gentleman. Keenan Wynn psychoanalyzes himself as having been jealous of his father, but one might find other explanations.

There have been other accounts of these tragedians: Jackie Gleason, who got his comic start at the public school of which my father was principal; Groucho's marvelously nontragic story; Joey Adams' serial story; and so on. One would like to see an objective, slightly hostile biography of Charlie Chaplin, whose early classic pictures were great ballet, but never to me very funny, except in the pure slapstick, which is of course close to ballet. As a small child, I smelled Chaplin's tightly introverted contempt.

This is the figure, however, whom we must accept as the public tragic hero of the future—a rich and neurotic mountebank Pagliacci who only affects to hide his broken heart. He may not look very promising for the purposes of great dramatic tragedy for Arthur Miller or Tennessee Williams; and yet I suggest that these gentlemen at least look him over as a possible subject. He is already the main tragic prototype for the whole American people.

1960

THREE

SURVIVAL

SURVIVAL IN THE ZOO

ONE NAME officially given the present period, if we go back perhaps 70,000,000 years, is the Age of Mammals. This Age is still going on. However, a single species or genus of mammal has quite recently appropriated the whole planet and while bemoaning its own imminent extinction (at its own hands) is bringing to a rapid close the Age of (all the other) Mammals and some birds. At the very worst that can happen, Man is going to do better than the passenger pigeon, Labrador duck, Indian two-horned rhinoceros and quagga. These are already extinct, kaput, finished; and several vanished with a strange, blackout celerity, as the bald eagle and osprey may be about to do. These last try to breed, but suddenly find they cannot. One can imagine a sort of genetic disdain of living in this world of Man's.

In the last forty years, conservation in the United States has saved many species. The primary credit for ending the massacre of other species is generally given to the New York Zoological Society and its director, the late William Hornaday. Whether his policies, now enacted into United States law, will be accepted by the politicians of Africa, South America, Asia and the South Pacific in time is of course purely speculative. And so is the practical feasibility of ceding to the other animals large enough areas even of North America, which are coveted by the dominant animal, Man.

The official intermediary in this situation is the zoo, here defined as maintaining an international collection of live animals. In the United States, there are thirty-eight first-class zoos, of which the leading three are the New York Zoological Society's Bronx Zoo, Chicago's Brookfield Zoo and the San Diego Zoo. The Bronx Zoo, for example, maintains 3,006 animals divided into 1,099 species. It has 193 species of mammals, 640 of birds, and 266 of reptiles and amphibians. (Fish, of course, are in its Aquarium in Coney Island.)

The other zoos cover most enterprising American cities, with oddly blank areas in New England outside Boston, the Southern states down to South Carolina, and the plateau states excluding Colorado. It might be deduced that where people feel superior, they are less interested in the lower orders. There are also innumerable small or specialized exhibits of live animals. Some, as at Bear Mountain in New York and outside Tucson, Arizona, are excellent. But most show unkempt animals, often not identified, and sometimes inspiring more pity and revulsion than interest. The greatest concentration of these amateur collections is in Florida, followed by Southern California and Canada.

The end of the Age of Mammals might be put into perspective by the response: "Who needs them?" It is true that nobody wants a wolf in the neighborhood, and U.S. wolves are down to around 1,000 survivors. But the ancestor stock of all our cattle, the aurochs, is extinct, and if we should want to breed from the original strain again, we simply could not do so. All we can do is debate whether the purer aurochs strain is the Spanish fighting bull or an English park breed. Before we say of any species, "Who needs it?" we might do better to give it several centuries of thought.

Some fairly radical new answers have been developed by the Bronx Zoo, particularly by its young director, William G. Conway.

One is to use theatrical devices to present the animal in a likeness of his natural environment. Another is to research and

proceed with the breeding in captivity of species that are endangered in the wild state.

The second is not as futile as it may sound. In fact, two
mammals that are extinct in the entirely wild state have prospered for some time only in zoos and parks. These are the
Père David's deer of China, extinct in China, and the wisent,
or European, bison. The Bronx Zoo has eight breeding Père
David's deer, and imported a pair of wisent from Holland.
(Incidentally, a few Père David's deer have at last been sent
back to China.) Other species of mammals undoubtedly have
a majority of their surviving populations in zoos; but the element of hope in this depends on their propagation in captivity.

"Survival Center" is the name of a projected new division
of the Bronx Zoo, for which it is now campaiging for $12,-
000,000. The name sounds melodramatic, but it is justified for
species for which the outside world is an extinction center. Some
of the species that will be studied and bred here are bald eagle,
nene goose (Hawaii), barnacle goose, sacred crane (northeast
Asia), imperial parrot, imperial ivory-billed woodpecker (Mexico), prairie chicken, Asiatic rhinoceros, giant sable antelope,
okapi, black-footed ferret, Komodo dragon, tuatera (New Zea-
land lizard, with which the Bronx Zoo has already set a longevity record—in captivity—of five years). The zoo has succeeded in breeding the pigmy hippopotamus, black-necked swan,
Barrows goldeneye and eider (from eggs imported from Iceland). A Bronx Zoo man was the first to rear whooping cranes
in captivity, in 1957.

Most mammals—cheetahs are an odd exception—will breed
in captivity; but birds, particularly waterfowl, tend to turn
celibate. Mr. Conway and his men want to know why; and,
more important, how to change the picture. The female swan,
for example, will sometimes breed if she has been captured very
early, preferably before hatching. Other waterfowl are sometimes persuaded to breed simply by raising the water level in

the enclosure, but why this works is not understood. Much more must be known, and in a hurry, about the breeding patterns of endangered species. In the rearing of whooping cranes, Mr. Conway discovered a great deal about their procedures (*Animal Kingdom*, August, 1957), such as that early feeding is solely of proteins and minerals, grain is first offered the young after a week or so, much food is carefully washed by the parents, the mother was the more conscientious brooder, the father the better feeder, chicks did not respond to parents' calls but waited to be found, the father stays awake all night guarding the nest, and so on.

The first reform mentioned, that of presenting every creature *as if* in its wild home, is in large part pure theatricality, and was invented by Carl Hagenbeck in Hamburg over fifty years ago. Neither the animal nor the visitor will be entirely deceived by the new artifices contemplated; but both will enjoy the encounter more than when they stared at each other through bars or wire mesh. And perhaps some of the wild creatures *will* be deceived.

In the new aquatic bird house, the shore birds will be seen on a beach retreating before incoming artificial waves; the cliff birds will cling to the face of a sheer cliff with a simulated surf booming below; and the visitors will find themselves looking at eye level into treetops (the tree trunks descending into a pit beneath) where herons are roosting.

The most extraordinary display will be that of those creatures that sleep by day and live by night, and hence are always seen sound asleep by zoo visitors. By keeping the lights up all night, the zoo will persuade them to sleep at night. When the visitors arrive by day, the lights will be dimmed sepulchrally, so that owls, bats, flying foxes, night monkeys and rattlesnakes will all spring into action. A minor difficulty in this program is getting an import permit for a flying fox, a big bat that feeds on fruit and terrifies the U.S. fruit lobby, no trifling lobby.

A Kodiak bear, which stands twelve feet tall and is the world's largest predator, will really get his message across to the visitor when he is met at arm's length through a pane of special glass, in a giant den.

The giraffes will at least appear to be feeding naturally on treetops, for their food will be placed there, instead of on the ground in a bucket.

Emperor penguins will be seen in an Antarctic scene, and air conditioning will throw a reasonably cold blast on the visitor.

The present system of putting all the kangaroos together, all the big cats in one house, etc., will eventually be replaced by geographical groupings such as Africa, and this will be sub-divided into habitats, such as the forest, veld and bush. In each, the associated animals will be seen together, though separated by hidden moats. Thus, in the American plains scene, the bison, wolf and prairie dog will seem to be associated on the terrain they actually occupy in common. All these rearrangements, of course, will cost a lot of money, while the results give people a vastly truer and more dramatic sense of how the rest of the animal kingdom lives.

This zoo of the future will also multiply its own headaches in an already complicated operation. A zoo commissary makes a United Nations dietary look simple, with over 1,000 species plus cranky individuals to feed. Supervising the rearing of young can require twenty-four-hour-a-day surveillance by scientists, who are paid by the New York Zoological Society. (Keepers, food, fuel and half of building costs are provided by New York City.) The new arrangements will certainly present unpredictable difficulties. An example is that if you drain the penguins' pool and then scare them they are likely to dive in on the concrete bottom and brain themselves. The mortality in even well-run zoos is distressing, and usually inexplicable; the aim of the Bronx Zoo is to reduce the inexplicability. New animals are paid for by the New York Zoological Society, not the city.

The Bronx Zoo now attracts 2,500,000 visitors every year. These represent its opportunity to tell the story of the animal kingdom, sympathetically, inspirationally, unforgettably—or dully. Its present management acutely feels the double responsibility—to teach the people, and to save the other species: two interlocked objectives.

The renaissance of the zoo, not a moment too soon, is not confined to the New York Zoological Society. In both Washington, D.C., and Los Angeles, citizens' committees are agitating for better zoos. Los Angeles' Mayor Poulson said, "We are still working toward a world-famous zoo. We haven't lowered our sights." In the same area an amateur, Maurice Machris, is trying to set up a conservation research ranch of about 400 acres to breed rare animals. He has already bought fifty species, mostly still in quarantine, and hopes for the incredible total of 900 species. He too has discovered that some important species are down to one or two hundred individuals. He is especially interested in the little-known kouprey of Cambodia, which may possibly be a true wild ox.

The spirit of such enterprises is admirable. One measure of the decency of a society must be whether its members care, or even affect to care, about the welfare of other species of no immediate benefit to them. It is not really an insult to mankind to admire a hummingbird, an albatross or a lion.

It may be noted that the zoos of Communist Russia are grim, old-fashioned jails. That of Communist East Berlin, however, is excellent, comparable to the fine zoos of Basle and Frankfurt. Such data are surely useful in cultural studies of these countries.

In America, the reporting on zoos by the press is invariably more or less "cute," and does not seem to me truthful. The theory may be that the press is addressed only to mammals that can read, and cannot resist giving its readers the assurance that, compared to themselves, okapi and whooping cranes are idiots. The press reaches for the winning side, the procreatively successful animal that can read and has the price of the paper.

1961

$\mathcal{S}$URVIVAL EVERYWHERE

$\mathcal{W}$HAT WILL be the emotional effect on the average person of learning that the measure of his lifetime probably lies in the 60,000 miles of blood-vessel capillaries in his body? What is anybody to do with a conscious responsibility for a system that would run quarter-way to the moon? Would we want to know the facts of life, even if they were really available?

Yet the whole matter of the aging and then shutting off of life is perhaps the central one for everybody. Since one can hardly put absolute trust in doctors or scientists, it may be as well for the rest of us to look over the data given in Robert de Ropp's *Man Against Aging*. One may have an occasional reservation about de Ropp, an English biochemist lately turned American, but his data are fascinating and worth summarizing.

Why death is inevitable is not yet understood, though we seem to be getting close to some answers. There are things like the sea anemone that may perhaps live forever. The swamp cypress and sequoia live for three or four thousand years, their centers dead, but the sap zone inside the bark perpetually renewed. Some tortoises and sturgeon live up to 200 years (growing continuously to the end, their flesh remaining tender); a crow and vulture have lived over 100 years; the Asiatic elephant 70; a particular horse to 62; and so on. (These latter early attained their full growth; and their flesh grew dry, tough and fibrous.)

Man has done best, of all the hot-blooded creatures. Old Parr in Charles I's time was making love at 140 and lived to 152 on a diet of cheese, milk, coarse bread and some alcoholic sour whey. He was then given a lord's dinner by the Earl of Arundel and immediately died of it. The Dane, Christian Drakenberg, lived a very hard life from 1626 to 1772—146 years. The Turk, Zaro Aga, claimed 156 years on his death in 1934. The Venetian, Cornaro, lived from 1464 to 1566, on a diet *per diem* of twelve ounces of food and fourteen of wine.

The parts of the human body have different calendars. The ear is mature and begins to decline at the age of ten, the eye soon after, the male sex function at 18, the muscular system at 25, the sense of taste at 40, the sense of smell at 60; while the liver and adrenals normally show very little degeneration. The whole show depends on the arterial system and heart. Their job is impaired by hardening of blood vessels, narrowing of blood channels and the drying and hardening of the jelly-fiber mixture that lies between the cells. This is what makes old chicken or beef tough; it evidently does not take place in fish.

Various experiments and observations cited by de Ropp would lead one to summarize a formula for long, or even eternal, life: be born of a young mother; grow slowly (unlike American children who are overfed for rapid growth); grow continuously until death (impossible for mammals); hibernate a part of every 24 hours (impossible for humans: at a temperature of 80° F. the human heart may get out of rhythm, "fibrillate"); have unspecialized cells with a big nucleus and small cytoplasm; keep moist; take juvenile hormones (tried on caterpillars successfully); take sex hormones (but side-effects may include cancer); feed on something like royal jelly that multiplies the queen bee's life tenfold; breathe only pure mountain air. Each has worked for something somewhere.

Raw nature does not tolerate any senescence at all; it quickly kills off the animal with slowed reflexes; only a tiny fraction of the animal population is granted a full life-span. But even prehistoric man probably had a life expectancy of 20 years; Hindus in 1910, 23 years; Ancient Romans, 25 years; Yankees in 1789, 35 years; and Americans today 73 for women, 67 for men. In 1950, in any large group of Americans, 78 percent could expect to be alive at 60, 59 percent at 70, and 30 percent at 80. These are very desirable figures, though they include no Old Parr, and they suggest that man may yet further defy cruel nature.

This recurring dream of rejuvenation, as de Ropp gives its history, provides some solid if heartless laughter, for here is man at his most humbly pathetic. Most recently the dream has taken the form of cytotoxic serum or ACS, novocaine therapy (dangerous), injection of cells from newborn lambs, and the hormone replacement therapy, which might be promising for women, who cease, after the climacteric, to produce the hormones estradiol and progesterone.

The dream is still a dream, but its solid rationale is that most organs remain good enough for another 50 years of life, if only one factor in the body could be changed; and the problem is to find that factor. It may lie in the pea-sized pituitary at the bottom of the brain, whose output gives key signals to other organs; or perhaps even deeper in the brain, in the hypothalamus, which may give the signals to the pituitary. It may lie in the pancreas' enzyme secretion, elastase, which may control the vital elasticity of the arteries; the young pancreas produces 208 units of it per gram of tissue; the old pancreas only nine units. De Ropp grows excited about the drug companies' race during the fifties to develop a safe adrenocortical hormone: "Lederle chemists took up the ball. A hydroxyl group was tacked onto the Squibb hormone. Result, triamcinolone, Aristocort, the aristocrat of the hormones." His feeling is legitimate, since he is a chief of chemistry research with Lederle.

Toward the end the book suffers from a failure to review these half-charted trails toward eternal life; instead, it monotonously reviews ways of dying, of which nobody will sample more than one or two. Interest is revived by a description of the brain nerve cells, which require a quarter of all the oxygen used by the human body, and depend on the presence of vitamin B^1, niacin, riboflavin, piridoxine, and glucose.

In this final chapter, "The Art of Aging," I was somehow exasperated by an impression of contempt for people so stupid as to have been born before 1900; yet Dr. de Ropp is already 47 himself. On a second reading, I find few actual statements to support the impression, except that generally grandparents are terrible people, and "the golden age for creative achievement appears to be the thirties." My own opinion is that children without living grandparents have been deprived of something very valuable; the golden age may be the twenties, forties, fifties or sixties, but probably not the thirties, at least not for a family man or woman.

In the matter of how the aging should handle their lives, he is apparently sensible but also objectionable: forget sex and concentrate on "gardening, horseback riding, swimming, and suitable gymnastics." After the numerous delights of the first 200 pages, we find ourselves in a newspaper advice column; Dr. de Ropp is simply not qualified for this metier. Perhaps an editor insisted on these unfruitful conclusions, which are not at all what a reader of the first 200 pages is looking for.

Certain readers will have been waiting for this book, for it consolidates material that is generally fragmented. The author keeps referring to Aldous Huxley's *After Many a Summer Dies the Swan*, perhaps the hoarsest laugh ever guffawed at old age and its lecheries; and the faint echo of that guffaw is perhaps the flaw in Dr. de Ropp's tone of voice; he is not naturally a joker.

1960

SURVIVAL IN THE WHITE HOUSE

THE PRESIDENT of the United States, first minister of the American people, is hired subjectively, almost by acclamation, after a partisan personnel screening, and is answerable to nobody and hence to everybody. But once their act of faith is consummated, the people now seem to develop misgivings. By way of their press representatives, they have taken to inspecting their new property, less as man, brain and character than as an animal, to look at his teeth, rap his knee and chest, listen to his heart, take a throat smear and perhaps read his horoscope.

After eight years of President Eisenhower's ailments—and they seemed to me serious enough to keep me from voting for him a second time (but that is also a political opinion), we are again in the midst of a national anxiety bee over the President as an animal. One hears one's lay friends issue portentous medical opinions, not wholly out of step with their known political opinions. Even doctors indulge in this kind of forensic medicine. Washington reporters demand firm answers to medical questions they have never asked their own doctors. And what exactly is it all about? Did we elect the man for his physical prowess? Are we going to impeach the President every time some doctor gives him a poor prognosis? Do we want to rush this news to our allies and enemies? For it is often true that powerful interests would much prefer the Vice President to be President, and would like to hamstring the President's effectiveness by crying over his imminent demise. We will return to a historic case of this kind.

In the current flap about President Kennedy, we are after all discussing a vigorous young man whose whole family has a fine health and longevity record. He has, it is true, a history of severe back trouble, malaria and adrenalin deficiency. And what, pray, is your history? The President must deserve from his fellow citizens a little of the same rights they claim. Nobody else would let one walk up and ask, "And how is your gastrointestinal tract today?"

At last, for the first time on record, this whole matter of our Presidents as clinical cases has been researched and recorded in Rudolph Marx's *The Health of the Presidents*. Dr. Marx is an ex-officer of the World War I German Army and an immigrant to the United States in 1922. One would wish that old Americans, or even the members of the John Birch Society, could work up a little of the deserved affection, admiration and pride this relatively recent American feels toward our past Presidents. For all these men, with the possible exception of Harding, stand up as remarkable, and often amazing, men, whatever history's considered opinion of their political value. On their medical histories, one cannot see that they were either qualified or disqualified for the Presidency as animals. Sickness was often the making of them, as in the case of Washington. Four died in office of natural causes: W. H. Harrison, Taylor, Harding and F. D. Roosevelt. The first two were tough old soldiers; and we could not have denied Roosevelt his right to finish the greatest war in history. Three others were assassinated, Lincoln, Garfield and McKinley, as the world entered the age of mass hatred, but surely this cannot be construed as a betrayal of trust.

Seven Presidents died in office, but the lesson is not that we should try to abolish Death in the White House. It might be that more care should be given to the selection of Vice Presidential candidates. Even such foresight can only be imperfect; when a new man comes into that office, the nation takes a new gamble.

The present survival of three ex-Presidents (who, because they are alive, are not considered in Dr. Marx's courteous work) suggests that the Presidency is not, even now, an automatic death sentence.

The evolution of the Presidency has been paralleled by the evolution of the science and art of medicine. The medical treatment of Washington and of Garfield seems today horrifying. A large part of Dr. Marx's problem was to find the old records and to reinterpret them in terms of modern knowledge. Where there are no records, he has described the customary therapies that were probably applied, over the period of two centuries on which he is reporting. He believes that Garfield and McKinley might possibly have been saved by modern medicine; Lincoln's wound would be mortal today.

Essentially, every chapter is an account of the progress toward, and the final arrival at, death. Since the author has first described the real man to whom this is happening, the account is heartbreaking, again and again. It is not nice to watch Lincoln die, or Garfield or McKinley or anyone else; but as the two old ex-enemies and friends, Adams and Jefferson, both hold onto life until the fiftieth anniversary of the Declaration of Independence, a glory and tragedy are unwittingly acted out by these two rotting and wonderful carcasses.

The White House, with the Potomac swamps, and a sewage ditch running across the backyard, was for long perhaps the unhealthiest spot in the United States. The endemic diseases of the South were brought in by all the Southern Presidents, yet they were remarkably long-lived. The longevity of the Presidents declined after Lincoln, until quite recent times. The life expectancy seems now to be on the upswing, considering the three living ex-Presidents. Some of the best risks, like Polk, died early; some of the worst, like Cleveland and Taft, passed seventy. The "cause of death" should never be taken literally, since most people die of the complications that, simply, one way or another, stop the heart. Sometimes, as in the case of W. H. Harrison, it is the doctors' treatment that kills them.

Dr. Marx's visceral point of view has the effect of bringing these men to life in a fresh and valid way. Our two greatest Presidents happen also to have been the two strongest: actual physical giants, wrestlers and rail-splitters. The smallest was Madison at 100 pounds, the biggest Taft at 330 pounds. Grant until he grew his beard looked like a slim, graceful, feminine youth; his voice was sweet.

The present demand to know everything about the President's viscera seems to me a decadence of the democratic state. When the people elect a President, they have taken a risk. Within reason, this risk must be accepted to the end. The public process of nagging at the President's health has political undertones, or feminine overtones, or the smell of the back fence. The nominating convention is a good time to discuss a candidate's medical history; his Administration is not. In the case of Eisenhower, this principle was exactly reversed.

Once there was an instance when it was of utmost importance to the prosperity of the nation that a President's potentially fatal illness be completely concealed. It was at the beginning of Cleveland's second term. The Sherman Silver Act was ruining the American economy, and there was a world crisis. Cleveland wanted the Act repealed. As he set about arranging this, he discovered that his upper jaw had developed a cancer, which had to be removed at once. What made the situation sticky was that his Vice President was Adlai Stevenson, a silver man. The operation was performed secretly, July 1, on a yacht moving slowly in the East River off Manhattan. The House repealed the Act on August 28. The next day the medical story broke in the papers, supposedly inspired by the dentist on the operative team. But since Cleveland by then looked and sounded better than ever, the denials were believed until the authoritative story was issued twenty-four years later by the doctor in charge.

What should have been the citizen's moral attitude toward this flagrant deception? The citizen had elected the whole man, Cleveland, complete with his cancer, then unknown even to Cleveland. Cleveland's value to the citizen was to get the Sherman Silver Act repealed, rather than to be a perfect physical specimen. The first value would have been seriously compromised, if the second value had been proved false. Against the interest of the citizen who had voted for Cleveland, the mere rumor of Cleveland's cancer might well have ruined the nation. Should the citizen still demand this titillating bit of information?

All science, all civilization, is dedicated to the reduction, if possible to zero, of risks, of unpredictable outcomes. But ultimately, in every aspect of society, in our dependence on other human beings, some risk must always remain. The risk inherent in electing a human being to the Presidency is not eliminated by nagging him about his imperfections.

1961

CIGARETTES, CANCER
AND THE CAMPUS

*T*HE PRESENT moment in cancer research yields a certain amount of material that the layman can grasp, but it is hard to find, despite recent cover stories on cancer in *Newsweek* (June 22) and *Time* (July 27). The big news on cancer was a July 9 dispatch that British mice had failed to get lung cancer after five years of inhaling cigarette smoke. This was reprinted "in the public interest" by the Tobacco Institute, at small cost when compared to the paid propaganda of the cigarette companies.

As for this great victory of the mice, the dean of English cancer researchers, the late Sir Ernest Kennaway, said in 1957, "Negative results of smoke inhalation experiments on rodents seem to me to be of no significance, because the animals, unlike smokers, keep their mouths shut and pass the smoke over their turbinates." Mice, in short, don't really enjoy the cigarette habit. They don't pull the smoke luxuriantly into the lungs after it has been heated inside the cigarette, briefly, to about 3,000° F.

Newsweek's story recounts the "miracle of modern surgery" on lung cancer, and miracle it is, except that after the surgery most of the patients are dead in two years, and 80 percent in five years. "It seems unlikely," writes a great surgeon, "that further significant technical improvements will be forthcoming, nor can it be supposed that they will materially improve matters should they come." *Newsweek*'s handling of the cigarette-cancer connection is the familiar one of confusion by verbosity.

Time's story, much more thoroughly researched, nevertheless repeats this technique, burying the first mention of cigarettes under 650 lines. It also introduces the Master Molecule, the Secret of Life—a thrilling new character, if true.

What is the cancer picture anyway?

In 1957, 255,000 Americans died from malignant neoplasis, i.e., cancer, as against 197,000 in 1948. Of course the total number of deaths also rose in that decade (from 1,444,000 to 1,636,000) but even so the cancer toll increased from 14 percent to 16 percent. Put in another way, annual cancer deaths were up from 1.34 per thousand of the living to 1.50 per thousand (*Time* makes it 1.3). Yet as late as 1930, cancer was considered under control at less than one death per thousand, and not provably on the increase except among older people. Something has been added since then.

Moreover, the present total figure conceals a lot of changes. Mortality has been reduced where the cancer occurs in "accessible sites"—skin, lip, tongue and mouth, bones, uterus. Breast cancer has remained about the same; but there has been improvement in such inaccessible sites as the esophagus in males and the stomach and intestine in females. Stomach and bladder cancer is generally on the decrease. Increases have come in pancreas, kidney and suprarenal cancer and in leukemia. But the massive increase has come in cancer of the lung and bronchus, a disease almost unknown fifty years ago, now accounting for nearly 15 percent of all cancer deaths, and moving up fast.

The earlier idea that cancer might be a "spontaneous" growth disease has been abandoned; and hundreds of cancer-causing agents, or carcinogens, have been isolated. Some of these are 4-aminodiphenyl, asbestos, benzidine, 2-napthylamine, certain mineral oils, chimney soot, coal-tar, radioactive materials, sodium arsenite and cigarette smoke, all effective in man.

A carcinogen evidently changes the nature of the cells some

time after the host has been exposed, but cancer will not appear for some further time up to twenty-five years. The carcinogens are of an immense variety of chemical types and operate by very different biochemical routes. The question is whether they do not all at some point bring about a change that is chemically and genetically the same, leading to the wild, untamable growth of the cancer. After the change has taken place, it does not seem to save the individual to avoid further exposure to the carcin- ogen. By then the cancer, though not visible to the microscope, is irreversible.

This mystery is at the agonizing center of cancer research.

Can anything be done until it is solved? Well, we can at least keep carcinogens away from people; and the primary one here is cigarette smoke.

Various statistics on the percentage of heavy cigarette smokers in total deaths from lung cancer put it from 40 times to 60 times as high as for nonsmokers. Light cigarette smokers and pipe and cigar smokers (who do not inhale) fall in between. In all diseases except lung cancer, heavy smokers are only slightly worse off than nonsmokers. All men get over six times as many lung cancers as all women; but nonsmoking men have the same rates as women.

Don't you begin to see a suspicious connection between lung cancer and cigarettes?

What is smoking? Here we may quote Kennaway again:

The smoking of tobacco involves a number of fundamental processes which all give rise to products found in the smoke. These are: (1) com- bustion, producing oxides of carbon and water; (2) thermal decomposi- tion, occurring in or near the hot zone and giving rise to a number of products which are either subsequently burnt or distilled away into the mainstream smoke; (3) distillation, proceeding in close proximity to the smouldering zone and giving vapours that condense in cooler zones; and (4) steam distillation, occurring mainly during the suction period and responsible for carrying quantities of tobacco constituents and ther-

mal decomposition products into the smoke at a relatively low temperature. It therefore follows that many of the more volatile constituents of
the original tobacco are found in the smoke and that, in addition, products of combustion and thermal decomposition are present. With the latter
must be included subsequent reaction products which originate from
primary decompositions.*

He appends a list of more than 110 elements and compounds
found in tobacco, and 150 found in tobacco smoke, including ten
proved carcinogens.

The English are particularly interested in lung cancer because it kills two 55-year-old Englishmen out of every 1,000
living, as against only one American male of the same age and
slightly higher percentages for the Danes, Swiss, Dutch and
Germans. One clue to the difference may be that the English
throw away a much shorter cigarette butt—23 mm., as against
an American's 33 mm. It has been proved that the higher the
materials are heated, the more potent are the carcinogens that
are ingested. Most of those in tobacco are polycyclic hydrocar-
bons of aromatic type. Acetylene is a product of the decomposition which forms carcinogens.

The fact that many doctors smoke cigarettes has an effect on
popular opinion. In recent interviews with men-on-the-street,
one of them answered, "I think all this lung cancer talk is a
lot of baloney. If it was really true, you'd see a lot of doctors
quitting smoking, and this I have not seen." A doctor is not
immune to habit; and by no means will all heavy smokers die
of cancer. Still, the profession ought to set an example. Most
young doctors are said to have stopped smoking.

If it is true that the lung carcinogens require about twenty-
five years to mature a cancer (and that is the period of wide-

* "Some Possible Exogenous Factors in the Causation of Lung Cancer" by
Kennaway and A. J. Lindsey. Published in British Medical Bulletin, "Causation of Cancer," May, 1958.

spread cigarette smoking), we may be on the threshold of a still more formidable explosion of lung cancer. Some bloodstrains seem to be relatively impervious to cancer: this reflection is the last recourse of resolute optimists. Indeed, it is my own. Middle-aged smokers must now take their chances on having some hereditary immunity to lung cancer, or dying of something else first. The young, however, can still be free of such weary thoughts.

And so the tobacco industry is proud to report an increase in youthful smokers, so that total U.S. consumption of cigarettes is up 20 percent in five years, though many adults have quit smoking. In view of what has been given here, this tactless brag is equivalent to announcing a war that will kill off more American men than World War II did, and on the average more painfully.

Somebody reacted properly to this threat. In Jacksonville, Florida, school principals, the medical society and the American Cancer Society combined to put on an antismoking educational program in eighteen high schools. The effect can be judged by the pupils' favorite question: "How do I get my parents to quit smoking?" Similar campaigns will be put on next fall in the schools of New York City and possibly some other Southern cities. New York has even asked the tobacco industry to contribute its support.

In Canada, a movement to ban cigarettes entirely was converted into a more realistic campaign to require cigarette advertising to state the tar content of the cigarette (the tar content of the hot smoke is more important) instead of "conveying the erroneous idea that filter tips can protect the smoker against lung cancer."

Where, then, would you expect the cigarette companies to aim their heaviest barrage of advertising? Where else but at the colleges, since nursery, grammar and high schools are evidently out of bounds? And, in fact, the main support of college newspapers and magazines in America is now, and has been for many years, cigarette advertising.

Tareyton tells the colleges, "Hooray for college students! They're making new Dual Filter Tareyton the big smoke on American campuses! Are you part of this movement? If so, thanks. If not, try 'em!" (Do today's college boys think in exclamation points?)

Viceroy develops "Do You Think For Yourself?" with a quiz, e.g., "Do you believe that the expression 'Every cloud has a silver lining' is (a) sticky sentimentality? (b) optimism with a poetic license? (c) faulty meterology?" and "In choosing a filter cigarette, would you depend (a) on the claims you read and hear? (b) on satisfying *yourself* that you're getting the right filtration and taste? (c) on the recommendations of your friends?" If you answered (b) to both of these, you think for yourself and ". . . usually smoke Viceroys."

Winston shows dressed-up busts of Napoleon and Archimedes. Thus: "The mystery is solved! Napoleon's famous gesture was just to reassure himself that he had plenty of cigarettes." And of Archimedes: "You can reproduce the experiment. It's easy as pi. . . . Simply light your first Winston and smoke it. . . . Eureka!" And then, of course and inevitably, "Winston tastes good—like a cigarette should!"

Equally brainy, Lucky Strike runs a contest for examples of "Thinklish." In this game, Viking oarsmen are Norsepower, dog pound is muttropolis. Of "delegates to a jazz convention," Lucky Strike deposes, "the hepresentatives come from all schools of jazz: hot, cool, and room temperature. But they're in perfect harmony on one point: the honest taste of a Lucky Strike. Get Luckies yourself. (You'll trumpet their praises.)"

In a matter that concerns the preservation of the race, such a narrowly aimed advertising campaign, for all its genial jokes and exclamation points, can easily be regarded as a frivolously treasonable conspiracy.

The tobacco industry, despite its sales figures, has actually been frightened by the Jacksonville school children. It had already tacitly admitted, with filter cigarettes, that all was not well. The use of the dread word, "tars," in advertising narrowed it down further. Now the propaganda issued by the newly formed Tobacco Institute may even mention cancer.

Half a dozen new filter cigarettes with beautiful, clean names will presently be on the market—Life and Belair and Spring and Alpine. They have caught the point that the heat of the cigarette increases the carcinogens and so try to cripple the draught with various filters, baffles, dampers and porous papers.

Into this desperate arena has strolled a joker worthy of Hans Christian Andersen. Under the name of Bantob, contracted from ban-tobacco, he has issued a cigarette called Vanguard, tested in Dayton, Ohio. This solves the whole problem by using something other than tobacco, a heavily guarded mystery "natural fiber." The best part of the jest is that it pays no taxes and thus gives the retailer a gigantic profit.

It is a pity to have to point out that even burning hay undoubtedly produces carcinogens, and that they might be even more deadly than the tobacco tars. It is to be hoped that the citizenry will not try rolling their own with shredded wheat or corn flakes.

Faced with a satirist of the caliber of Bantob's inventor society comes to an end of the small jokes. The next step is an imaginary cigarette.

1959

REDUCING AD ABSURDUM

*T*HE PLEASURE of eating to repletion, once reserved to the very few, is so available in America today that millions now are as bloated as a senior wife in a Sultan's harem—and hating it. The statistics say that half of American men, and three-quarters of American women, are overweight; this would seem an exaggeration, as one looks about. Still, a lot of people have no more figure between chest and hips than a market hog; and a lot more insist that they are too fat. This condition has led to the result that about half the population will read anything on how to reduce.

In this context, what everybody knows is never mentioned, and should be. First, one of the major anticipations that keeps many people going is the next meal; it is a large part of what they mean by happiness and they should not lightly be deprived of it. Second, an adult's ingestion and enjoyment of food is not especially attractive to other adults. Some "backward" peoples, such as the Balinese, recognize this by politely turning their backs on the other diners when they eat. In short, human beings tend to be enthusiastic about their own eating, and quite unenthusiastic about other people's eating, unless they are magnanimous chefs or great-hearted mothers of families, for whom the consumption seems a compliment to their product.

The Puritanical disapproval of fatness in others is especially forthcoming from people who are themselves fat. This performance, both funny and saddening to thin people, says something about man's helpless inhumanity. But I also suspect an element of the same thing in the specialists' advice to the overweight on how to reduce. The most superficial review of publicized reducing diets will confirm such suspicion.

This matter has gone so far and wild that should I now cruelly invent a farce diet (say, caviar for protein, peanut butter for fat, buttered popcorn for carbohydrates, vitamin pills and plenty of bourbon sour mash whisky), any publisher could easily sell 50,000 copies of the book. If there is any deficiency in this diet (journalistic, not dietetic), it would be only that it is not funny enough.

The cruelty and irresponsibility of offering one single, standard dietary solution for everybody is obvious. What a person eats is, in many important respects, his life. But every individual is different from every other individual. No doctrinaire solution will work for them all. Each individual has conditioned habits of eating, of taste, of appetite, of expenditure of energy, of nervous rhythms and, most important of all, of metabolism. Few modern doctors have the interest, time or genius to find out all about any one individual; and many are themselves overweight. But the individual has the time and interest and, at least about himself, perhaps the genius. After all, it's his life.

If he still prefers professional advice, here is what he will find:

Avoid fats, says Dr. Stanley M. Garn in *The Nation's Children* (Vol. II). "I am struck by [children's diets'] resemblance to the diet . . . used to create obesity in rats. Frappés, fat-meat hamburgers, bacon and mayonnaise sandwiches, followed by ice cream."

Eat fats, says Dr. Richard Mackarness in *Eat Fat and Grow Slim*. "Fat is the least fattening of all foods because it turns the bellows on the body-fires in a fat person and enables him to mobilize his stored fat . . . helping him to burn up more efficiently the food he eats."

Avoid potatoes, says practically everybody since the pioneer William Banting in the nineteenth century.

Eat potatoes, says Dr. H. L. Marriott in the *British Medical Journal*, so long as they are boiled, steamed or baked in the jackets.

Don't mix foods, says Dr. William Howard Hay, in such "appalling mixtures" as bacon and eggs, meat and potatoes, bread and cheese or toast and marmalade. This monotrophic diet has its most devoted followers in Hollywood.

"Nonsense," says Prof. John Yudkin in *This Slimming Business*, to the foregoing. Foods, he says, are not exclusively protein or carbohydrate. Bread has some protein; and the amino acids from both bread and meat simultaneously are required to convert the protein into good tissue.

Avoid plain water, say Gayelord Hauser and some doctors. Says Hauser: "Plain water is responsible for many overweight, puffed-up bodies." Instead, he advises lemon juice, cider vinegar, etc., "to dissolve the fat."

Drink lots of water, says Dr. Mackarness. Dr. Yudkin adds: "All healthy people, even fat people, have a pretty perfect mechanism which regulates very exactly the amount of water and of salt which the body retains." Apparently the body is extremely insistent on maintaining a certain proportion of fluidity and salinity.

Avoid alcohol, says nearly everybody.

Drink alcohol, says Dr. Mackarness. "There is the intriguing possibility that alcoholic drinks . . . may step up metabolism to an extent which more than compensates for the calories taken in as alcohol. . . . Probably all alcoholic drinks except those like beer, which contain large amounts of carbohydrates, are slimming."

There is no need to take sides in any of these religious wars. The layman, however, would be justified in thinking that somebody didn't know what he was talking about.

The most suspect are those who treat the human body as if it were a standard blast furnace, where certain elements in fixed proportion are poured in, subjected to a uniform process and culminate in a uniform product, absolutely and precisely predictable.

If this were true, reducing diets would long since have become a dead subject. But it is said that they are instead the one subject guaranteed to bring any social group alive and quivering. Actually, this must apply only to groups conversationally dominated by women. I hear very few men seriously discussing reducing; I have never done so. But it is true that one must be ready to discuss the weight of any lady one knows well; in America one must never say, "But I like you fat." To an American woman, flesh means only carbohydrates.

The subject is so entrancing that it is likely to appear in any issue of *Woman's Day*, *McCall's*, *Reader's Digest* and most recently, of all places, in *U.S. News & World Report*, whose April 11 issue gave eight fairly unprofitable pages to an interview on reducing, with a specialist who looked overweight, if not quite obese, to me.

His comments can be divided between the debatable and the undebatable. Of the latter: "Overweight people are more likely to die of heart disease. . . . A young man doing light work . . . probably should get around 2,400 calories a day. . . . It's a mistake to go on a stringent reducing diet. . . ." Of the debatable: "It is very desirable to divide your food supply approximately equally in the three meals. . . . Any amount of alcohol is bad. . . . There are only one or two explanations of the man who stays thin. One is, he isn't absorbing the energy, which is unlikely; or two, he is expending more than it looks as though he's expending. . . . To use up one pound of body fat, you have to walk about thirty-five miles. . . ." He is absolutely opposed to eating meat fat.

Meat fat is to me a prized delicacy; I also love quantities of beer; peanut butter and mayonnaise are the blessings of civilization; and I have weighed about the same for thirty years. Furthermore, any urbanite who suddenly walks thirty-five miles is going to lose a lot more than a pound; he may lose consciousness, too. The doctor and myself are evidently not members of the same animal species. Anyway, he certainly doesn't know anything about my species.

But an experiment was conducted in England by Sir Charles Dodds of Middlesex Hospital which moves this subject up to a height where we begin to get a view. He rounded up two groups of people, one whose weights had been increasing, the other whose weights had remained fairly level for some years. Both groups were asked to double or triple their intake of food for a period.

If you believed *U.S. News* & *World Report*, you would expect both groups to gain some weight. The first group, indeed, did. The second gained not at all.

There are better lessons here than the mere destruction of dieting theories. The first group, one must conclude, could deal with a surplus of calories only by storing them as surplus fat. For some this may have been aggravated by a suspected abnormality of being unable to convert any carbohydrates at all into energy, so that all bread, potatoes and sweets turn into fat and never do the body any good. For these people, the result of eating is still an unsatisfied feeling, more eating and more fat.

Of the second group, it must be assumed that the challenge of surplus calories put their metabolism into high gear. The juices were present, ready and willing to tear the stuff apart. They rushed to the attack with a cheer and the self-confidence of Caesar's legions on a good day. The first group's legions were nonexistent (unlikely) or disorganized or asleep. (I will add my suspicion that the second group, feeling an uncomfortable loginess, also increased their overt exercise, while the first group succumbed to the lethargy, to which they were already partly habituated.)

The useful point of this experiment is that it demonstrates that different people are different, and shifts the emphasis to metabolism, the subject doctors do not like to talk about because they scarcely understand it.

Metabolism is a very interesting subject. A shrew, for example, must eat every few hours or die of starvation; it has a maniacal metabolism. Some passerine birds eat several times their weight every day, but an obese wild bird is unthinkable; it would not be able to get airborne. Strains of wild birds and animals with inefficient metabolisms have long since been eliminated. In domesticated animals, metabolism controls production of milk, eggs and *pâté de foie gras*.

It is, however, possible for a human being with an imperfect metabolism to survive handily, since human brains have almost eliminated the challenges to physical efficiency. Two sets of cells in the brain of all mammals are concerned with appetite. If these are destroyed in rats, the rats do not know how to stop eating. In other words, these nerve centers transmit the news from the stomach that it has had enough, and turn off the appetite. It is possible that an excess of alcohol and cigarette-smoking deadens the message from the body that it would like some food now, please.

A decent respect for the mysterious orchestrations of the body was a remarkable quality of a recent three-part serial on alcoholism in *The New Yorker* by Berton Roueché. This quoted a Chicago doctor on some individuals' peculiar sensitization to particular foods, especially the grains, wheat, corn and rye, that incidentally provide most alcohol. These become "addictive" foods, like alcohol. It also relates alcoholism and other food addictions to defects in the endocrine gland system—thyroid, parathyroid, pituitary, adrenal, gonad, pancreatic islets of Langerhans. The adrenals, for example, are essential to carbohydrate metabolism; their failure creates a body need for blood sugar. The failure of other ductless glands seems to produce other compulsive food needs. This kind of talk gets us somewhere.

But the individual need not become the guinea pig of science; what he most needs is to find out about himself, empirically. In ordinary common sense, the individual ought to increase or decrease his allotment of only one food for perhaps a week at a time (potatoes, bread, sweets, fats, meat, etc.), leaving the rest of his accustomed diet exactly the same. During this period he should weigh himself every day at the same time, preferably just before breakfast. If he does not soon know what his particular metabolism can handle and what it cannot, he must be very peculiar. The lessons he learns will apply only to himself; he should not be encouraged to write a book advising anybody else how to get fat or thin. Especially if he has an M.D.

But the individual weighing himself in the morning and trying to remember what he ate yesterday ought also to weigh two other factors. The first is whether he feels well. If he does, the reason may be that what he ate yesterday was good for him. (Or it may simply be that it's a beautiful morning or he's in love or he's due for a raise.)

He should also try to remember how he enjoyed what he ate. An animal makes the best use of what it likes, i.e., what seems to taste good, what is all-around welcome news to the mouth, nose, stomach, brain, glands and nerves; but of course if this also adds weight, he had better do without it, if he really doesn't want to add weight. Otherwise, excluding what he knows very well he ought to avoid, the individual ought to eat precisely what he likes best, if in reasonable quantities. All his life he is going to think about the next meal. Very well, let him think about it pleasurably and selectively and intelligently, and then eat it.

Too many of the diets I have looked at seem to me to reflect the prescriber's antisocial disapproval of other people's having any fun. This pompous sadism, of which we are all a little guilty, is a philosophical, sociological and dietary disaster. To tell anybody to drink only skimmed milk is a dirty, rotten trick.

1960

FOUR

NON-ATHLETIC
ACTIVITIES

_T_HE CROSSWORD
ADDICT

_T_HE NEW world is already one where the American adult's leisure time, including sleep, is over three times his working time. He has typically been groomed for all this leisure by a fair amount of education, and it is often happily reported that in his leisure he is giving his expensive brains to intellectual pursuits.

And so one naturally inquires: which intellectual pursuits? A little observation soon shows that there is only one fairly universal form of intellectual activity pursued by at least one person in every second family. And that is crossword puzzles. Since this is indubitably true (and probably invisible to a conscientious foreign student of America), it is remarkable that the literature on the subject is frivolous, indulgent and cute.

Crossword puzzles are a little too big for that, since virtually every major newspaper in the United States today runs a daily crossword—after nearly forty years of what was once 1924's foolish fad. The thing has penetrated most civilized countries, including the Communist ones, where the clues embody the party line, and a puzzle constructor can land in jail for plotting a crossword by which "Socialist statesman" comes out unavoidably "Tito."

In America the main problem is familial. If two members of a family do the puzzle, they need two copies of the newspaper. One would suppose that the first solver could erase his answers, and pass the paper over to the second, but this is impossible, for interesting reasons.

People do crossword puzzles for somewhat the same reason they become mathematicians and scientists: they know in advance that there is an answer. The rest of us steadily stare at problems for which, for all we know, there may be no answer at all, or one so unpleasant we do not want to know it just yet. We may suppose that this is a peculiarly contemporary climate, but it is probably eternal.

To the puzzle-solver, the existence of a perfect answer is guaranteed. In solving his problem, he rises entirely above the real world, where most problems have no perfect answer. Having filled in the last square, he can indulge a small sneer at all the unfinished puzzles around him, and perhaps bring to his own real problems some of the puzzler's patience and self-confidence. Or he may ruin his life by resenting the disorder of real problems, so slovenly and unfair as compared to crosswords.

But once the puzzle is solved, it is a dead issue. Nobody else in that family group wants to step in the first solver's dirty footprints. The fantasy that perhaps nobody else in the world could solve that puzzle has evaporated. It is now obvious that anybody could solve it. It has become an old joke, an obsolete issue, a used paper plate, a filled vacuum-cleaner bag.

This may be part of the reason why mathematics and science sometimes bore the brightest students, the ones who want to invent their own solutions, and are depressed by the puzzles their predecessors have already solved. They want fresh crossword puzzles.

To people at all sophisticated in the language, crosswords may actually be an injury. When I am asked to give a four-letter word for "unusually great," my feeling for the language

is not sharpened, but corroded, when I confront the answer
"rare"; or for "absurd," "inept"; or for "eradicate," "epilate";
or for "recites," "says"; and so on. This is not a language one
wants to use, and some of this debris may remain in the mind.

But surely some useful information is leaked out by crosswords. One can learn that a mythical king of Britain was
Artegal, an ancient British historian Bede (again and again),
the Asiatic goat antelope is a serow, church-land a glebe, a
merganser is a smee or a smew, that cavalry is a deep chrome
yellow, corporal an altar cloth, leister a fishing spear, a fanon
is an orale, dorado is cuir, and so on.

Everybody has had the intuition that crosswords do not
wholly explore the full possibilities of the language. The reason
they do not has much to do with the construction of English
words, which begin with a great variety of combinations. Short
words also end with considerable variety. But medium and long
words tend to end in a monotony of relatively few forms, the
terminal letters being, E, D, H, L, N, R, S, T, W and Y, as
can be seen in any paragraph in print. If one writes down four
equal-length words offhand, the terminal letters are likely to
form the word, eeee, or ssss, or seed. Thus a puzzle's least inspired words are to be found at the bottom and right-hand side.
Here, in a recent New York *Herald Tribune* Sunday puzzle
were the words, seeders, tensest, endless, tigress and regents.
But in this one, nearly every word ended in the easy letters,
especially s and d, in a total surrender to tired professionalism.
In such a morass of clichés, it does not save face to insert out-
rages like mantra ("devotional formula"), sulcus ("furrow"),
labile ("plastic"), dalles ("canyon walls"), cassonade ("musco-
vado sugar") and tascos ("clays for melting pots").

The more notorious clichés come from the puzzler's need for
numerous vowels in the middle of his words. And so we get
Aaron, taal (Boer), arara (macaw), abaca (hemp), aga, kayak
and umiak, taa (pagoda) and all the Latin genus names.

Now how do words begin? About half the words in a big dictionary begin with just five letters, S, C, P, A or T. A sixth of all words begin with S alone, more than the combined total of the eleven least-used letters. Possibly because the popular letters are heavily loaded with prefixes, sub-, con-, pre-, a-, trans-, they do not get proportional representation in crosswords. Instead crosswords tend to begin with the popular terminal letters.

The curious fact is that the cliché words have overrun all parts of the crossword puzzle, even where they give no special advantage. The jargon has very largely displaced the language, quite unnecessarily. For one must remember that there are a great many crossword reference books, listing the clichés in every convenient way. Of course, there comes a day when the puzzler is ashamed to use the cliché again, and it drops out of sight, as did aardvark. A new word like odometer will sweep all the puzzles and soon be beaten to death. It will have its life after death in the duller puzzles.

In a difficult puzzle, it certainly spoils the fun to go to a reference book before one has given one's memory every chance. But the old hands profess *never* to consult the dictionary or encyclopedia. This attitude has for me the color of a futile and diddling literacy.

First, in this way, these people make certain that they will never learn anything new. Second, such a pose is disrespectful of knowledge, or wholly cynical of the knowledge offered. Third, it is often unfeasible, as can be seen in several of the words given above. Nobody knows that reveille drum rolls are dians, nobody but Webster. Novices like myself (I ignored the intellectual life until several years ago) hold the vision of the perfect solution and also hope to learn something. All my solutions were for a time checked and perfect, but that glorious morning is fading. When one lacks the first letter of a three-letter word for yellow ocher, and combs through the dictionary to find that the word is sil, one is never quite the same again, quite so eager for the frontiers of new information. As the closets of the mind fill up with this rubbish, one may be troubled by one's inability to forget it all, to forget sil and elater and ret and tor and sorb and adit and seesee or ort and abb.

It is merely suggested that the puzzle constructors show some enterprising respect for the big dictionary, that is, for the whole language and tradition. For example, the word "great" is an amenable word for crosswords, and the dictionary offers such educational combinations as Great Assembly, The Great Beyond, great blue heron, great circle, great climacteric, great crested flycatcher, great enlightenment, Greater Mysteries, Great Goddess, Great Horde, Great Interregnum, Great Mother, Great Rebellion, *et al*. The dictionaries, the histories, the encyclopedias are filled with suitable and interesting words that have never been seen in crossword puzzles.

Perhaps crossword constructors are not paid enough—from $10 to $25 a masterpiece. Perhaps the fault is that a quarter of the constructors are killing time in federal or state prisons, and the rest feel as if they might as well be in prison. Or the futility of crossword puzzles may stem straight from their origin.

This came in 1913 when an editor on the old New York *World* Sunday magazine section, Arthur Winn, decided to fill a little space with an adaptation of the old game, word squares, viz.:

```
W O R E
O P E N
R E A D
E N D S
```

To Winn had come, after several thousand years, the revolutionary thought that the down words did not absolutely have to be the same as the crosswords. He developed a puzzle page filled with word squares, enigmas, hidden words, rebuses, anagrams and his specialty, the "Cross Word Corner," a crossword puzzle that looked very much like those of today, and seems now fairly difficult and amusing. The clichés were already in evidence: ret, ode, aver, haha (hedge in a ditch), Eli, etc. Some of his clichés have since been outlawed. But his colossal discovery slumbered for eleven years.

Then in 1924 two Columbia graduates, Simon and Schuster, wanting to be book publishers, wondered what to publish. An aunt of one, perhaps a stockholder, insisted on crossword puzzles. The boys called in Margaret Petherbridge, who later married John Farrar, another publisher, and she elaborated and formalized the crossword puzzle as it is known today. But it had been launched as a publishing gimmick whose success enraged old-line publishers. After nearly forty years it is clearly something more than that, it is much more "national" than baseball, but the cuteness, the dilettantism, the banality, the fun-fun-fun, still hold the crosswords in their grip. Mrs. Farrar, the editor of the most literate and unpredictable of the Sunday puzzles, in *The New York Times*, is a lone chatelaine of high standards. The *Times* did not give in to crosswords until February, 1942; perhaps as a reaction to Pearl Harbor.

The *Times* puzzle can be, on a given Sunday, easier than the *Herald Tribune* puzzle, but the former will always be challenging, the latter stupefying or exasperating. The construction of a crossword unconsciously reveals the maker's whole mental furniture, his reserves of knowledge and insight. If he is a victim of rote ("sound of the surf"), he will be inept ("absurd").

But, aha, there is another sort of crossword puzzle. One is in the London *Observer*, another is to be found in *The Nation*. They are supposed to be fiendish, but this is not fair. They simply do not work on a single set of rules, and they do not warn you which of their numerous sets of rules any given clue is geared to. The word fiendish describes more accurately the mood of the solver.

I am happy to say that I have licked *The Nation*'s crossword, partly because I am good at anagrams and have some feeling for the language, but more importantly because I have a brother who is good at puns (but not anagrams) and sundry tricks. Beyond these assets, my recourse is to peck *The Nation* puzzle to bits. The subjective malevolence of the puzzle must be equaled by the solver's activist malevolence; no quarter is given, or should be expected. The immorality of this all-in combat might seem shocking in such a magazine, but there, inside the back cover, the combatants stagger with net and dagger. (Somebody took twelve years to solve one puzzle in the London *Observer*.)

The worst problems in *The Nation*'s puzzles are those where components of the answer word are hidden seriatim in a sentence or phrase of apparent gibberish. In these one-syllable or even one-letter components, for example, thousand is M, 54 is LIV, witticism is mot, mother is dam or ma, examine or look over is con, layer is hen, air is tune or song, interdiction is ban, debts spell IOUs, belief is ism, type is en, politician is MP, main is ocean, sea or mare, very loud is ff, turn is u, damage is mar, missing is shy, concerning is re, unknown is x, no longer or formerly is ex, etc.

Or the key words in the clue may be barely noticeable words, like in or about or around, signaling that the letters of one word are to be put around the letters of another.

Or the word up, or hoisted, may signal in a down word that the answer should be printed from the bottom up, that is, reversed. Thus, "hoisting the canvas possessed the blooming things" tells you frankly to run up the synonyms, sail and had, which, read down, spell dahlias. Or the word back, or return,

on a crossword, clearly tells one to run the clue words backwards. What could be fairer?

Half a dozen answers in any *Nation* puzzle will be anagrams
formed from one or more words. Sometimes these are signaled
by the words mixture, makeup, battered, false, bad, confused,
unusual, version, variety, in a way, possibly, a sort of, the hard
way, etc. Thus, "cocaine mixture" candidly conveys "oceanic."
How obvious can you get? But just as often there is no signal
whatever. "To Caliban" equals botanical; "not solemn"
somnolent; "limit is used, I'd" dissimilitude, "midair, etc."
diametric, "if the orchestra's" ostrich feathers.

Or the answer word may lie outright in the clue, though
hidden (as in the old New York *World* puzzle page), as the
word eyesore is hidden in "maybe, yes, or even no."

Or the clue may be a reference to a famous quotation.

Or an outrageous pun, or combination of puns.

Or it may even be a straightforward, unbelievable statement
of fact. And so on. But one does not know which set of rules
obtains with the particular word.

My own procedure is to run down the clues looking for anagrams and obvious jokes. These give me a few letters with
which to peck the crosswords out, trying various letters in each
vacant slot. Often one has the right answer, and must then
spend another half-hour figuring out why it is the answer.

Everybody who works *The Nation* puzzle knows all the
above. But I would like to say that its exhilarating feature is
that it teaches one not to accept as final one's first rapid impression of what a combination of words seems to mean. It inculcates
a savage suspicion, and a doubt of one's own impression. It trains
one, after exhaustive research, to throw an eviscerated hypothesis
out the window, and embrace, unexhausted, a new one. And in
this puzzle the answer words are a compliment to one's normal
intelligence and usually interestingly abnormal constructions in

the language, e.g., usurper, eggcups, husband, and typically words beginning with vowels, but too often ending in -ing.

One might say that such puzzles are virtuous in demonstrating that the answers to anything are, properly, hard to come by. Once come by, it is true, the answer has no use, but one tends to keep it around, as athletes keep their trophies. At least I can get insane laughter out of almost anybody by quoting the clues and answers of *The Nation*'s puzzles; and in this way I spread some happiness.

The Nation's crossword puzzle is a better puzzle because it excites more emotion. But any crossword puzzle can be a superb triggering device to interest the human mind in a word, name, or phrase which may open a door into the real world, present or past. It is no criticism of this device that it opens doors at random. In my opinion, there is no better way than by the accidental door to enter the area of human knowledge. My primary objection to the current crossword puzzles is simply that they open no, or few, doors.

So long as this remains true, it means that America's leisure life of the intellect will be transacted as a stale jargon in an airless room, in a conceited parade of a futile literacy. Hard words, alas!

1961

*I*N SEARCH OF ATHENS, U.S.A.

*T*HE ATHENS of America!" What a boast! What a cultural climax! What a tourist attraction! Before many more years, we may expect a national brawl for the title. In the past, various "Athenses" of this and that have included Cordoba, Copenhagen, Edinburgh, Cork, Belfast and finally Boston, Mass., in tribute to its Harvard graduates. A number of college towns—in Georgia, Alabama, Tennessee, West Virginia and southern Ohio—actually have the legal name of Athens.

Any American "Athens" has got to have a university, so that our scouting for material must center on the 2,000-odd universities and colleges, senior and junior, in the United States. And these beautiful college campuses are certainly among the least ephemeral institutions in America and may have some survivors even 500 years from now. However, the "Athens" we are looking for is not one of suitable architecture or ripened ivy, but of dynamic, sophisticated people.

Before we inspect the whole university picture, notice must be taken of the claim of Princeton University that it is already "The Athens of America." The boast was invented by its former president, Harold Dodds, and was repeated as recently as Nov. 14, 1958, in the Princeton *Alumni Weekly*.

Princeton's principal claim to the title is based on an institution—the Institute for Advanced Study, endowed by the Bambergers in 1930—which is not officially connected with the university, though it is nearby.

Princeton was not yet a university in 1896, when it changed its name from the College of New Jersey. Several things began happening to the institution just before and during World War II that took it off the ground. The most important was the arrival at the Institute for Advanced Study (thus, "at Princeton") of Albert Einstein, fleeing Hitler's Europe. And presently the plainclothes generals from the Pentagon began arriving incognito, and Princeton was involved in the nuclear-research team at Brookhaven, New York.

The second was the installation in and around Princeton of miscellaneous research, industrial and foundation outfits, for mixed reasons. The pioneer was evidently George Gallup's Institute of Public Opinion (polls and Madison Avenue market research). Princeton, connected with the Pentagon, the nucleus and Madison Avenue, began looking in the mirror more often. By now there are over seventy research establishments in the town, including the Sarnoff Research Center employing over a hundred Ph.D.s, the Industrial Reactor Laboratories, the Turbo-Motor Division of Curtiss-Wright, the Electronics Associates' Computation Center, the Applied Science Corp., Aeronautical Research Associates, etc.

The third development that intoxicated Princeton was the settling-in of a mixed bag of writers, journalists, big-thinkers and exurbanites generally, for the university is almost midway between New York and Washington. The significant arrival was the novelist John O'Hara, a noncollegian who had all his life looked to Yale College as the seat of power and posh. His switch to Princeton, since he is known to be hypersensitive in these distinctions, is catastrophic for Yale. To O'Hara's keen nose, the smell of posh now blows off Princeton.

It may be said that the arrival of Einstein scotched the ghost of Princeton's own F. Scott Fitzgerald. It may also be said that Einstein's death and O'Hara's arrival ushered Fitzgerald's ghost back again. Princeton has gratefully given O'Hara the Princeton Tiger watch charm and the Princeton Right Wing Club tiepin and attends his annual big football party. O'Hara brings out the worst in Princeton.

Princeton may yet become the Athens of America, but probably not so long as air generals walk in and out and huge corporations hold seminars in the Princeton Inn and military Congressmen can pillory Princeton professors and ignorant playboys can cuckold the associate professors. Princeton, no more than any other, cannot render to both God and Caesar.

The institution's actual status in the Athens sweepstakes will fall into place, by no means disgracefully, if we enlarge our view to take in the whole splendid and various company of distinguished American universities, once we know which they are.

If not to Princeton, to which of the first twenty or so American universities ought the title to be awarded? And this question brings up the much more useful, preliminary question: which are the first twenty or so American universities?

One would think that any such list would be controversial to the point of multilateral civil war. Just as no one wants his mother classified socially, no alumnus likes his Alma Mater realistically rated. But in fact the list is a commonplace among experienced educators; it is one of the daily reaffirmed facts of life to administrators of the fellowship foundations. Many a man would like to insinuate his own school into the list, but he is prevented on two counts.

The first count is that it would be hard to omit any of twenty-one universities. The second is that the great mass of American colleges, senior and junior, are crippled by a small endowment, dependence on either church or state, a brief past, a small library, poorly paid teachers and a poor ratio of teachers to students. Certainly hundreds of schools boast some fine teachers, fine departments and fine students and alumni, but their limitations are all too well known to their own faculties. If the list of twenty-one is politely suppressed, it is out of a sense of consideration. Yet this gentle conspiracy is no help, and may be a distinct hindrance, to our urgent intellectual advance. It throws the whole matter of higher education into a generalized, hopeless twilight where no names are named, no faces are seen and all the cats are gray.

One booby-trap will be avoided here. The twenty-one will not be named in order of merit, but merely in order of the size of the endowment, excluding the value of the campus installation. The twenty-one are to be taken simply as a group. They are: Harvard (including Radcliffe), Yale, Columbia (including Barnard), Chicago, M.I.T., California (at Berkeley), Stanford, Rice, Cornell, Princeton, Minnesota, Pennsylvania, Washington (at St. Louis), Dartmouth, Caltech, Tulane, Michigan, Virginia, Wisconsin, North Carolina and Colorado.

Anyone whose university is omitted ought now to consider the parallel list of the twenty-one *richest* schools in America, for fourteen of them are on the first list. The big endowments are (in millions): Texas $287, Harvard $278, Yale $174, Columbia $147, Chicago $123, M.I.T. $88, California $86, Northwestern $82, Rochester $79, Stanford $75, Rice $65, Cornell $65, Johns Hopkins $63, Princeton $62, Minnesota $59, Pennsylvania $56, Washington $48, Dartmouth $48, New York University $45, Vanderbilt and Duke both $41. Caltech is at $37. A sensitive alumnus of many a university could put his school into contention very soon with a gift of $20 million.

Big money, in short, may have qualified two-thirds of our list but failed to qualify the richest of all, Texas, while Rice in Texas, with one-fourth the endowment, made it.

Well, what is wrong with the other seven? Texas' endowment is not solid capital like Harvard's, but consists of the appraised values of oil properties—the gifts are generally hedged and restrictive. The board of trustees, dominated by politicians and the tight Texas community of millionaires, wins every battle with the faculty. The contrast with Tulane is significant.

Northwestern is overshadowed by the University of Chicago.

Rochester is under suspicion of domination by Eastman Kodak.

Johns Hopkins is thought of, most unfairly, by matriculates as exclusively a medical school.

N.Y.U. is overshadowed by Columbia (see Northwestern).

Vanderbilt and Duke remain Southern schools commemorating dead millionaires, though both have some fine faculty members and Duke a good library.

Well then, what is so good about the other seven that made the twenty-one without big money?

Caltech has an all-male student body of only a thousand on which to spend its $37 million. Perhaps nowhere else are brains so pampered.

Tulane ($28 million) has a beautiful campus with the fragrance of sweet olive, and a cultivated board of trustees who, in New Orleans' Latin-European tradition, believe that brains are aristocratic.

Michigan ($25 million) has a very high even value through all faculties; a handsome, well-treed campus, and acceptance by the Ivy League group as virtually one of themselves.

Virgina ($18 million), which is practically state-supported like Minnesota, Michigan and some others, is what is meant in much of the South by "The University." The real reason is that the late Thomas Jefferson is still in residence. His name is used every day and settles all arguments. Virginia has been a

true university since Jefferson planted it in his own native foot-
hills of the Blue Ridge Mountains.

Wisconsin ($12 million) and North Carolina ($5 million)
once claimed the most progressive elements in their sections.
The politics of the McCarthy era cut cruelly into faculty pride
and independence.

Colorado sits high in the Rockies and gets status from its
annual World Affairs Conference, held without press-agentry.
In spite of low salaries, an able faculty is drawn by the fine
living quarters. Its character is a tribute to Colorado politicians
who have made no effort to ruin the faculty.

The top twenty-one are not named without some criticism.

Chicago has the most rigid faculty caste system in America,
giving it a distinctly Madison Avenue tone. It once offered to
change its name to Rockefeller University in view of the $170
million received. It doesn't seem to want to be loved.

Stanford, a plutocrats' school in red-tiled Spanish Mission,
aspires too frankly, like Princeton, to the Athenian, but the
weather is right.

Cornell has another overpowering board of trustees.

Minnesota, it has been said quite seriously, would be more
Athenian if it were not quite so far north.

Washington, sitting at the center of the heartland where
within a radius of a hundred miles a dozen rivers flow together,
is listed with no qualifications at all. The extraordinary community of St. Louis believes, like New Orleans, in an elite of
brains and manners. A man can safely wear a silk hat on a St.
Louis street. Washington has almost as many Nobel Prize-
winners as California and Columbia. It has its own TV station,
headed by Arthur Holly Compton.

Dartmouth: see Minnesota.

Most of the first twenty-one are too committed to conformism
and the search for "acceptability."

In case the Athens of America should turn out to be a primarily undergraduate school, a top list of these is given, with endowments (in millions); Wellesley $33; Vassar $29; Oberlin $27, Brown including Pembroke $26; Amherst $24; Wesleyan $24; Williams $20; Smith $20; Bowdoin $14; Bryn Mawr $14; Swarthmore $13; Haverford $10; Mt. Holyoke $10; Carleton $8; Davidson $8; Hamilton $7; and, with still smaller endowments, Antioch, Kenyon, Lawrence, Reed and St. John's (Annapolis), plus the three military academies. In this area, the coincidental appearance on one campus of half a dozen fine teachers could be decisive, so that the list is subject to change.

A physically stupendous new candidate is the Air Force Academy at Colorado Springs. Its site gives the feeling of looking out across all America. The vast buildings appear to float on their walls of glass, a material which has a deplorable way of exploding outward in the steady seventy-mile winds. The place cost nearly $200,000,000, not counting the carloads of fresh glass. Greatness here depends on the future of air power, currently more debatable than the lethal power of flying glass.

Another test is age, which allows money, ivy and loyalties to grow. These dates of founding also give a series of footnotes to real American history: Harvard 1636, William and Mary 1693, St. John's 1696, Yale 1701, Pennsylvania 1740, Moravian College for Women 1742, Princeton 1746, Washington and Lee 1749, Columbia 1754, Brown 1764, Rutgers 1766, Dartmouth 1769, Salem (N.C.) 1772, Dickinson 1773, Hampden-Sydney 1776. Only six of these are on our first list. Two others are Moravian; Dickinson went in for Indians.

In the next fifty years, twenty-four more schools were founded, but only three reach our first list: North Carolina 1795, Michigan 1817 and Virginia 1819. There were bursts of college-founding before and after the Civil War and again toward the end of the century, when *nouveau riche* Texas, Stanford, Caltech, Rice and Chicago arrived. One can spend fruitless hours brooding over the effect on a college's ultimate character of the historical period and place in which it began; but there is certainly an effect.

Another factor in a school is the availability of knowledge, crudely expressed in the number of library books and the ratio of faculty to students. The library totals, in decimals of a million, are: Harvard 5.5, Yale 4.2, California 3.5, Stanford 3.0, Michigan 2.3, Columbia 2.1, Chicago 1.9, Cornell 1.6, Minnesota 1.6, Wisconsin 1.3, Pennsylvania 1.3, Princeton 1.2, North Carolina 1.1, Colorado .78, Dartmouth .72, Tulane .6, Virginia .6, Washington .52, M.I.T. .4, Rice .25, Caltech .09.

The lack of books is sometimes balanced by an excellent faculty-student ratio, as at Caltech 1-3, M.I.T. 1-5, Tulane and Virginia 1-8. The good undergraduate schools are surprisingly consistent at a teacher-student ratio of 1-9 and a library of around 300,000 volumes (though the libraries at Brown and Oberlin are above 800,000, while Antioch, Reed and Davidson fall far below the average). In the long run, the library may be the decisive factor. The future may be shaped by whether a university guessed right or wrong with its books, had good or bad luck. Was Harvard right or wrong in specializing in East Asia, Dante, Montaigne, Tennyson and Keats; Yale in Shakespeare, Boswell, Franklin, Walpole, Meredith and Judaism; Texas in Texas and English literature; Princeton in Jefferson, Woodrow Wilson and diplomacy; Columbia in Joan of Arc, Spinoza, Russia and East Asia? Who can tell? But once such a direction has been set, the university is forever stuck with it. The kind of people who would be interested in that field flock in and if they are dull boys, they stupefy the university. It is amusing to notice that Princeton's interest in Thomas Jefferson is competitive with Virginia's proprietary interest: good, sound, in-fighting, since the two compete for Southern students. This

whole matter of university libraries is worthy of review by a
critic of the first rank, not me.

Still another way of rating colleges was presented by the
Scientific American in July, 1951. It determined which colleges
had originally graduated the highest percentage of the male
Ph.D.s listed in *American Men of Science*. The first twenty
schools on a list of fifty were Reed (Ore.), Caltech, Kalamazoo,
Earlham, Oberlin, Massachusetts State, Hope (Mich.), De
Pauw, Nebraska Wesleyan, Iowa Wesleyan, Antioch, Marietta
(O.), Colorado, Cornell (Ia.), Central (Mo.), Chicago, Haver-
ford, Clark (Mass.), Johns Hopkins, Emporia (Kan.).

This list shows that the use of exact criteria in this matter
turns it into farce. Not one Ivy League school is on the entire
list; most of those that are on the list suffer from every teaching disability that the American college is heir to. This exhibi-
tion of degree-worship, or academomania, could equally be used
to prove that the Ph.D. is worthless.

Still another way of establishing a ranking was conscientiously
explored by the Chicago *Tribune* in the spring of 1957. Its reporters polled educators all over the country on their opinions
of their own and other institutions and somehow averaged out a
consensus.

This resulted in a list of ten top universities, given, as even
my courageous sources did not dare to do, in invidious order of
merit, as follows: Harvard, Yale, California (Berkeley), Chicago, Columbia, Princeton, Michigan, Cornell, Wisconsin, Stanford.

All this does is to take our top ten, virtually in order of endowment (with a little juggling), drop M.I.T. and Rice, move
up Michigan and Wisconsin. However, the *Tribune* quoted the
educators' doubts about Wisconsin as "lacking momentum . . .
it is not a dynamic school." Its brilliant past was probably what
got it on the list.

The cautious list of ten, with its incautious ranking, gives the peculiar result of breaking into two groups with a gulf between.

The *Tribune*'s sources also gave the first ten men's colleges as Haverford, Amherst, Kenyon, Wesleyan, Hamilton, Union, Bowdoin, University of the South, Washington and Lee, and Williams, and the first ten coeducational colleges: Oberlin, Swarthmore, Carleton, Reed, Pomona, Grinnell, Lawrence, Wooster (Ohio), Kalamazoo and Hope. (I suspect the sources of having believed the *Scientific American* story.) The omissions from these lists are even more astonishing than the inclusions, for some argument can be raised for every little college in America and one would be delighted to listen to it. I am not speaking of the women's colleges, for the *Tribune* gave a ten-best list especially for them, which was impeccably chivalrous.

Some people would have us look, for the Athens of America, to the industrial-research centers, such as Standard Oil's at Linden, N.J., the General Motors Technical Center ("The Versailles of Industry"), the complex of electronic works around San Diego, or that incredible Shangri La, Los Alamos, approached between mountains and over gorges until suddenly there it is in the upper airs, loaded with Ph.D.s whose luncheon conversation is unintelligible. But these are all engaged in applied science and dedicated to anything but disinterested thought.

There still remains the one place in America that superbly has no interest whatever in becoming the Athens of America, that regularly throws away its Athenian assets, that is loved and hated more sincerely than any other, the capital of the arts and professions, of the United Nations, of business and finance, the greatest port in the world, the self-made Acropolis, awesome, preoccupied, dead-pan and irresistible.

And so, of course, in all sensible probability, this has to be the Athens of America—New York City. There is essentially no competition.

On the university level, this would point us to Columbia. It began in 1754 with ministers of five different faiths, including the Hebrew, as *ex officio* governors, on the shore of the Hudson River between Murray and Barclay streets. In 1857 it moved to the heart of modern Madison Avenue and moved out again, under President Seth Low, in 1897, just as the advertising business discovered itself, to the hill of Morningside overlooking the Hudson.

Between these two dates a lot of Americans had discovered in European universities, chiefly German, that their own alma maters were hardly senior high schools. They came home to turn them, by a hundred different theories, into true universities. The practical theory of education had been applied by Benjamin Franklin at Pennsylvania and by Jefferson at Virginia; it was developed by Wayland at Brown, White at Cornell and Van Hise at Wisconsin.

Harvard and Columbia, having been true universities for some time, resisted this influence, though both introduced business schools. Harvard, however, remains in Boston, an enclave of the exhausted Puritan tradition in an Irish Catholic city. Columbia, having shaken off the dust first of Wall Street and then of Madison Avenue, had the advantage of being no one thing.

The Chicago *Tribune* survey, which was of course rooted in the Midwest, was "astonished" by the high quality of Columbia. This quality is indeed not ostentatious; it attracts very little attention even from New York City; the New York newspapers hardly ever mention Columbia. The great peculiar city hardly knows that Columbia University is there, somewhat as modern Greeks hardly ever raise their eyes to the Acropolis.

My biased choice of Columbia can be opposed by those who remember that the enduring heart of Athens was not really the Acropolis, but Plato's school, which was held a mile to the north of the city in the walled park of Academus. On this analogy, New York's Academe would be sited in Westchester or Staten Island, but surely not in New Jersey.

1960

*F*ACE-LIFTING THE GIANTS

*T*WO MASSIVE institutions, *The Saturday Evening Post* and *Life*, have recently agreed that *something* has happened to the American reader, and in consequence revised their format and editorial attacks. Meanwhile, their chief competitor, *Look*, stood firm. The *Post* and *Life* editors do not actually *know* what is happening in the American mind; neither do I.

One theory is that the reader had grown seriously tired of being kidded and conned by the mass magazines. This theory seems to be generally accepted, since most general magazines have recently made an attempt to be more intelligent, or more sophisticated, or more something. The desire to compliment the reader on his or her superiority runs the spectrum from *McCall's* to *Woman's Day* to the syndicated newspaper columns.

Everything the mass magazine can conceivably say it has already said a thousand times over; it can hardly think up a new recipe. The triteness rings especially loud when a mass magazine takes up one of the standard strong stands. For many people, the solution has been to stop reading magazines entirely on the discovery that the benefit of reading a mass magazine is a fringe benefit, and a very raveled fringe. The sequel is that the nonreader finds himself suddenly in a purer, rarer air, alone with his own thoughts, which he may even find surprisingly interesting.

A related theory is that there are times to read, and times not to read. The depression, the New Deal and Hitler gave a lot of people the reading habit. The Eisenhower era killed the habit for many. Today a reader may feel that once he has got the point of The Bomb, further social commentary is superfluous. He may see the earth as simply spinning, like a gambler's coin, whose destiny is to come down either heads or tails.

Corporation board rooms are not so philosophical. So people don't read, they say—make 'em buy the magazine, anyway. To this riddle there is indeed an answer, and the answer is pictures. If they won't read, they can at least look. And pictures are today the lifeblood of the mass magazines, including of course *Life*, *Look* and the *Post*.

Photographs dominate the field, because a photograph is much cheaper than a painting. And by a complicated process of personalities and procedures, the photographers employed by *Life* early convinced the journalists who employed them that they had an art and a mystique that Time, Inc. people could never understand. I can say, with some aura of authority, that most *Life* photographers are idiots, and most of their pictures are pointless. The fact is that almost anybody can take a pretty good picture if he will use as much film as a *Life* photographer uses and try enough angles and exposures and keep his thumb off the lens. (I have probably looked at half a million pictures by *Life* photographers; these heroes are indefatigable.)

Since professional photographers tend to be a little bit stupider than the rest of mankind about almost anything, their pictures reflect this disability. The problem of a *Life* editor is that he is stuck with the pile of pictures that the *Life* photographer has brought back from Samarkand or Timbuctu.

Some genius at *Look*, probably Daniel Mich, saw the flaw in the *Life* procedure. *Look* exhibits a total mistrust of photographers. It assigns a "producer" to spell out to the photographer what the point of the story is. A worse insult could hardly be imagined, but of course the photographers accept it. Nobody without a very thick skin should aspire to this art. The result in *Look* is that each of *Look*'s pictures is *working*. They are not brilliant, but they are humane and intelligent. The magazine is loaded with individual faces, and the faces are expressing something. They show what a photographer can do if things are patiently spelled out for him, and he is given hard orders, with no allowance for his genius.

Look's secret is still invisible to *Life*, but the reformed *Post* has made an effort to adapt it to its own uses. The "old" *Post* worked on some amazing fallacies, besides the blind faith in photographers. In the issue I looked at, it showed men's garden clubs, TV education, African hospitals, a town's Paint-Up Festival and tourists. These are all communal activities, blotting out the individuals. Russia is even more communal than America; and so are caste India, tribal Africa and semifeudal Europe. The communal American, with his shirt hanging out over his pants, getting into the spirit of things, may be useful, but he is not interesting. Another peculiarity of the "old" *Post* articles I read was that there was not one single fight in the issue, in violation of the oldest law of journalism or even just storytelling.

The "new" *Post*, beginning Sept. 16, 1961, apparently abandoned these three fallacies. Communal life gave way to interesting individuals. Some articles showed some fight. And art directors were put in charge of the photographers and artists.

A reasonable improvement, this bore little relation to the *Post*'s advertisements: ". . . blazing new spirit. Color runs riot. Imagination is king. The printed word rises to new glory. A new creative freedom comes to magazines—and the roar of excitement can be heard. . . ." Why do publishers have to talk as if they were hiding a new Voltaire, Swift, Baudelaire and Goya, when they have only hired some new art directors? The blaze, riot, imagination, freedom and roar dwindled down to an amusing picture of Casey Stengel prissily sniffing a red rose.

Maybe the *Post* editors feel as if they had set fire to the sofa, but the blaze is simply the European format that has been leaking into American magazines since World War I: bleed pages, lots of wasted white space and sans-serif type.

Art directors, the monopolists of these tattered mysteries, are quite the equal of photographers as hollow bluffers and packagers of moonshine. They can turn a straightforward story into gibberish by putting the title and author's name on a preceding page, splashing the text with an ape's footprint around whose toemarks the paragraphs snake, and using three different type faces in three different colors. They like it best when these little tricks make no communicative point whatever, but cost a lot to produce.

As for *Post* fiction, new or old, its action reporting is excellent; its mood stories begin to be preposterous in the first paragraph. Somebody should explain about mood stories to magazine editors. You don't start at 20,000 feet; you start on the ground, unless you're writing exclusively for fifteen-year-old girls or drunkards.

A few figures will describe the *Life-Look-Post* race. In 1951, the *Post* and *Look* were about equal above 3,000,000 circulation, and *Life* was king at over 5,000,000. Today all three are around 7,000,000, but the *Post* is proud to claim that it is in no hurry to reach that figure, while *Life* and *Look* guarantee it for early next year. These swollen lists have been achieved by cut-rate subscription prices in the following percentages: *Life* 78 percent, *Look* 48 percent, *Post* 44 percent. Meanwhile, back on Madison Avenue, *Life* and the *Post* have lost in advertising pages, *Look* has slightly gained. Nothing conclusive there, except that *Life* and the *Post* are scared, and the latter at least has been losing money.

A very recent *Life* statement that its revenue increase in the third quarter of 1961 represented two-thirds of the whole increase by general magazines in that quarter exasperated *Look*, which could point out that its increase in the same quarter was nearly the same as *Life*'s. "Well, that's *one* way of putting it," said *Look*'s counteradvertisement, as a charming euphemism for the short word, lie.

More complicated words are required to describe the "new" *Life*, advertised June 1, 1961, as committed to beauty, understanding and wisdom. The claims were in a lower key than the *Post*'s, but were still fairly pretentious. As an editor, I can find in the "new" *Life* only pure chaos.

In the issue of August 4, 1961, one suddenly comes on a chinless, pout-mouthed, barebacked citizen, about a quarter life-size, patting sun-lotion on his fat wife's back, on the beach at Atlantic City. One starts back in revulsion. For somehow one has been tricked into identifying oneself with this repellent scene. The reader is suddenly a sun-baked slob married to a fried blob. The flick of self-horror passes and as one peruses the whole eight pages of people sun-bathing—not beautiful people, just unidentified people with skin—the numb boredom sets in. The message of these eight valuable pages is no more than: people have skin. A mosquito would be delighted by this message, but nobody else.

The theory of editorial lunacy is never a safe one. One must suppose, instead, that in this foolish story *Life*'s editors thought they were capturing *Look*'s common touch, or the identification in the *Post*'s Norman Rockwell illustrations. The utter failure of the attempt has a lot to say about the limitations of uninspired photography. It was an insult to the reader. But the intention of this unnewsworthy, banal and offensive story must have been nobly ambitious: to speak to the readers' instincts rather than to their brains. If this is true, it bespeaks a profound repudiation of *Life*'s original function as a fact outfit, telling about what it knew something about.

Another story, Sept. 8, 1961, on the monsoon in India, compounds the *Life* chaos, and this time gives it twenty pages in color. These expensive and beautiful pages said something less subtle than that people have skin; they said that it rains in India. I think I know that; if they had told me that it rains in the Sahara Desert, I might have been susceptible. The Indian rain is displayed with plenty of white space, bleed pages and sans-serif type set like a disordered, illegible poetry. The point of these pages is so vague in the editors' minds that it is supported by quotations from Hindu poets, not the ideal caption-writers for *Life*. The whole story does make a kind of music, but it says absolutely nothing to a Western reader and whirls on out of the top of one's head.

If one takes it that the story tells us how we should feel (rather than think) about India, the ugly thought rises that the present *Life* editors are not competent to tell us that, and were not hired for that job. It is often said outside the organization that the present survivors on *Life* from 1940 are precisely those (with one or two exceptions) who would in the different climate of 1940 have been unanimously voted least likely to survive on *Life*. This is probably a compliment to them, but its relevance is that it is a *unanimous* compliment. Even more significantly, a majority of the survivors are products of the picture-handling, or photographer-handling, department. These include the present editor, Edward K. Thompson, who comes from South Dakota, not far from Harold Ross country. In his choice of personnel, the proprietor, Luce, exhibits a decided preference for hicks, for after all he was born outremer, in China. By upbringing, Luce has almost nothing in common with his fellow-Americans; he is an *Auslander*, a very unusual thing in America. This makes for some confusion in the Time, Inc. operation. Nobody understands Luce. In fact, Luce likes to affect that he doesn't understand Luce.

It is not realized how massively *Life* has moved in on book publishing. It circularized 10,000,000 people for its *Pictorial*

Atlas of the World, a handsome but error-ridden work, of which it sold 310,000 copies and printed another 100,000. Its *Russia* sold 475,000 copies. Its *The Sea* (an un*Life*like book because the consultant insisted on accuracy over the protest of the *Life* staff) has sold 250,000; *The Forest* has sold 200,000, and others are rolling off the presses. To believe everything in these books (except *The Sea*) would probably be naïve. They are hasty organization jobs, concentrating on making a good general impression, regardless of "small" errors.

Life seems like a blinded giant. It staggers blindly, with its hands before it, through a fog it has created itself. Will-o'-the-wisps, like beauty, understanding, wisdom, are dancing somewhere in the murk ahead, and it stumbles on—not forgetting the advertisers and subscribers—trying to remember the dictionary definitions of those great words. But for *Life* editors they are only words in the dictionary, and it is often terribly difficult to remember.

1961

A DEFENSE OF TIME, INC.

*A*RTICLES LIKE the foregoing have created a false impression that I am indiscriminately hostile toward Time, Inc. The truth is somewhat more complicated, and may be signaled by my reactions to a book about Time, *Name and Address*, by a former *Time* managing editor, T. S. Matthews.

This book summons me with a blaze of trumpets to a novel and overdue function—the defense of Time, Inc. When Matthews writes: ". . . strutting little venture . . . scarecrow style . . . snook-cockery . . . ludicrous, exhibitionistic but arresting dialect of journalese . . . slickness, smartness, bluff . . . ," it is time for the ranks to close. He tells us that at every stage of his career on *Time*, he blushed, flinched and held back, hating each more elevated prostitution while bowing to his shameful fate, like a character in *Candide*.

This is a slander on a number of able, honorable men of the thirties who liked their *Time* jobs. It assumes the virtue of the American intellectual position that *Time* was a tissue of deliberate lies. The difficulties involved in persuading these men to compose a book of lies would have been so enormous as to be laughable. The American intellectuals of the thirties were themselves confused; and this confusion itself determined much *Time* policy, made of it a choice of opposites. *Time* naturally tried to speak with one voice, or at least seem to. But it candidly reflected the world of the people who wrote it—young, talented, irresponsible, upper-middle-class, somewhat pompous. They were generally left to their own devices; certainly I was.

I speak here only of what I know; I haven't read *Time* in

fifteen years. But Matthews' maudlin confession can be put more fully into perspective. What he did not know was that in those days one small, prolific core of writers, who never mentioned the fact, were thoroughly aware that a larger group had no idea what Time, Inc. was all about. The larger group, headed by Luce, included Matthews. The smaller numbered at least Martin, Billings, Busch, Fraser, Gottfried, *et al*. Others fell partway in both. These others were nice people; nobody wanted to hurt their feelings; and they were loaded with feelings.

Time was directed at the literate Philistine reader, who was assumed to be in such a hurry that only great charm and provocativeness could stop him long enough to read anything. The reader's attention was all-important; the subject quite secondary; and it was best if the writer, until just before he read the research, had been as ignorant as the reader. The success of this method derives from the psychological truth that the first impact of information on any mind is always more vivid than any follow-up. For example, if you have never before heard that Nero was a much-beloved Emperor who for a thousand years was expected to return to the Romans, this news will astound you and would be considered "*Time*-worthy." But if, as a historian, you had always known it, you would not even think to mention it. And yet it is a very instructive, if highly cynical, fact.

Matthews' error is shown quite clearly when he describes his operations as editor of the "back-of-the-book" critical departments of *Time*. He promptly inquired into the souls, sincerities and scholarships of his staff and set about making these departments really professional. This sounds all right but it was in fact all wrong. He was merely proving that he thought he was still on *The New Republic*.

The true secret of Time, Inc., if anything so blatant can be called a secret (and yet this one evidently still is), is that it must remain ignorant, soulless and amateur. When it tries to be professional, it violates its own format and becomes an enormity. Matthews' resolve to please God and the professionals could lead nowhere except to *Time*'s decadence. And one cannot suppose that he got God and the professionals to read even the back end of the magazine.

Matthews' group were so intent on the soul business that they even descended on Luce to inquire into his soul. Matthews describes this wonderful scene (a pack of naïve hounds baying on the trail of an invisible or nonexistent fox) which, in fictional form, appeared in Wertenbaker's *The Death of Kings*. I need hardly add that as an amateur I laughed all the way through both versions of the scene, but not quite happily, for it is saddening to watch decent men pour their hearts down a drain. Their only sin had been to miss the whole point of Time, Inc., which did not want their souls.

The word "amateur" here is not used disdainfully. I accept Peter Viereck's use of it in *Contact*, February, 1960: "An amateur is the non-technician: not yet deprived of creative imagination by expertese." He invents a Professor Albert Rapp, a professional scholar in the field of humor (!), who accused Al Capp, the creator of "Li'l Abner," of "amateur statements" about humor and a lack of "professional status."

A professional is either a parrot or a sphinx; he knows either "everything" or "nothing." An amateur is somebody you can talk to; he has no excuse for pomposity, and very little for obscurantism. He would just as soon tear up the textbook. To a professional, that would be like tearing himself apart.

To a professional like Matthews it was necessarily important to know how Luce's soul read. The amateurs wanted to know as little about Luce's soul as they could possibly arrange. The amateurs were always working like hell; the professionals were arranging little meetings of minds. And so, no doubt, it always goes everywhere. And the amateurs generally go home at 6 P.M. on the dot with a clear conscience.

Maybe it was not too important that Matthews, the professional, was managing editor of *Time* from 1943 to 1949. Consider the period: wartime censorship, the massive crushing of the Axis, the boasts of the Pentagon, the cross-eyed dealings with Russia, the liquidation of the British Empire, the loss of Central Europe and China; what a moment of untruth! It was not a time for amateurs, as Churchill retired. Significantly Matthews does not mention any great journalistic decisions, triumphs or defeats. Probably there were none.

There is, finally, one other way in which the amateurs and professionals divide. After the professionals leave Time, Inc., they usually suffer a bitter trauma. They all have fascinating, if confusing, stories of how they were betrayed. The amateurs, on the other hand, have dry eyes. They feel that Time, Inc. owes them nothing; and they owe Time, Inc. nothing. When they meet, they do not repudiate the past but neither do they linger on it. They can distinguish between God and Caesar.

1960

THE "NEW YORKER"

HICK

*I*T IS incredible and outrageous, but nonetheless a fact, that the generation of American culture between the world wars was strongly affected by the character, manners and will of one Harold Ross, late editor of *The New Yorker* magazine, the nominal wheelhorse of American sophistication. He is now the hero of a book by James Thurber, *The Years with Ross.*

Ross in the early 1920's, that period when the machine age was expected to overwhelm the individual, seized on the discovery by *Time*'s Briton Hadden that "writers are a dime a dozen." Ross, an *Auslander*, conceived of a magazine for the "sophisticated" New Yorker, a creature he saw somewhat as a grub sees a butterfly. In New York, the writers and artists were superabundant, the audience was not quite ready, the magazine was inevitable.

At first both audience and contributors were largely confined to Greenwich Village. The future was black. Then an article about debutantes by Clarence Mackay's daughter, now Mrs. Irving Berlin, put it on the front page of *The New York Times*. The first financial success of *The New Yorker* was arrived at, simply, by taking over the old *Vanity Fair* crowd—Dorothy Parker for books, Robert Benchley for plays and Alexander Woollcott for "Shouts and Murmurs." In that period, people of a kind could not safely go out to dinner without having read that week's Parker, Benchley and Woollcott; not the cartoon jokes yet; not "Talk of the Town." *The New Yorker*, a weekly, became a stronger habit than *Vanity Fair*, a monthly.

The depression benefited *New Yorker* advertising, as a depression always will a closely read magazine as against superficially read magazines. *The New Yorker* and *Time* in those years pulled together the American elite, with some pretension to brains, and naturally knifed each other at every opportunity. Part of *The New Yorker*'s character was defined by the need to be the opposite of *Time*. Yet the same people went back and forth between the two magazines. (This is not in Thurber's book.)

So far so good. But in the heart of this ripening apple was Harold Ross who is defined, but not depicted, in Thurber's book as a lovable, crotchety, beneficial force in American culture. Ross did indeed have the dream of a magazine, but he was utterly incompetent to produce it. He had to bring in other people whom he immediately feared, suspected and hated, i.e., according to Thurber, "loved." Thurber's book documents the terrible truth that Ross had no valid relationship with any creation excepting only *The New Yorker*; if you were the lifeblood of this creation, he "loved" you. It is not disinterested for an editor to be nice to Thurber. Ross did not care about the money in the enterprise; he cared only about the perfection of this insane impersonation of the sophisticated New Yorker, as a Norman in the year 900 might have wanted to look like a Gaul.

Ross, in his own person, stubbornly remained the most uncompromising lout, hick, clod and boor I think I have ever met, and Thurber, an honest man, completely documents this.

But in fact he was a successful editor. Why? He was a Philistine; he instinctively despised everything *The New Yorker* had to stand for; but somehow he was convinced that, no matter how he felt, it was the greatest thing in the world. As a barbarian from outside the gates, he resolved to bring perfection to this thing he did not understand, even though he would not know perfection when he saw it. Suspicious and baleful, he scrutinized the copy and the art, looking for who would betray him. Probably the manic scrutiny stimulated some of the people involved; it may have paralyzed and disgusted others. Who can say? But Ross was not sure of himself. If his opponent kept his composure, Ross would back down, because to him the whole thing was a mystery, as the whole world of ideas and intuitions must be to a convinced Philistine.

Ross was not peculiar in himself. He was only shocking as the editor of *The New Yorker*. He was a standard American type: the mother's boy who takes it out as a profane talker, a loud-mouth, a sulker, a bluffer, a practical joker, a fake tough guy, a Legionnaire at a convention, a lousy poker player, a goddamner of women schoolteachers (his mother was one), a paranoiac, an inveterate outsider, a human being who knows he cannot handle his own emotions and decides to have none.

Mr. Thurber, a brave as well as a gifted man, evidently kept his composure and even, together with E. B. White, injected into the magazine an antineurotic creation of his own. But Ross had to try to turn these proved men into formulae or fixtures, owned by him.

The New Yorker's problem was that no magazine can live on sophistication alone. Like refinement, which the daily press peddles, sophistication as an end in itself is vulgar. One solution lay in repeated formulae: "Talk of the Town," the departments, "Infatuation with Sound of Own Words," "Neatest Trick of the Week," "Social Notes from All Over" and such tips to the reader on how to feel superior. The fiction had to stylize itself, first getting more and more elliptical and factual, as in the work of O'Hara, Wenning, *et al.*, and later interminably long and often amateurish. In nonfiction, too, it became the policy that there are very few good subjects, and when one comes along, wring it of the last drop.

Thurber points out that the "Where Are They Now?" formula was lifted, without a nod, from Elmer Davis. In 1931, Ross printed a page of poems called "U.S.A. Blues" by me (I am not a poet). I sent in a follow-up set, but these were rejected as too serious, or something. To my understandable amazement, a similar page of poems called "Red, White and Blues" by another writer presently appeared. Most magazines stick at doing this sort of thing, but never Ross. Perhaps he was envious of the legal mass-piracy of *Time*'s system. His burglaries were altruistic, not for money but for the magazine. He was stealing, like any burglar, for his very life, or as a mother would steal for her starving children. Ross was indeed a she-wolf in a perpetual famine year.

There can be two points of view about this; but neither can allow that Ross was a respectable, lovable human being.

The first point of view would be that a really first-class editor must be a she-wolf. Perhaps he must also be a Philistine, who is ashamed of Philistinism and lusts for the creative world from outside the store window. Perhaps like a great surgeon or priest, he must be somewhat hard-hearted. Perhaps like a great general or football coach, he must be somewhat corny. Perhaps like a great chairman of the board, he must have the one-track mind of a mother and homemaker. All traits of the she-wolf, if I may be allowed the Philistinism.

I think this point of view is possible but not certified. Actually I think that the first requisite of a great editor is magnanimity, and the second that he have the luck to have good writers and artists, and the third that he have an audience. Ross had the last two.

The second possible point of view is that Ross canalized and loused up the talent that offered itself and was just another of the numerous American editors who have brought us into our present Sargasso Sea, in a dead calm. For this he deserves no unique blame; but he was also offensive about it, and a discredit and embarrassment to any company he was in.

To say that Ross was a great editor seems to me like saying that Rome became great only after it was overrun by the barbarians who hated, feared ("loved") Rome. Spare me this kind of ("love"). I put Ross at this end of Rome's history rather than as the suckler of Romulus and Remus.

I think most literate people would be fascinated by this book. They will meet many delightful people, including the author, and I believe their judgment of Ross will be, at the end, substantially what mine has always been. Oddly, such is the seduction of Thurber's craft, my eyes watered at the end, at the death of Ross. I don't know how Thurber did it to me; perhaps it was because some good men and women felt something for Ross that they interpreted as ("love").

1959

FIVE

ESCAPE

*A*LL THAT SPACE

A LONG LOOK at the night sky makes most people feel kind of holy. When the full moon slides hugely up, this mood swells into a gentle carnality, and at this time of the month the police departments of the world are alerted for a burst of senseless violence. The moon has always been with us; it belongs to all of us; it seems to have power over our tides and our women; it is the something extra that gives a special enchantment to life on earth; it is the one completely apolitical thing in the world.

But suppose, one night, as the big, red moon looms, we know that there are two Russian soldiers on it. What difference will it make?

The following study, based on published material, looks into this possibility.

There is a story out of West Germany that three Russian men and one woman have already perished in space. The source located the Soviet space base as "near the Elbrus Mountains" (the 700-mile Elburz range of Iran, running from Caucasia to Afghanistan). Since a moon shot is improved by getting as close as possible to the equator, I could have invented this piece of intelligence myself, but would have felt some obligation to choose between Caucasia and the Karakum Desert. Logistically, one would prefer Caucasia to the Ashkabad area.

A Russian scientist told the American Rocket Society meeting that Russia has at present absolutely no man-in-space program whatever.

So the very same Russian scientist had his name signed to an article, again reported out of West Germany, predicting (1) that two Russian men would orbit the earth in 1959 (too late now); (2) that two men with TV cameras would orbit the moon in early 1960; (3) two men and two women would spend six months orbiting the moon in late 1960; and (4) rockets to Mars and Venus, and then Mercury and Jupiter would subsequently go out.

Whether or not any of this transpires, it is all—except (1)—perfectly possible for the Russians now, and largely possible for the United States National Aeronautics (not Astronautics, as one would suppose) and Space Administration or, as hereafter designated, NASA.

The reason for the Russian superiority is disgustingly simple. It has nothing to do with military potentials. Both Russia and the United States now have enough operational ICBMs to fight a war, with the United States still having a superior strategic air force, and probably greater electronic accuracy in laying down ICBMs. Most present United States programs are developing weaker but more accurate rockets. The problem of shooting half-way around the earth has long since been solved by both sides and become merely operational.

But the great propaganda thrusts into space are dominated by Russia's greater readiness to accept gigantism in rockets. Their basic rocket has a thrust of six to eight hundred thousand pounds. Our Atlas has a thrust of only 380,000 pounds, compiled from two engines of 150,000 and a central sustaining engine of 80,000. We are developing the Delta (150,000-pound thrust), the Vega and the smaller Scout. Later will come the Titan, with a first-stage thrust of 300,000 pounds, a second stage of 200,000. By 1965, we will have the Nova, 300 feet high at takeoff, with a cluster of four or six rockets, each giving 1,500,000 pounds of thrust. Weighing 2,000 tons at takeoff, it would still weigh four tons when it started back from the moon. That's all in 1965, maybe; not Now.

Quite possibly Now is not really important, except to the kind of mind that cares whether Columbus is called Italian or Spanish, or was almost French, or should be called American (a term that would have insulted Columbus).

Our moon program is like Russia's, but probably more dilatory: a photographing of the far side; a soft landing of instruments, by means of braking retro-rockets; later, a soft landing of a small instrumented "tankette" to roam the surface, if possible; and finally, perhaps in 1965, the round trip for American men.

Preparatory to the final step, Mercury Project, priced at $250,000,000, may well begin to shoot men up 120 miles in an X-15 rocket plane, with the Vega. Shorter flights will use the reliable small Redstone and the powerful, less reliable Atlas. The men will be recovered in the South Atlantic as was Sam the monkey. The later objective is to orbit a man around the earth. His capsule will have walls of nickel-cobalt and titanium, separated by accoustical insulation, and two windows. The man can either do his own steering or rely on a horizon-scanning system which automatically sets off pitch-and-yaw jets and roll jets. Retro-jet will slow down the capsule enough to drop it into the earth's atmosphere where, twelve miles up, a small drogue parachute will open, and then, at two miles, the main parachute. The military men selected for these chores have been quoted as unimpressed by the hazards. They apparently are not worried by Congress' having cut NASA's appropriation by $30,000,000.

Their ultimate destination is of course the moon. And what exactly will they find? The moon has either no atmosphere at all, or very, very little. By day, the temperature is 248° F.; by night, —200° F.; and the change of temperature is very abrupt.

Without a pressurized and insulated suit, the human body would first explode, then freeze or boil. A man on the moon will see the horizon sloping out of sight two miles off. The sky will be black. There will be no sound, no wind, no fire, no possibility of blast effect. Meteorites will be bombarding the surface constantly, as they have for three or four billion years. Naturally, as a result, most of the moon's surface is probably a deep sea of pulverized light dust, in which one might possibly be able to swim. Since the moon's gravity is very weak, a fairly small push will send a return trip back to the earth. This, apart from its mineral resources, is the one great beauty of the moon: it is easy to leave it.

In this lunar race, why should the Russians go ahead of us? I believe the reason is that their talent for lunacy is greater than ours, and I mean this in much more than a ribald sense.

If Man can get out into space, he must. That is an obligation built into us by our nature. (We can all skip the 100,000 words proving that this is so. Large blobs of them are for sale on every newsstand.) But to land on the moon is not exactly the same as Columbus' landing on America. In a practical sense, a man on the moon has moved from somewhere to nowhere, and has to come back. In a few decades, we will have found out all we need to know, and the space shots will end.

In this finite period, space exploration will give us a critical body of information about the universe and our own planet. The costs are so great that government must finance them. The democratic taxpayer may well in this juncture drag his heels, just as he did when Hitler was developing the tank, the plane and the V-2, for this is also the nature of a free society. If space exploration is a race, the totalitarian country will probably "win" it.

The prevailing thought in America seems to be that it is not a race, but a serious search for the truth. Most scientists agree

with A. R. B. Lovell, director of England's giant radar telescope, who said, "In terms of satellites, America has got back
many more results than the Russians." The head of NASA has
said that space exploration should be a joint effort of all earth
nations, and has offered the use of America's world-wide track-
ing system to the Russians.

The opposite point of view, that space is *per se* a serious
battlefield of prime importance, is shared by the Kremlin and
some American lunatics. The actual battlefield, of course, would
be the earth. Dr. Lee Du Bridge, president of Caltech, says,
"I do not want to get into a nuclear war over who owns the
moon." But the Russians have assigned space to their military.
They impose complete security measures. Their own training
pamphlets for their own missile crews use photographs only of
American missiles. They really think they are in a race of war.

This war into nowhere may be precisely the sort of war the
Russians will be good at, and ought to be encouraged in. To
maintain a small crew on the moon would require a series of
follow-up shots that would bankrupt most nations. And all the
materials used are gone forever, into "nowhere." One question
is what we would call the moon migrants—whether lunarians or
by the more familiar word, lunatics. Such an empire one would
devoutly wish on one's worst enemy.

Now, who wants Venus?

And so we read in *Time*, Nov. 23, 1959, the grimly greedy
blueprint for annexing the moon: how to store the daytime heat
to moderate the nighttime cold, how to get oxygen from the
rocks, etc., to master this "classical high ground" to monitor
everything going on on earth and take potshots at it. The sources
were an Air Force lieutenant colonel and a brigadier general.
When you have stopped laughing, notice that this marvelous
extravagance with energy seems to be a built-in brain-ganglion in
Pentagon big-thinkers, at least among the younger, more steely-
eyed boys on the way up. *Time* concludes: "And the nation that

first lands men and instruments on the moon will be the one whose political and economic outlook becomes the dominant force on earth. . . . Prestige for unnumbered years. . . ."

The Vikings first landed men and instruments on North America; the years of their prestige were decidedly numbered. When the investigation of the universe is turned into a college boy's game and Pentagon sprint for promotion, both monstrously magnified by space euphoria, we must begin to look for the sane and pure men. The universe was not planned to make Luce Republicanism the dominant "political and economic outlook." Such efforts to subvert the unpredictable, open-minded, magnanimous adventure of space exploration into a little greedy iron fist bouncing off the table must seem uniquely repugnant and, for our own interest, undesirable.

The title of the book, Martin Caidin's *War for the Moon*, sounds like more of the same, but the book is not that at all. People like Caidin, actually involved in space exploration, seem to become both pure and sane; and the great excitement of his story does not overthrow his reason. Incidentally, he conveys an impression of the very formidable American competence in rocketry, despite Department of Defense indecisions. Thor-Able, for example, had 300,000 parts and brought in fifty-two scientific and industrial firms. The great American team is well into this thing.

Caidin's story concentrates on the Air Force's three moon-shot failures in 1958 and the Army's one failure, climaxed by Mechta, the Russian success Jan. 2, 1959, and the Army's Pioneer IV success March 3, 1959.

Beside the date of Jan. 2, 1959, all other rocket dates fade away: Goddard's first rocket failure on March 16, 1926; V-2's first flight from Peenemunde in 1942 with a 56,000-pound thrust; the Army's shot with a V-2 plus WAC-Corporal up 252 miles in February, 1949; the first (vetoed) American moon project in 1955 with a Navaho booster (270,000-pound thrust), a Redstone (75,000-pound thrust) and two solid-propellant rockets; the first Sputnik on Oct. 4, 1957; the first dog-manned Sputnik, Nov. 3, 1957; the first American moon-shot try, Aug. 17, 1958, with Thor (127)-Able I, which exploded; Pioneer I on Oct. 11, which went 72,000 miles (one-third the way to the moon). For Mechta, like Pioneer IV, and many more to come, took the whole solar system for its yard.

Caidin has a little bias for the Air Force and is not nearly so heartbroken by Army failures, but this can surely be forgiven, though my bias is the other way. He describes the work of the brilliant Russians who have contributed to rocket development: Tsiolkovskii, Tzander, Kondatryuk, Rynin, Perel'man, Fortikov, Tikhonravov, Pobedonostev, Merkulov, Glushko, Dushkin, Korolev, Semenov Zel'dovich, Khristianovich and Shedov—and let us by all means honor them all.

It is foolish to expect that anybody can tell the true, whole story of rocketry today, since Russia conceals all its failures and nearly everything about its successes, and the United States too keeps many of its shots secret. The capitalistic nation is much the less monopolistic, however. *War for the Moon* does not attempt the impossible, and probably unwise, chore of diagramming all our rocket program, but it tells enough to give the Russians cause for thought.

I am greatly cheered by two other American probings into space. One is the eighty-five-foot radar telescope at Green Bank, West Virginia, which on January 1 began listening on the frequency of hydrogen, twenty-one cm., for orderly radio sounds from two "near" stars that probably have planet systems—Tau Ceti and Epsilon Eridiani, "only" eleven light years away. The other is the eighty-five-foot radar telescope (Goldstone) at Camp Irwin, California, which in 1960 will be able to track a messaging object four million miles, and in 1961 four billion miles.

The current shots toward Venus cannot be tracked all the way this year, but can next year, since the solar system is only eight billion miles across.

Of more immediate use to earth men will be the so-called "stationary" satellites, orbiting only as often as the earth rolls over, and so "standing still" in relation to a given earth area. These will be up 22,300 miles and can do all sorts of useful jobs, in war or peace, for the country that gives them the jobs and can read their reports. Naturally we can put them up over the USSR and they can put them up over us, monitoring at far closer range than men on the moon. This sort of inevitable, mutual peek-a-boo, probably counterpointed by diplomatic protests and scientific disclaimers, is at least neighborly, and may very well suggest the preferability of world collaboration in these matters.

Exhilarated by the eerie beauties and epochal discoveries of outer space, we ought nevertheless to remember that our home planet is undoubtedly one of the most beautiful and richly endowed in the universe. Anyway, it is our first order of business; space is a poor second. This much will remain evident to the pure and sane.

The universe, we have already learned, is viciously hostile to earth men. It will not tolerate them. At the first trifling mistake, it destroys them; there is no mercy whatever. This unfathomable cruelty will not deter us for a moment. But will it not, as the first casualty lists come back, bring all earth men a little closer? As the survivors return from the wars with the bewitching and implacable bitch, space, all men must know forever that our great mercy does not reside in nations, laws, gods, religions, but simply in the glorious atmosphere of this home planet—essentially only the one element of oxygen. In the no-quarter war on space, which makes all human differences frivolous or, rather, invisible, earth men may just conceivably unite.

1960

$\mathcal{F}$LYING SAUCERY

$\mathcal{T}$HE "FLYING SAUCERS" or "soucoupes" or "discs" or "Ufos" (unidentified flying objects, in military jargon) were first seen during World War II over Sweden and Germany, and afterwards practically everywhere, including the Antarctic. But they seem to have concentrated over the southwestern United States, making their earthly capital Los Angeles.

They are usually reported as round or eye-shaped, sometimes as cigar-shaped. Dissimilar visions seem now to have been consolidated to give them all the abilities to race at up to 10,000 miles an hour, zigzag at this speed, stop on a dime, hover, accelerate at impossible rates, appear and disappear at whim. They range in size from a watch-face to a warehouse, and one "observer" claims a 9,000-mile-long Ufo. When the occupants decant themselves, they are seen as dwarfs or giants, beautiful or ugly, human or monstrous, sometimes lemurlike, sometimes insectiform. The beings, as well as their transport, are often composed of pure fire or light, but without any combustion.

Some of the reports come from sober, reputable people, especially commercial airline pilots who did not expect, and were not pleased by, the spectacle. One pilot on the Puerto Rico run had to pull his plane into a steep climb to avoid a fiery mass hurtling at him. (And this seems to be a new problem for pilots.) Seven other pilots that night saw a similar object. Pan American pilot George Wilson watched one large, bright light followed by four small lights in regular formation bear down on his plane and make a sharp right turn at impossible speed. These are probably honest reports. Yet it should be remembered that intermittently through the ages, sober, reputable people have been "seeing" things that weren't there.

The United States Air Force regularly evaluates the Ufos. Of 143 reported in the first half of 1959, 7 were balloons, 23 aircraft, 65 astronomical phenomena, 19 birds, hoaxes and searchlights, and 26 were dismissed for insufficient data. That left three "unknown." For a while there were about 100 "unknowns" a year. They had dropped to 20 in 1957, 7 in 1958. However, the reports are again on the increase.

Still, it is true that "unknown" is a big, awesome word.

And so, bathing in its eerie light, a new elite of hysterics and mountebanks has appropriated the world of the future. Ingenious plot gimmicks used for years by science-fiction writers are now put forward by a Fools' Festival as science-nonfiction.

And respectable people do not laugh. Everybody today is afraid of being caught smiling at Jules Verne, nearly a hundred years late. Everybody's naïve belief in the incredible, whether scientific or supernatural, is in peculiar contrast to everybody's decadent cynicism about all human affairs, even the most credible. And this takes us back to the dawn of the Christian era and a similar phenomenon, alchemy.

Alchemy began as an honest philosophy of chemistry. It soon turned, in Alexandria, into the making of imitation jewelry. This small success for profit turned into the age-long attempt to transmute other metals into real gold and find the elixir of immortality. By then the alchemists had been in touch with the gods, and the fallen angels, who had interbred with mortal women, published magic formulae under false names and glorified the "philosopher's egg" which is now in the sky, in a distinct comedown in nomenclature, as the "flying saucer" or "Ufo."

Today, the elixir of immortality has been vouchsafed to one George van Tassel by friends from Venus. He has collected money and actually built the concrete foundation for a "human regenerator laboratory" at Yucca Valley, California, and wants to run for President on the Space ticket. A Missouri hillbilly, Buck Nelson, returned from Mars, reports that there the schools are all happily segregated among white Gentiles, Jews and Negroes. "Long John" Nebel, who has a post-midnight radio program on New York's WOR, suspects the visitors from outer space may be actually enemy agents, and counts himself the Paul Revere of outer space. One Orfeo M. Angelucci has published a book describing his intimate relations with the outer-space people. Probably a real visionary, he has seen the gods in their fiery light, drunk their beverages ("delicious"), heard their galactic music ("etheric"), visited the small planetoid ("celestial") where his friends live, and unhappily made a disgusting mortal "pass" at his friend's girl. Orfeo sounds like a good running mate for George van Tassel, better than Nixon and somewhat similar. "Long John" would be Secretary of State, with a somewhat enlarged jurisdiction. Surely we could overrun three or four other solar systems in four years, with such an administration.

Tomorrow, the galaxy.

My favorite argument against manned flying saucers must be discarded. I had thought that all mathematical odds would be against other planets' inspecting us at just the moment we conceived an interest in them—sixteen years out of the 4,000,000,000 of our planet's existence, or .0000004 percent. However, mathematicians say that the odds would remain the same—very long —through all time, since there can be no relative probabilities on an event for which there are no data. Alchemy, astrology, the Hitlerian "big lie," and all such legends as Prester John, the non-existent Christian ruler of Asia, meet this fine definition: "the event for which there are no data." When the sane begin believing in such events, the holiday is on and eventually it must be paid for.

Still, one may be attracted to the Fools' Festival. Very well.

But let us set some standards. Please don't give us any more of this stuff about the objects' weightlessness in the earth's field or immunity to atmospheric frictions. If the objects are made of fire, they must singe or ignite what they approach, and the fire must smell. I beg the addicts not to speak of "visitors from other galaxies": the word galaxy seems to be new and lovely to them. They cannot realize how large our own galaxy is—a diameter of 100,000 light years, each light year being six trillion miles. Our sun requires about 200 million ordinary years to make one revolution around the center of the galaxy and is only one of at least 200 billion stars. At this stage of the myth, the saucerites would be wise to confine themselves to this galaxy. The odds against any one "visitor from another galaxy" being able to find our little solar system are really astronomical; and here the mathematicians agree.

A layman can add, without presumption, the note that about the time flying saucers were first seen, planes had just begun to fly at 20,000 feet. At these heights there may be rare light phenomena, like the Aurora Borealis, that can do all the unnatural things flying saucers do—hover, turn at right angles, disappear, accelerate. Or meteoric or electrical or magnetic phenomena. Unfortunately, a pilot is not in the most objective possible mood after he has been flying for hours alone through a nightful of sky; his psyche can become very active.

And so the second great zone for flying saucers, outside Southern California, is the couch of every psychiatrist whose patients see flying saucers in bed.

Dr. Carl Gustav Jung has just published a book on the subject, *Flying Saucers*. Surely subject and author have rarely been more happily wedded. The genius for ambiguity or "double talk" conceals whether or not Jung believes in flying saucers until, on page 149, we have: "The only thing we know with tolerable certainty about Ufos is that they possess a surface which can be seen by the eye and at the same time throws back a radar echo. . . . Their movements indicate volition and psychic relatedness, e.g., evasion and flight, perhaps even aggression and defense." He believes in them, though in the preface he denies it.

To give the best first, Dr. Jung takes these phenomena, or possibly visions, as proof of the end of an era. (You see, this subject is not a waste of your time at all.) He writes:

> As we know from ancient Egyptian history, they are symptoms of psychic changes that always appear at the end of one Platonic month and at the beginning of another. They are, it seems, changes in the constellation of psychic dominants, of the archetypes, or "gods" as they used to be called, which bring about, or accompany, long-lasting transformations of the collective psyche.

Human history, Dr. Jung tells us, has moved from the age of Taurus into Aries and then into Pisces (around the time of Christ) and is now going into Aquarius.

This rendering of history must make us all wonder where we have been and sorry we were away. It is exciting to hear about eras ending and new archetypes forming; one of us may be the new archetype. If this is astrology, eight signs come between Aries and Pisces, and Aquarius is before, not after, Pisces. If it is astronomy, it is true that the constellation Pisces, in our view of it, is next to Aries; but astronomy seems even more remote than astrology from these matters.

Eras are, of course, ending all the time, for somebody or something. The question always is: whom or what? For the West, I had thought an era had ended in 1914–18, and surely this present one must run on a little longer before it matures.

Jung's cheering implication, in hiding his history in the ciphers of numerology or alchemy or astrology, is that the kind of era, the kind of archetype and the date of the unveiling have all been decided in advance by forces far beyond human control. But perhaps we do not want so much irresponsibility. He will say a very good thing, such as that numbers were not invented, but discovered, and then add that the number four represents totality: three plus one, or Father, Son and Holy Ghost plus the Devil; and that all life is dominated by this overriding "truth."

With this sort of cabalism, he interprets some dreams and some paintings of unidentified flying objects. If I understand him, the flying saucer represents the whole soul or anima or rotundum or mandala (neither word in my dictionary) or God's eye or philosopher's egg or *yang* and *yin* or *complexio oppositorum* or Primordial Man or *chen-yen*.

He also cites mass visions of something very much like fiery flying saucers in Basel and Nuremberg in the 1560's, when the Counter Reformation was hitting these two rich and sophisticated cities. It may also be remembered that the Moslem *djinn* were of pure flame, good and evil, beautiful and ugly, and appeared and disappeared at will. The fantasy part of the flying-saucer business is spectacularly not novel; and Jung is right to associate it with the dark side of human tradition. Still, one wonders about his reasons for choosing this disreputable subject and, as he himself says, putting his "reputation . . . in jeopardy."

There may be a clue. All sorts of people, from Toynbee down, are sitting around waiting, in this period, for the revelation of a new universal religion. Among them, in a thoroughly relaxed mood, is to be found myself. It is obvious that since the masses are being constantly reminded of higher forms of life across hundreds of thousands of light years, God must soon be revamped to take in more territory; a great revelation on this one little planet seems suddenly, to say the least, disproportionate. This crass intuition appears to have come to several of the flying saucerites who report that Christ and Buddha were actually born on Venus. This must appear as pure sacrilege to any church, since it would imply that the two must have been moving from planet to planet, repeating the same message and the same experience, to propagate truly galactic faiths. On the stage of the universe, communications of this nature present logistical problems that a one-planet religion is not prepared for. The Salesman's itinerary would have to be coordinated with each planet's successive arrival at the desired stage of cultural evolution. If the waiting list grew too long, some cultures might have to be "frozen," like Egypt's, until there was time to get around to them. A little less than 2,000 years after Christ had called: the atom bomb. To millions of people, such thoughts must soon become a consequence of any attempt to think of a godhead that is, in the astronomical sense, universal. And this universe is already one of the world-wide political facts of life. The contest between the United States and the Soviet Union is scored by two billion people on which will get out into the universe first. Even pigmy Negritoes who do not know about either Christ or gravity can see the stars and perhaps the satellites. The consideration that now confronts earthly organized religion is the night sky.

The flying saucer visions are a vulgar solution of this problem, humbly proffered by the ignorant. The new religion, if any, would have to come from someone with a better grasp of astronomy. Dr. Jung, however, has put in his claim as a prophet of the new religion. He simply decided that an epiphany is well worth a reputation.

1959

SIX

A LITTLE EXTRA ADVANTAGE

WOMEN AND POWER

THE GENERALIZED image a man has of a woman is of a soft, smiling, generous potential of bliss, the one who can make a man feel wonderful, and in some fractional sense, this is a true image.

But most of the women one actually encounters in life seem hard-faced, selfish, suspicious, stingy, misshapen, overweight, ill-tempered, self-righteous, touchy, hysterical and generally such an insult to one's dream of a woman that one would like to kick them in the behind, on general principles. And yet, buried somewhere in each of these harpies, is the angel of the dream.

The reason for this familiar and painful paradox is that the gentle, nubile, protected young woman grows older. The girl who would be delighted to inhabit a dream is obliged, with her stock of instincts, to inhabit real life. And her reaction, it will here be proposed, is to retrogress in evolution, to reverse phylogeny (instead of to recapitulate it), and to employ her human brain to achieve the kind of victories natural to a female spider or wasp or mosquito, while lacking their superb natural equipment.

Of course there are glorious exceptions to this statement, and I hasten to add that they include every woman I know, but I have been fortunate.

Like the female arachnids and insects, however, the human female has a feeling, or at least a sex memory, of power, which she generally conceals. And this contributes largely to the man-made legend of the mystery of women.

222 *A* LITTLE EXTRA ADVANTAGE

The mystery is based in men's preference for imagining that a woman is virtually of a different species from a man, and in this philosophy there is happiness (and also trouble). Men's failure to understand women is very simply explained: they like only women they do not understand. They do not marry the numerous women they understand all too well. Thus their chief experience of women is of precisely those they never wanted to understand. (Understanding is not a synonym for familiarity or predictability or mere knowledge, veteran husbands should be reminded.) It is much more fun to possess a woman whom one does not understand, even when she is entirely familiar. The best intercourse is not a meeting of minds, at least so far as I have ever heard.

Whereas men positively do not want to understand the women they love, the women do want to understand the men, but their capacity for understanding is astonishingly limited, for reasons that may become evident. The chief reasons are that women are perpetually power-hungry, while settling for very little power, and that they can never see the obvious in a man. The first disability may perhaps blind a woman to the actual quality of "her" man. For the incredible fact is that a woman's sense of power convinces her that she "owns" a man, who doesn't feel owned at all. This lunacy of course adds to the mystery of women. But it is possible, after a certain age, to think clearly about women, after one has emotionally realized that they are of the same species as men, a depressing discovery but one that must ultimately be faced.

Women's fondness for gossip and moralizing only shows that they understood the power of a good propaganda long before men did; and all women are born propagandists, from childhood on. A good home is in fact founded on a subtle and unwearying propaganda by the mother, who thus becomes the center of a power complex. Women gravitate to all propaganda institutions, to the churches, to teaching, to political organizations. Any propaganda whatever will fascinate some of them, and this includes Communism and Fascism. Most of our more celebrated male traitors were in fact introduced to treason by their womenfolk, but chivalrously suppressed this information. (As did, for perhaps the same reason, the press.) Yet, as Theodor Reik has pointed out, women do not enjoy abstract thinking though being, as members of our species, perfectly capable of it. The clue is very strong that they are attracted to doctrinaire propaganda because they smell the reek of power. On the more usual level, every woman invents her own local, personal propaganda and becomes the Law-Giver in the home, explaining how life should be run to a man who can usually think better, yell louder and invent moral laws faster than she can. The more power a man gives a woman, the louder she yells.

A recent, well-documented series in *Life* magazine on American love and marriage ruefully agreed that the worst human relations in polite America today are those, in private, between husbands and wives. The screamer is typically the wife. These jangling decibels secretly condition the modern American. It is therefore vital to get to the bottom of this unnatural hubbub. And one way to do so is to consider the eternal female as the evolutionary product of a large picture.

The theory would have to be that as life has evolved from the lower phyla and classes up toward the warm-blooded creatures, the female egg has always retained a domineering power or atavistic memory never entirely overpowered by the male sperm. Nature, for excellent reasons, may be, or rather, most certainly is, partial to the eternal female, the only real champion of life, and far less interested in the male differentiations of species, genuses, families and orders, or in the splendid male specializations. Nature primarily, it would seem, wants to keep that egg going. And even the modern cerebral woman seems to know this. She knows that she is indispensable, and the man is expendable. Historical periods when too many men had been expended, as in the year A.D. 1000, have always been rare, tragic and disgraceful, because the women were in power.

It must surely astonish anybody to be told flatly that the overwhelming majority of animal life on this planet is absolutely dominated by females, but this is the case. The first ten phyla of the evolutionary table, up through the annelids or segmented worms, have no separate males. The creatures, being capable of reproduction, should in my opinion be called versatile females (rather than, as they are, hermaphrodites) having their own built-in male attachments. They are simply sophisticated and independent females having no need of males, which, in their time of origin, did not exist, and were not, I must suppose, missed. With the arthropods, the eleventh of the 13 phyla, the male parts at last managed to secede from the terrible female into independent identity.

The male parts, in the greatest revolution in all animal history, invented and became the sex that can only be described as the second sex.

Before this great invention there could not, of course, have been any of what are now called "relations between the sexes." But now at last the female, the queen of creation, could look at the male, her lover, see him clearly, and establish the glorious relationship. And what did she see? An ignominious little jerk. Love? Good God! Who could love this? This is going to be *some* relationship. For the female of one species of spider is 1,300 times as heavy as the male; for her to look up to him would be impossible and unnatural. The romance is transacted by his sneaking onto her premises without her knowing it and making a hasty getaway when she begins to realize what is going on. Female spiders occasionally manage to catch and eat the males after the ball is over, but the males seem to know the peril and usually escape in good order. The male tarantula, however, dies immediately after consummation, whereas the female lives to the ripe age of twenty years. Some small male spiders have cultivated the tact of first tugging at the corner of the terrible female's web, to test her mood. If she comes roaring out on a bad morning, he disappears. If instead she exhibits a ready languor, he cautiously approaches. Love on this level takes courage, or the sense of expendability. And what about the human level?

In the praying mantis family, the larger female starts eating her lover from the head down as the marriage is consummated, thus assuring him that he is useful not only as a father but also as foodstuff, in that order. Meanwhile rival Lotharios watch the procedure nearby, their antennae trembling in anticipation, but of what? This awful and awesome scene is shown in full color in Robert Snyder's *The Hidden World*, a beautiful movie in which one sees a female praying mantis ten feet tall, a sight to shake the stoutest heart. For this serene cannibal lady has a certain haunting relevance to the human condition. She reminded me of somebody.

The whole insect world gives all the talent and power to the female. The only mosquito that bites is the female. The only bee that stings is a female. The only wasp that stings is a female. For humans the bad news in nature, on a picnic, is exclusively female. Has this fact no significance about the female principle? Male spiders, it is true, have poison sacs but they are not worth thinking about because the males are so small and their poison sacs are so diminished.

The female talents, it should be noted, are not dilettante but thoroughly practical. The female mosquito needs animal blood to become fertile; her buzz is a signal to other females that blood is on the table, and come and get it. The male has no biting apparatus. The worker and warrior bees are all female, obedient to the more fully developed queen bee, the pampered propagator and the symbolic ideal of all feminine women, who are perhaps irritated by their lack of equivalent status. The female wasp that survives the winter is the sole propagator of the race. She alone builds the papier-mâché nest and produces her first (female) young parthenogenetically, that is, without any male assistance. Late in the season she lays a few male eggs which mature into males which fertilize a few females in a curious sky-flight, and then die.

For at least half a billion years, the male was superfluous. In certain insect families, such as the aphids, he is still superfluous, for the females forget about males for several generations and reproduce parthenogenetically. As an afterthought, they then produce a generation of males, say briefly, "Hello, Daddy!" and get themselves fertilized afresh. These on-and-off males seem merely the female's occasional status symbol, as if to show the world she is not a hermaphroditic roundworm or animalcule or starfish. For many women, a husband too is a status symbol, and very little else. If they could procreate parthenogenetically for several generations, they would certainly do so.

This is the female's eternal insult to the male. The male's reply has been: very well, so I am expendable. In the human form, and even before, he has inclined toward a habit of experiment, risk and creation, and also of warfare. Sensing that he is expendable, he has naturally expended himself to some purpose. At least, he seems to say, I will not be expended in vain, since I am going to be expended anyway. And so, by male experiment, risk and self-expenditure (perhaps a synonym for "work"), there has emerged a civilized world, over the horrified lawgiving of the females.

And what was the law of the female-dominated world? Spider silk would be industrially useful, but if one puts two female spiders in one container, the larger will kill and eat the smaller. There went female civilization, and also the spider silk industry. Yet some people think women should run this world.

Nature, evidently dissatisfied with the females' habits, allowed the males to grow bigger and stronger. The biggest bullfrog in the pond may still be a female but paleontologists are hard put to identify a fossil dinosaur as male or female. The male had at last won physical equality. The terror of the dinosaurs, Tyrannosaurus, was as often male as female.

Our own "relations between the sexes" become clearer with the warm-blooded creatures which were at first very small and naturally furtive. Why their blood heated up is a mystery I never have seen discussed. A good explanation is that their hearts began beating a great deal faster than those of the dinosaurs, and the reason for the more rapid heartbeat may have been something so obvious as continuous, hysterical fear. In the later age of the great dinosaurs, perpetual silent terror would have been the proper and sensible emotion for a little creature.

The creation of warm-blooded animals with enlarging brains presented nature with a new problem. Hot blood goes with temperament. Suppose the females were just too damned temperamental and choosy to mate with the available males; suppose they had opinions. There would go evolution. Surely here, in these early marsupials, we find a parable for the dilemma of the modern American married couple. It must have been a shaking period as the two sexes struggled for dominance, with the bigger males winning the argument, and the less powerful or aggressive males and more difficult females dying fruitless. And so seduction, and if necessary rape, entered the natural scheme of things.

It is to be doubted whether male superiority is automatically accepted by the female mammals and birds. Even at this late stage the female frequently has the decisive power. The oldest female frequently leads the flock or herd because it includes more of her personal, loyal, cared-for descendants. The female still rules in the less intelligent families and orders. But in the higher forms the capacity for affection and magnanimity makes male wolves and elephants, for example, loyal to their mates and ferocious toward their mates' enemies. We are obliged to think that this represented an advance over the females' world.

In any case, the rise of the male ended cannibalism between the sexes, as a rule, and introduced the beginning of chivalry, or the protection of the weaker. This improvement has been repealed by various German philosophers, leading to Fascism and Communism.

A seduction ritual is always a compliment to the seducee. Such rituals are used by the egrets, cranes, loons, swans, mergansers, ruffs, plovers, and so on. These males sway the females with a display of energy and splendor. Other forms such as the hawks and owls apparently mate for life, thus sparing themselves all the springtime fuss every year.

Among the birds the female, though no longer all-powerful, still has most of the talent while the male has learned how to sing, woo, fight and explore. The female must feel some degree of admiration, awe and intimidation. She has an opinion, as usual, but the male now also has a right to an opinion.

The new relationship produced an interesting variety of social arrangements. The male house wren, wild turkey and some grouse are polygamous. The ani are communistic, a whole colony nesting and breeding collectively and indiscriminately. Cowbirds do not mate at all, but simply philander at will, the female depositing her "accident" in the nest of another species.

A special word is earned by the phalaropes, whose females are bigger and handsomer than the males, and do the courting and egglaying, and nothing more. The males build the nest, hatch the eggs and rear and feed the young. The female is polyandrous, and may lay several batches of eggs, foisting each off on another discarded lover. The males are at first very diffident but grow more sexually brazen as they get the idea. Their later adventures with the incorrigibly sluttish females, however, are not usually productive after they have begun brooding one set of eggs. There would seem a possibility that female phalaropes are unique in getting some positive pleasure out of intercourse.

The human judgment would be that the phalaropes must be a decadent line. But these are completely fearless little birds, able to swim and feed serenely in an oceanic gale or a crashing surf, perfectly at ease in a very hazardous situation. The male, it may be noted, is the indispensable one. The female, after she has laid the eggs, is expendable. This was the most complete reversal of nature's pattern until human civilization arrived.

Primitive men, lacking our larger knowledge of the female's place in the evolution of life, firmly assigned the female an inferior position, from which she has by no means entirely escaped. The physical power is (generally) on the male side, and so in self-defense the female cites moral and spiritual and doctrinaire laws that work to her benefit.

But beneath all this nonsense, perhaps far beneath, lies the woman's unconscious knowledge of the past queendom of the female and her old powers, and her outrage at confronting a world of male sovereignty. Her reaction, after her early beauty and her effortless power over men has gone, is understandable; and her forgiveness of the male for his sovereignty makes her adorable. Like members of ancient and overthrown royal dynasties, she knows that she is "better" than the members of this parvenu second sex, which she is still bringing to birth. Her desire for power is betrayed by her delight in male children, whereas the female pattern and atavistic function is to produce primarily females. Remember, the females are indispensable, the males are expendable; and women are not in the business of wasting their time, yet they have so far succumbed to a male world as to want sons. There are exceptions, such as my own mother who wanted a daughter, but all she got was five sons. But she was a remarkable woman. Most women want that extra little possibility of power. She did not. There are these exceptions.

As we have seen, evolution has progressively dethroned the female. The result is a character combining the impotent snobbery of uncrowned Habsburgs and Romanoffs with a basic lack of self-confidence. And this character drives a female all her life to try to be a good little girl or, insofar as she knows she has not been, to look like a good little girl. This passion for virtue is what chiefly occasions her lying, tantrums, smugness, extravagance, stinginess, as well as all the wonderful, gracious and beneficial things she does for other people.

For of course the latter are what our nerves rightly expect from our women, and when we get the former we are proportionately offended. Monks have God to bring out their energies; most men have only women. But any man who feels bigger because his woman has no confidence in herself is a damned fool; he ought to try to build up her self-confidence. Some cultures do it by letting the women do the hard work.

But the self-distrust goes very deep. Reik gives the example of a single man and a single woman separately passing a handsome young couple on the street. Everybody will agree that *both* barely glance at the man, but inspect the woman in detail. The man reacts naturally; the woman inhibits her natural impulse and reacts almost defensively, as a competitive professional. She must check her self-confidence against the other woman's charms and also pick up any available tips on beauty. But in thus forfeiting any natural pleasure in the encounter, she remains virtuous and superior.

A woman who understands power is rare indeed. Women's idea of power is of something that can be shown off. They wear all their jewels, whereas men of power prefer to be thought a little less powerful than they actually are. Women like to be associated with rich or powerful men; some are even sexually stimulated by being with a man who is rich, or even just acts rich. They get another kind of power from an aura of respectability, that is, by being a member in good standing of the worldwide secret society of good women, and they are constantly giving the countersigns of this great club. (Every member's credentials are suspect.) By extension, they love groups of any kind, and love to "bore from within."

In their very different ways they have in common the desire to be, in their terms, on the winning side. This visceral need to win all arguments, even with the wrong case, is so foolish that one is thrown back on the generalized explanation of the eternal female as the deposed queen of our creation. She starts screaming when she is completely in the wrong, perhaps remembering whole geologic eras when the female could never be wrong. But even allowing her her great past, how can a woman argue with me? I mean, in the English language, and by the laws of logic. Unless I am a male praying mantis.

On the other hand, a woman with a beautiful pair of breasts must be judged innocent of any crime whatsoever, for the dream of a benefit that her person conveys offsets the damage of the crime. This law is in fact operative with male grand juries, with rare exceptions. To remove such a woman from society seems to men an enormity; but to the female jurors it always seems a very good idea, and so they vote.

For the female juror's power is much like that of a female spider, mosquito, bee or wasp. She is serious about life; she has work to do; she has to make harsh judgments; she is in dead earnest; she has to look ahead and conserve; she wants satisfactory results; she prefers a monopoly; and when she has achieved one, she is complacent. If a member of her sex has so far violated the rules as to be in the dock, she should be destroyed. For the female is indifferent to beliefs and values not her own, hostile to alien forms of life, and unable to tolerate contradiction.

One had better accept most of this femaleness as is. For when a woman tries to repudiate her femaleness, she begins to feel that she has lost her "identity," certainly a very difficult thing to do. (This has evidently replaced the loss of virginity as a disaster.) The attitude was expressed in an anonymous letter to a magazine: "Women who marry and have children today are trapped and largely swindled out of their lives as adult human beings. They become appliances—one of the most versatile and convenient appliances ever devised by man. . . . In real life it is degrading. There is no future in it, no success in it, very little dignity in it and in many cases no thanks for it. . . . Most modern wives have the same education, the same ambitions and interests, and even have held the same level jobs as their husbands."

This woman has clearly been educated to believe that she has the same kind of identity as a man, and was born for higher things than child-rearing and homemaking. In finding her identity as a free citizen, she has lost her identity as a female; and this latter is about 75 percent of a woman's identity. She is evidently miserable, and a disaster for everybody around her. And this letter could have been written by several million American women, exactly the ones who have been most expensively reared. The more women are emancipated, the more convinced they become that they are enslaved.

Yet just by being a woman, *sans* identity, *sans* education, *sans* opinions, she is indispensable. On the other hand, except for fertilizing the female, man has himself invented all his innumerable jobs (such as my writing these generalizations) and they could all be abolished. Out of man's job-inventing, experimentation, brawling, fooling-around, exploration, idle curiosity, recklessness and wastefulness, dreams, abstractions, and impractical interest in the truth, has come civilization, for good or ill.

In this sense, the typical woman progresses from the gentle, sentimental barbarian to the breeder-monopolist to the clubwoman and so on back through the phyla, perhaps as far as the black widow spider. One might suppose that one should withdraw education and the vote from women, but I think not: I have not enough faith in men's civilization. Women are a won-

derful restraining force on the male's headlong idea of civilization; they should be cultivated and protected. Still, the fact remains that the most intelligent women I have known well, in
an active life, have not gone to college. (Exception! Exception!) Education does make women less violent in an overt
way.

This essay pretends to explain women: not a very difficult
feat. But since men do not want to understand women, the
effort has been wasted. One would suppose that the "relations
between the sexes" would therefore be much more difficult than
they actually are. Fortunately nature still runs the show. The
other sex is infinitely fascinating because it is, in one's own
terms, quite insane, while still using the same words one uses
oneself in apparently a totally different sense.

The climactic paradox of the "miracle of love" is that each
partner receives something the other hasn't given, and never
had, or will have, to give. The something, however, is actually
received, and each is much improved. The epilogue of love,
which is marriage, may be the realization that the giver was
giving something wholly different from what was received but
in its different way worth accepting.

Some husbands and wives may think they understand and are
understood. If they are right, there cannot be anything much
to understand.

1962

$\mathscr{W}$ATER AND DESPOTISM

$\mathscr{M}$ANY DESPOTISMS, according to some historians, have developed out of control of the water supply (see Karl A. Wittfogel, *Oriental Despotism*, 1957). One can speculate further that the battle for the oasis comprised most of prehistory. American freedom is based in part on the cheapness and abundance of water. But the news is that we are running short of that element, and a gleam has entered the potential despots' eyes. That is the theme, sometimes unknowingly, of all four of these books.*

The story of violence begins in the book by Senator Kerr of Oklahoma; it is a work dressed in *Reader's Digest* style by Malvine Stephenson and Tris Coffin (their names appear with the Senator's on the title page but not on the cover). The grand stupidity of the hopeless determination in the 1920's to control the raging Mississippi with levees alone is described again—and Herbert Hoover bobs up again on the wrong side, the infallible engineer. The Senator, of course, is on the right side—a network of small dams on the tributaries. But the Maginot Line theory for taming an angry river persisted for some years.

Senator Kerr gives the land area of the United States as

---

* *LAND, WOOD AND WATER.* By Senator Robert S. Kerr. Fleet Publishing Corp.
WATER SUPPLY. By Jack Hirshleifer, James C. De Haven and Jerome W. Milliman. University of Chicago Press.
POLITICS AND GRASS. By Philip O. Foss. University of Washington Press.
NEW WATER FOR A THIRSTY WORLD. By Michael Salzman. Science Foundation Press.

234

1,900,000 square miles, when it was 3,000,000 (before Alaska and Hawaii). This might be forgivable from anyone else, but not from a U.S. Senator: it is as if he does not know what he is a Senator of. In every second chapter Senator Kerr (via his writers) shyly drapes a wreath on his own forehead, then another and another, until one wonders how he can still stand up under the weight of the awesome modesty plus the wreaths.

He works up to "The Kerr Plan," which is simply to persuade all the agencies concerned with the basins of the Arkansas, White and Red Rivers to sit together on an Inter-Agency Committee and publish a report. This has opened the way for various projects, some undoubtedly useful, some probably pork-barrel, and for a Senate committee on national water problems whose chairman, Senator Kerr, promises a report in January. Well, let's wait for the report.

The second book, *Water Supply*, really knows what it is talking about. The authors point out that Kerr's beloved reservoirs evaporate vast quantities of water, and that this water may never fall again on land. Evaporation rates in the United States range from 15 inches to, in the Southwest, 130 inches a year. Lake Mead, behind Boulder Dam, loses by evaporation 800,000 acre feet a year. Thinking like bankers, the authors prefer the water underground until it is needed. The porous or creviced underground strata, called "aquifers," greatly complicate so-called "water rights." The authors are skeptical of the value of many plants, especially the phreatophytes (those with deep roots), which trap water only to transpire it back into the air.

Allowing for the industrial re-use of water, they figure that production of a ton of finished steel could involve the loss of only 1,400 gallons of water, as against Kerr's 65,000 gallons, and a ton of butadiene (synthetic rubber), 26,000 gallons against Kerr's 600,000 gallons. With such economies in mind, they say: "We have . . . not attempted . . . to predict what the supplies and uses will or should be in 1980, 2000 or 2200. We regard such forecasts, commonly based upon crude extra-polations of recent aggregate trends, as usually mistaken and even dangerous. The forecasts are typically mistaken because they ignore the factor of . . . erroneous public policies that will not be easy to maintain in the face of growing real cost of water."

But such optimism, based on faith in free market competition, runs head-on into the growing despotism, executive, legislative, or judicial. Local politicians want to give their own voters water to waste (as two studies in this book demonstrate for New York City and Southern California) and reject the most obvious economies.

A reasonable allocation of water should, these economists say, be based on the marginal values in use—that is, the value of the last units used. The first value of water is obviously as a drink, but people can drink only so much; the second use may be for agriculture, but that too has a limit; and so on down the line. An intelligent society gets all the values it can, within reason in each value. But this philosophy of water is at odds with most government action, which accepts each declared "need" as an absolute, not recognizing it as only a relative "desire." On the insatiable need basis, I could argue that I need all the water in the watershed for my own personal use, and you could argue the same.

Water Supply adopts a novel skepticism toward many reclamation projects. The benefits, it is suggested, of irrigation projects in the basins of the Missouri and Upper Colorado rivers can never equal the public expenditure, totaling in these cases more than $3 billion. As for the Chief Joseph Dam Project in Washington State, the authors quote an authority as estimating the national subsidy per farm in that area at about $22,000 —certainly a lot for the rest of us to contribute to one family.

The bookkeeping approach to water may seem cold to some tastes, including mine, but it earns respectful consideration.

Coldness stops when the book comes to the law of water. The states, in more than half the area of the country, claim to own all the water. The authors ask whether the language used in these statutes "is an innocuous form of words to indicate that the state has an interest in water-resource development or whether the language actually means what (in extreme cases) it says. . . . That there are defects in present systems of private water rights is very clear; but to abolish property rights rather than cure the defects is a drastic and, we believe, unwise remedy." The despotisms are under way.

The federal government has also cut into the water game, and some crucial cases are now going through the courts. Indian reservations (with no Indians) give the government a handle to claim limitless water for "ultimate development." "Navigation," elastically defined, gives federal authorities still another gimmick to claim any water that can float anything bigger than a duck. And so on. It does not look good for just ordinary citizens or, as I like to call them, the sovereign power. Water will soon be a more powerful lever to power than even national defense; and the politicians are catching the heady scent.

The third book, *Politics and Grass,* was so painful that I could not read it thoroughly. It is the tragic story of why a quarter of America has been left a desert by the Western stockmen who, as "advisory boards" in control of the open, public range, have thwarted Roosevelt's attempt to save the plains. One also begins to understand why the plateau states, instead of breeding a free, adventurous, pioneering race, generally vote for black reaction and "to have and to hold." But of course: they too are getting something for nothing. One can only wish all these clever little cowboys a good night's sleep. Though the tone of the book is pedantically factual, it should be read only by people who do not mind getting mad and disgusted.

The fourth book, *New Water for a Thirsty World*, takes a biochemist's approach to oxygen and hydrogen and proposes that the crust of the earth is constantly combining those elements as *new* water and secreting it. It also asserts that if this process were not going on, the break-up of H_2O molecules by such operations as photosynthesis would long ago have emptied all the oceans. I do not feel competent to discuss either of these propositions, which have evidently been rejected by almost all the schools. But I am not so naïve as the professors; I would not presume to dismiss Michael Salzman's evidence that there is good water down under layers of hard rock, where it is not supposed to be. The writer has gone far to justify his title, and the ignorance of scientists is nothing to surprise or dismay anyone.

My objection to this book is perverse: the people who now refuse to look at Mr. Salzman's proofs (mostly the work of Stephan Reiss) are exactly those who, a little later, will make use of his solution to evade all the other solutions. For the new, or "juvenile," water can be only a partial solution. The curse of man is that nature again and again gives him something for nothing, like Reiss's new water; and suddenly he is spoiled, like an apple that is spoiled.

All truly great issues, like water, reach honest men as a confusion of hatreds. In much the way that I once hated both Fascists and Communists, and indeed still do, in this matter of water, my rage goes out in all directions, and my pity for the posterity. People read fiction nowadays to feel miserable, but they do not need to. These books will make them feel much lousier.

1960

$\mathcal{T}$HE COMMUNIST
PERFORMANCE

$\mathcal{I}$N THE 1930's Americans were given, and accepted, a good deal of information about faraway nations, usually related to whether these would be gobbled up later, or sooner, by the various conquerors. But when the Fascist menace ended, the curiosity ended, and it was not revived by the later fear and hatred of Soviet Russia.

That apathy has lately been jolted, almost irrelevantly, by the emergence of a free Black Africa, partial, confused and somehow urgent to the American reader. Ordinary people are looking at the map again.

There are some small books called *Common Sense about Russia, Common Sense about China*, etc., that attempt, and very largely do, the job that the American press should have given its talents to during the past somnabulist decade. It is important that none of the authors (all but one are English) is *against* the area he is writing about. What a comfort this is, when one comes to Russia.

This book peers as closely as possible, painstakingly, rather sympathetically, at the USSR and sees things that might astound even a well-informed American. There are about 52,000,000 workers in Russia, and since the state is their boss, they get no protection from their trade unions. They earn perhaps 700 roubles, or about $10 a week, while the big shots take in 20,000 roubles, or about $300 a week. They each have less than sixty square feet of living space all to themselves, just enough for one bed and one bureau. Judging from newspaper stories, they have nevertheless remained like people elsewhere. They get drunk (the big binge is the rule), buy bootleg vodka (the state makes a 7,000 percent profit on vodka), indulge criminally in jazzomania and rock 'n' roll records, bribe and embezzle, buy and sell privately ("speculate"), murder, beg, worship God (about 40,000,000 actively) and have somehow failed to be successfully indoctrinated in all these years by an exclusive Party propaganda.

The implication that the Communist revolution has been a disaster for its people requires some examples and some explanation. Robert Conquest gives both, but with much sympathy and some hope.

One thing is certain: everything that is good in politics is written out plain in the Soviet Constitution; it is all there. Reading from documents, a Soviet partisan can rightly say that Russia is the most democratic country in the world, as the Webbs once said, after reading the documents. The only catch is that the Soviet leaders are not bound by the constitution, the laws or the documents, and they do not publicly announce their acts.

For example, Soviet minorities have always been given complete constitutional protection. Nine nations, embraced in seven autonomous republics, the Crimean, Kalmyk, Chechen-Ingush, Volga-German, Kabardino-Balkar, had, before World War II, given almost unanimous yes-votes in all Stalin elections, and were advertised by the state as veritable tigers waiting to rend the foreign foe. Their people had never received any but Soviet information about the Soviet or about the foreign invader. Nevertheless, they all went over en masse to the invader, evidently any invader, even before the foreign army had overrun them. Nine nations were rounded up by the MVD and deported to Siberia in cattle cars, being largely exterminated on the way or on arrival. All histories, maps and encyclopedias were reedited so that it was as if these nine nations had *never* existed. The blackout was complete and remained so until five nations were restored to their rights by a decree of February, 1957. Most Russians had never heard that they had ever disappeared.

How do we know even these "facts"? Only because the Khrushchev regime wanted to blackguard the Stalin regime. But a "fact" in the USSR is a peculiar monstrosity no honest man who ever lived would recognize. It is now a fact in Russia that the great Soviet leaders, Bukharin, Zinoviev, Kamenev and Rykov, never existed; all histories and encyclopedias omit their names. Ordzhonikidze's death in 1937 was recorded as from a heart attack; in Khrushchev's Secret Speech of 1956, this is corrected to his having shot himself, at Stalin's request. In 1950, a prominent Politburo member is executed; nobody is told, but in 1952 his policies are publicly attacked. Then in 1954 the prosecutor of the case is himself executed for having "faked the evidence"; and the original victim is "rehabilitated." This story lasts two years; then Khrushchev announces that Stalin had done the faking; after a year's reflection he amends this to extend the guilt to Malenkov. Actually, members of the Politburo were in even worse peril than disloyal minorities. Almost all died violently.

The author warns us against concluding that all Soviet statements are lies; and develops a reasonable hope that things may be improving in Moscow. The revolution was achieved by three types: the theorist, the bureaucrat and the humanist, the last having especially appealed to sympathetic democrats. But the others soon eliminated this type; and then the bureaucrats swarmed over the theorists. The sort of man drawn into Russian government is ambitious, ruthless, realistic, obedient and iron-nerved. He has also memorized Marx and Lenin. He early learns the organization trick of looking good when everybody else looks bad; and naturally applies this skill to foreign affairs.

These gentlemen, and millions more, devotedly try to make the planned economy work. Yet private farms produce more per hectare than collective, and collectives more than state farms; and the plan is to turn everything into state farms. Russia's grain per capita, and cattle absolutely, were greater in Tsarist times than in 1954. Many factories are virtually idle for twenty days in the month, and have to produce 70 percent of their quota in the last ten days. This is "rushing" (*shturmovschina*).

On politics, we can simply quote: "It can be deduced that the constitutional arrangements of the USSR are not, at present, of the slightest real significance. We should seek the realities of rule, and of power, elsewhere." Such a society produced in the peacetime of the thirties about 10,000,000 deaths. The Forced Labor Camps always held around 3,000,000 people, as against a high in Tsarist times of 183,000.

The "thaws" after Stalin's death briefly revealed the dissents of the people. The writers said that party membership brutalized human beings, and that "a tribe of bureaucrats has seized power in our country." University students issued underground papers called variously *The Fig Leaf, Culture, Fresh Voices, Heresy, The Bell,* and in answer to speeches for "democracy" chanted together, "From below! From below!" One story told of the practice at Komsomol rallies whereby one boy would shout, "Hear that? Patriotism!"—to be answered from another corner of the hall with "Stormy ovation! All rise!" There were student riots at least in Stalin University in Tbilisi, Georgia, in 1956.

Khrushchev crushed these performances and in 1955 began reducing the number of full-time students, "to give a rebuff to unhealthy phenomena."

But Conquest's reason for hoping for better things from Russia is that these hushed voices can no longer be entirely stilled, without a resumption of Stalin's total terror, now probably unfeasible. If the humanists can reclaim an influence in Russia, they may be able to make it "one of the finest components of a world community." Who would not wish for that?

The book on China is as revealing as that on Russia. It is split in two: "Before Communism" and "Under Communism." The fatal flaw in Sun Yat Sen and the later Kuomintang, it is suggested, was an insipidity of ideas. The strength of Mao Tse-Tung is his freedom from dogma. "Marxism," he has said, ". . . has neither good looks nor magic. It is only very useful. . . . Those who take it as dogma . . . we ought to tell that their dogmas are more useless than cow dung." Marx would have despised a peasant revolt, and that was what Mao planned and brought off, while quoting Marx at every turn.

Nor did Russia arrange the Chinese Communist revolution. Stalin recognized Chiang Kai-shek as late as 1948, and ridiculed the Chinese Communists during the War.

In China the Communists have used carefully encouraged peasant hatred to smash the expendable classes, in a series of rehearsed campaigns given such titles as "Cutting off the Feudal Tails" or "Fill the Holes and Level the Tops." For some years China was convulsed by violent fevers of hatred and fear, leaving the middle peasants in control of the land. Meanwhile the strongest state apparatus in all Chinese history was built up, numbering now more than 12,000,000 Communists. And the Reds accomplished many things that old China hands would call impossible. Corruption has ended. Cities are clean; often without flies or mosquitoes. Dogs have been eliminated from Peking. Even spitting has been practically abolished. Furthermore, China has produced the innovation of industrialized villages, so that there are few atom bomb targets. Sixty million children are in primary schools. And China is science crazy, though Mao neither likes nor understands science.

Where this story loses its grip is in the last stages. For in six months in 1958, the peasant holdings were abolished and all China was turned into communes. Astonishing claims were at once made for increases in production of nearly everything. Simultaneously, the Chinese family was denounced as primitive, and broken up insofar as possible. This account does not cover the famines and floods of 1960.

In short, no judgment can now be made on China. It is true that its official enemy is the United States; but its greatest benefit would be friendship with the United States. It is true that the regime's feared and respected enemy is the scholar-gentry; but these may yet take over the regime. In fact, most of the Communist elite are the sons of scholar-gentry; the mass of the lower echelons are illiterate peasants.

I would say that these books are indispensable reading for anybody in government, or for anybody with an irresponsible curiosity about his world. For in fact this is our world. These other lunatics are also patriots; they are sincerely fighting for their nations' glory. One may laugh, or congeal into contempt, or cry evil, but still the West must try to understand these powerful rulers, and also their difficulties.

1960

$\mathcal{V}$IRTUE TRIUMPHS, VERY LATE

$\mathcal{O}$NE DAY the bill falls due for the wicked—sometimes, it is true, a lifetime or a thousand years late, but all morality and hope disappear when people cease to expect that day.

It came, for thousands of people ruined in the 1950's, in New York Supreme Court, when the libel case of John Henry Faulk against Vincent W. Hartnett, Laurence E. Johnson and Aware, Inc. went to the jury on the evening of June 28, 1962, the fourteenth wedding anniversary of Mr. and Mrs. Faulk, and a bad six years since Faulk was cut down by the word "Communist," and brought suit. Since such maligners leave very faint tracks, the trial had dragged on, under Justice Abraham Geller, for eleven weeks, to pick up that sinister spoor. For Faulk, a man who was anything but a Communist, had been indelibly branded as one—and so ruined. As sensible people, we know that this is impossible; still, it happened.

Louis Nizer, author of the book, *My Life in Court*, was counsel for the plaintiff. His case was that an inhuman, un-American and tragic wrong had been done. The defense was that its acts had been purely American, and that tragedy is irrelevant and immaterial.

Around 1950, the defendants had discovered that close study of the Attorney General's list of subversive organizations and the files of the House Un-American Activities Committee gave one a tool against thousands of people, especially in TV and radio, which are supported by conservative and easily scared advertisers. You just had to do the homework. If you made it known in the right quarters that a performer or writer had "a significant Communist-front record" (the standard incantation), he was through. If he defended himself, it would cost him at least $6,000 in the courts, and he was probably still through. Many of the accused therefore took the Fifth Amendment. In that case, they were through, too. This glorious business flourished most briskly against the members of the American Federation of Television and Radio Artists (AFTRA), to which all performers in TV and radio had to belong.

What sort of American would stoop to this work? Hartnett, whom I watched for some weeks in court, is the type of the eternal, meticulous snooper and sneak, and even has the sunken, prissy mouth of the beldam gossip of caricature. Paul R. Milton, his associate in Aware, Inc., has a big, wholesale butcher's head from which peeps, now and then, a terrified little girl. Johnson, a Syracuse grocer who sold his chain of supermarkets in 1956, never appeared in court.

Hartnett profited by $25,000 a year for supplying the names of "Communists" to such clients as Borden's, Lever Brothers, American Broadcasting Company, Young and Rubicam, the Cutler Agency. Hartnett wrote a magazine article chiding Borden's for permitting "Communists" on its TV show, got himself hired by Borden's (for $10,000 that year), then added two paragraphs to his article, concluding that Borden's had now taken all appropriate steps to do better in the future. Milton accused a writer on the TV show, *Treasury Men in Action*, of being pro-Communist, got him fired, and then took his job. Ah, those were the halcyon days.

The defense described Hartnett as an "expert"—an expert on wicked people, like Bernard Guy or Torquemade, those masters of The Question. Hartnett himself testified that he had never blacklisted anybody; he had merely done objective research on "significant Communist-front records." This dazzling

new career was childishly, enviably easy: of course, one kept a
file of "names," subscribed to the *Daily Worker,* got on all
liberal and leftist mailing lists, saved old programs, eaves-
dropped on groups of actors with a microphone and hidden re-
corder, corresponded with the House Un-American Activities
Committee. None of his victims knew him, or remembered ever
having seen him, but of course he knew them all, since they
were performers, publicly visible or audible. Hartnett was, in effect, the invisible man, and he carefully kept it that way.

The flood of names he garnered he sold to his clients at $5
a head, a price that must make the ruined men rage when they
look at their wives and children. To find one's soul worth $5
must be terrible; the Devil pays better. But they can be con-
soled to know that for the same name Hartnett collected $5
from each of a number of clients. Arthur Miller's name was
worth $300. One joker got Hartnett to clear the name, Santa
Claus, and he did so for $5. It all sounds as petty as a spinster's
hobby in Keokuk, but it added up to $25,000 a year for Hart-
nett, the invisible man whom nobody ever remembered. And
corporations worth a hundred billion dollars trembled on his
telephone calls and jumped at his command. The thing is too
ridiculous to be believed; still, it happened. It was proved in
court. It was not even argued by the defense.

The defense emphasized that Hartnett's transcendent virtue
was that he did not, repeat did not, add to this income by
letting the accused buy their way off his lists. (But in some
cases, e.g., the actress Kim Hunter, he did coerce performers
into expressing opinions they hated.) It is an interesting aesthetic
theory that because he might have been blacker, and was not,
he must therefore be white. My observation is that he lacks the
guts and tact to blackmail; this must be face-to-face. Lacking
these, he convinces himself that he is filled with principle.

Hartnett's accusation was enough in the fifties, as everyone
knows: the corporations immediately panicked and disavowed

the individuals. "A sponsor is interested in selling goods; it is not interested in causes. Why buy a headache?" said a witness. But it is hard to prove this legally. Nizer had the utmost difficulty wringing any important admission out of the corporate witnesses, and we all understand why. The defense naturally counted on this.

In these matters, the Communists and the "anti-Communists" are agreed on destroying the only true anti-Communists, the decent people in the middle. Their very decency seems to enrage the two extremes.

The murderous arrogance of these "anti-Communists" was shown when a producer challenged the "non-clearance" of a woman entertainer who, he knew, had extremely conservative politics. He demanded at least an explanation, was refused, demanded it again, and found that the woman had been mistaken for another with a vaguely similar name; still, he was told to fire her anyway, because the public might confuse the two. He refused, and was informed, "Next time don't be so emphatic, or they say they might take an interest in you."

Looking back at Johnson, Hartnett and Aware, Inc. (the name itself is an understated threat), an historical memory comes to mind: the Reign of Terror of the French Revolution, Robespierre and the Committee of Public Safety: accusations without accusers, cursory trials or no trials, the Law of Suspects, the "clearing" by the local committees of surveillance. "Not cleared" is an inscrutable tag Robespierre would have liked. And the American people were hardly conscious that this Terror was in force. The American press did not report it; it was either sympathetic or terrified too.

And one mean little group of men were able to do this: Johnson combined with the grocery clerks' branch of the Syracuse American Legion, combined with Hartnett and Milton, whom we have seen, and the Aware, Inc., publications.

At the trial, Hartnett confessed that his alliance with Johnson, who could threaten any reluctant advertiser with the hostility of the retail grocers' association (maybe), "enhanced my value." That is, Johnson's operations could put teeth in Hartnett's most careless whims as to who had a "significant Communist-front record." Madison Avenue fell into line. If it did not, Johnson came roaring down from Syracuse, raging up and down Madison Avenue, to see to it.

The closet government of the United States for some years, while Eisenhower thought he was running the country, was this savage little cabal of very small men without talent, distinction or courage.

By 1955, however, the thing had grown over-ripe. The Robespierres had grown fat. And the decent Americans in AFTRA were ready to call a halt and crack down on both Communists and blacklisters. They voted to condemn Aware, Inc., and put up a middle-of-the-road slate of officers, including John Henry Faulk as second vice-president.

Hartnett wrote Johnson, "We have already lost Equity. We may lose our control of AFTRA." What? Neither was a member of AFTRA. What control? But of course, AFTRA had been both their victim and their puppet.

This John Henry Faulk had become a radio and TV personality with a great following, on the basis of a rich personality of effortless Texas charm, a liberal humanism and a built-in affection for the whole American heritage. He was wholly unlike and a better performer than Godfrey, Linkletter, et al. He liked to talk, and he had a lot to say America liked to hear. He was on the threshold of a $500,000-a-year career when he consented to try to impose a peace in the war of traitors in AFTRA, by running as a candidate. What a fool, I would say, but remember that he was a good-hearted, reasonable man from the country, who thought he was in a decent, reasonable world.

Hartnett, Milton and Aware, Inc., cooked up a bulletin, Exhibit 41 at the trial, purporting to show Faulk's "significant

Communist-front record." In view of the sequel, I don't expect you to believe this, but five of the seven items were outright inventions, and the other two were absolutely insignificant. If they were "significant," your mother is an Albanian Communist spy.

For example, the bulletin represented an interview by the New York *Herald Tribune* with Faulk as an interview with him by the *Daily Worker*. For example, again, the bulletin stated that one "Communist affair" Faulk attended was a Salute to the United Nations, where the speakers were Secretary of State Stettinius and Trygve Lie (these latter facts, of course, not mentioned in the citation).

The intent to destroy Faulk professionally, and no other intent, was betrayed by the twelve categories of recipients to whom this masterpiece was mailed February 10, 1956: newspapers, radio and TV companies, two national advertising associations, advertising agencies, association of retail grocers, motion picture studios, sponsoring corporations, law-enforcement agencies, four actors' unions, patriotic organizations, leading magazines, leading columnists. In this list, we can see the combined malevolences of Johnson, Hartnett, Milton and the others plotting to corner a man. It is not a refreshing sight.

From that day on, Faulk never appeared again on television, because he had no contract. But somehow the Committee of Public Safety had been unable to dislodge him from his 5 to 6 P.M. radio show. The people still loved him; and the Robespierres raged. What had happened was that Charles Collingwood, a CBS commentator and president of AFTRA, had told the president of CBS Radio that if Faulk were fired, AFTRA would subpoena and examine the advertising agency executives whose clients had canceled from the Faulk show. (Twenty-nine did.) Ed Murrow backed up Collingwood. But sixteen months later, Collingwood was no longer president of AFTRA; Murrow was no longer with CBS, and Faulk was on a Caribbean vacation; and now CBS fired Faulk, though his program had more listeners than any other CBS show.

However, the Terror had been defied, and was resolved to finish the execution. It followed Faulk to promises of jobs in Minneapolis, New York and San Francisco—promises which then "mysteriously" fell through. That is, the warm, loving conversation suddenly turned distant and evasive. Faulk told his friends in the business he would do anything, even to sweeping out the studio, for after all he had a wife and children. They tried not to tell him that the Terror had conveyed to them that Faulk was not to be hired in any capacity, or the terrible vengeance would fall on one and all. Behind the curtain, as this agony drew itself out, were Johnson, Hartnett and the members of Aware, Inc., smiling in the various ways they knew how to smile, or even laugh. I saw several of their smiles and they were frightening.

Finally Faulk retreated to his home town, Austin, Texas, where he and his wife, by both working, were able to bring in under $5,000 a year. In the industry he was a "walking corpse," but not in his own mind, for Louis Nizer had taken his case against the Terror. At the preliminary examinations Nizer, to his amazement, discovered that Faulk had never before laid eyes on Hartnett, who had so vengefully and wickedly chopped him down. Hartnett had indeed been "objective," as objective as Hitler or Stalin in their mass exterminations. Hartnett had not even paid Faulk the compliment of hating him viscerally. He had been far too busy with his little lists. The prim little mouth had bitten down on Faulk and spat him out.

I have in the above roughly synthesized the evidence at the trial with other information and "fair comment," a legal term. Now both sides rest. The defense attorney, Bolan, a partner of Roy Cohn (whom else?), argued in summation that Faulk was a liar, Hartnett was a more truthful and honest man than anyone you will ever come across, Faulk did better after the libel than before, Faulk never was any good anyway, Faulk had no future on TV and was just a self-aggrandized disc jockey. So much for Bolan's dramatic criticism. He also advanced the social theory that though the courts cannot object to a man's taking the Fifth Amendment, his neighbors can and should. A neighborly lynching, he said, is right and proper. Blacklisting is simply splendid and purely patriotic. (This was not an issue in the trial: Faulk never took the Fifth Amendment on anything, and was never technically blacklisted.) Bolan was in fact arguing some other case that existed in the dream world of Johnson, Hartnett and Aware, Inc., where so many other nightmares had indeed come true; but this was not the case being argued before Justice Abraham Geller.

Nizer's summation pulled out of the mass of evidence an easily read trail of conspiracy against Faulk, as given above. A peculiar incident here should have alerted me. I could not get into the courtroom before the first recess, but was at the head of the overflow line when a Yahoo type bulled his way through us and into the court attendants, snarling "I will not stand back! Tell the judge I'm here!" He identified himself as from the New York *Journal-American* and was allowed in. He seated himself at the press table, glowering about as if he were banked in Communists. The *Journal-American* had not reported the case; why this?

Defendant Johnson, hiding out in a Bronx motel, had just died that morning. This for the first time made the trial news to most of the press (though for the *Journal-American* not good news).

Nizer asked for a minimum $1,000,000 compensatory damages, and $1,000,000 punitive damages from each of the three defendants. The judge, however, told the jury that Johnson was dead and could not be assessed punitive damages.

Before midnight on the Faulks' wedding anniversary, the jury came in with its verdict: $1,000,000 compensatory damages, $1,250,000 punitive against Hartnett, $1,250,000 punitive against Aware. All twelve jurors agreed on the verdict, but one woman thought the amount too high. (In a civil suit, a 10 to 2 vote is enough.)

This story reached page one, column one, of the *Times*, which alone had reported the whole trial. The *Journal-American* headlined its story: "Faulk May Never Get His Millions For Libel—$3,500,000 Phantom Award"—another way of saying "Yah! Yah!"

In fact, lawyers agreed that Faulk and Nizer will get the $1,000,000 from Johnson's estate, and part of Hartnett's income for the rest of his life. The liability of the Aware officers is speculative; Milton has a good deal of real estate. Nizer in six years had had costs of about $200,000 and will get them back at least. The income tax on Faulk's share of the compensatory damages is subject to various deductions and should properly be spread over the past five years. The punitive damages are nontaxable.

It is to be hoped that the defense will appeal so that this largest award in the history of libel cases will be built into the legal structure of the higher judiciary. Already that $3,500,000 award has washed out a lot of mouths. Paupers may continue to gibber, "Significant Communist-front record," but anybody with a bank account had better not join in.

The second hope, which is already more than that, is that John Henry Faulk will now return to his talent for entertaining and instructing the American people.

1962

INTERVIEW WITH
213 BANK ROBBERS

*W*HAT IS WRONG with our society cannot be simple, for we are constantly confronted by new, unexpected and usually unpredicted problems.

One of the latest, according to the FBI, is the disappearance of the old, and the arrival of a brand-new, kind of bank robber. In one form he comes as a nice-looking young amateur who takes relatively small sums at gunpoint from suburban branch banks, makes his getaway on suburban side roads, and invests his gains carefully, sometimes with the very bank he has just robbed. In another form, he or she stands in line at a crowded metropolitan bank, passes a note indicating that he or she possesses a gun, grenade or container of acid, and disappears into the sidewalk crowd with the collection. The "notepasser" has become a police cliché, and is said to make up 70 percent of big-city bank robbers. It is often a woman, sometimes a grandmother. These money-desperate mice, so unlike Jesse James, John Dillinger, Pretty Boy Floyd, have nevertheless brought the annual totals of bank robberies close to the 1932 record of 740, before the Federal Bank Robbery Statute.

Insurance is, of course, the reason for the bank's vulnerability, just as it is for the automobile driver's recklessness. Neither the bank nor the insurance company is upset by the loss of perhaps $2,000. At the present rate of bank robberies, a given bank will statistically be hit once in thirty-four years. Over that period, the cost of the most obvious precautions would exceed by many times the loss by the eventual stickup.

The real financial danger for the bank would come from the killing or wounding of a bank customer or employee. The bank's attitude toward the bank robber is put into further perspective by the fact that its own trusted employees will quietly appropriate much more of its assets in any given year than any bold invader.

There is only one thing about holdups that bothers bankers. After a bank has been held up, depositors tend to shift their accounts to another bank. The bank seems to acquire a tone of raffishness which somehow offends the customers: it takes on a guilt by association with bank robbers. Customer reaction is no joke to bankers today, and so banks are beginning to take some precautions.

But neither bankers nor the FBI can give us the last word on bank robberies. For such insights in depth, we must go to bank robbers. And fortunately 213 of these experts, now in residence at the Leavenworth (Kansas) Penitentiary, have spoken in a recent issue (Vol. 15, No. 2) of the prison's undergraduate magazine, appropriately named *New Era*. These gentlemen, serving a total of 3,956 years for their views on bank robbery, include both old-style and new-style bank robbers, and we may all take off our hats as we listen to them on Their Subject.

It is a fairly shaking experience merely to get as far as the outside of the bank, on the road leading to the bank's doors. After the individual's varied and protracted preparation, his first important step is to get a gun. The fact that he is flushed with power by his gun ought to be a warning; a proud man would immediately throw it down the sewer. But it is agreed that the gun in hand, to both old and new bank robbers, is a marvelous tranquilizer. They like to handle it, and like the sound of the safety-catch snapping. Yet bank robbers as a class do not like killing, and do not often kill.

Secondly, usually after a series of preparatory crimes, the individual begins to see bank robbery as an "important" and self-justifying crime. Pointing a gun at a bank teller seems to this fraternity more significant or glamorous or awe-inspiring than pointing a gun at a storekeeper or paymaster. It seems to have a tragic nobility, very appealing to bank robbers who are nearly always idealists. A bank is centrally tied in to the capitalistic system; it is a symbol, to bank robbers if to nobody else. The setting is more grandiose than most, and to operate on that tiled proscenium, beneath the high ceilings and in the subdued atmosphere, must give the bank robber the momentary feeling that he is a Robber Baron or a Shakespearean actor on a fatal stage. This awe of banks ought to please bankers; it is merely inverted or turned satirical by the bank robber.

The older bank robbers who told their stories in the Leavenworth self-examination fell into the following types.

The Dreamer: "This phoney, tinselled, hypocritical, half-myth, half-lie existence that some people accepted as a worthwhile way of life. . . . The same intensity of purpose that I had once dedicated towards a worthwhile goal, I [now] dedicated to the gun. I hated everything. . . . I was a fool who expended a great deal of honestly misdirected energy robbing a bunch of hypocrites who were not worth the effort and energy I wasted on them. . . . I was a dreamer."

The Misfit: "I had had over sixty jobs in less than three years, lost them through indifference, fighting, absenteeism, lack of purpose, direction, and a sense of hollowness, that all this had no real meaning, that the world owed me a living. . . . I have felt a deep bitter need for revenge against life itself, especially authority. . . . Quiet desperation. . . . Visions of ecstasy. . . . The three R's: resentment, revenge, restraint."

The Doomed: (Product of a starving, drunken, thieving family and a brutal reform school, he straightforwardly took the only way he knew.) "After all, I wasn't being dishonest. Dishonesty implied deceit, didn't it? I certainly wasn't deceiving anybody when I shoved that pistol in their face."

The Professional: "This is the meaning of armed robbery to a professional stickup man: the robbery is his open rebellion against society, his declaration of denial, scorn and hate. . . . I pity the society of fools who advocate prison reform for my benefit. . . . To a stickup man, God is his gun, and when he forgets this, he's riding for a terrible fall."

The Cannibal: "To me the gun . . . is an end which satisfies all my insatiable drives for domination, power and sexual prowess." (His practice of love-making with a loaded gun lost him all five of his wives, for some odd quirk of womankind he does not understand.) "Nothing short of their complete terror-stricken submission to my power needs could bring me the necessary release of body and mind I was seeking. . . . It's very difficult to explain all the queer, fascinating sensations pounding and surging through me while I'm holding a gun on a victim, watching his body tremble and sweat. . . . I feel like God. . . . Right and wrong are the absolute commands of the man behind the gun. . . . It is like suddenly coming to the meaning of everything and you grasp this tremendous insight into absolute truth. . . . It was not uncommon for me to leave and forget the money. . . . My life has been saturated in envy and hatred of the accomplishments of others. . . . I've often thought that I would have made a great leader, with the ingenuity to introduce social astonishments as outrageous and fantastic as any conceived by great rulers."

This last impulse-boast deserves serious thought as defining the "greatness" of despots as that of inventing "social astonishments," whether useful or ruinous, and as relating the all-out criminal brain to the thinking of these celebrated and ill-remembered names. "Social astonishments" is a phrase that would have delighted Machiavelli. I pray that this is not the last that will be heard of it. The name of its author is given as James M., still a mute inglorious tyrant of the world.

So much for the old bank robbers. It seems to be true that they are no longer at work. The probability is that their type has died out, retired or gone into other lines of criminal endeavor.

The new bank robbers deposed as follows:

The Nice Guy: A good factory worker, he liked "the little things, like a can of cool beer, a swim in the ocean, a walk in the park, any show I wanted to see." To finance a marriage to a nice girl, he joined two neighborhood thieves. "I had been shy with girls before, but now I felt adequate and secure. I also didn't want to get married. . . . I sure miss the small things in life while I sit in this new stone home of mine."

The Proud Boy: "That night in that orderly room was just a little too much for me, and before I finished with one sergeant and two corporals, I believe I made believers out of them." AWOL from then on, he found sanctuary in whorehouses, and his living with the gun for fifteen years. "I had too much pride to go crawling back. . . . A man has to recognize something in the mirror he can respect. . . . When I look in the mirror, I see a reflection I can respect. . . . Today—to put it mildly— I am just a little bitter. . . . I've gone too far one way and I don't believe I have enough time left to get half back to where I veered off fifteen years ago."

The Comer: "I became an advertising account executive at twenty-five. . . . I even headed the Juvenile Delinquency Prevention Week committee of the Junior Chamber of Commerce. . . . The real central datum of my life is thirty years of controlled systematic hatred . . . an unlimited, nonspecific hatred of society. I do not hate individuals or certain groups or strata." At twenty-nine, he was senselessly beaten up by two policemen, and threatened with reprisals should he sue the city. He thereupon robbed three banks in a month. "I'm not sorry."

The "note-passers," specifically the women, are of course not at Leavenworth.

The new bank robbers seem to agree that robbing a bank is not a particularly big deal, but only an unconventional and potentially embarrassing way of putting one's personal books in order. And yet, if one tries to put oneself in the situation, one sees that bank robbery is a conspicuous, antisocial, revolutionary act, a short-cut so short as to amount to a generalized explosion against society.

The old bank robbers knew this; they were exhilarated by the fact. The Professional quoted above says of the new people, "I've never been able to take this postwar crop of bank robbers seriously. . . . [No] pride in their work. . . . [They] will admit that the purpose behind their jobs was to get enough money to set themselves up in some manner where they could look forward to a secure future and social acceptance. . . . I found it hard to keep from laughing. . . . They actually think that after seven or eight years, society is going to forgive them. . . . This bunch of amateur bank robbers are suffering from no more than the aftermath of World War II and Korea; they are confused, disgusted and bitter."

A statistical survey of the 213 bank robbers in the Leavenworth magazine generally confirms the Professional's opinion. It has the usual defect of averaging out old and new types, pigs and pitchforks. However, the majority make up a fairly superior, amiable and good-looking (judging from their photographs) group of American citizens. The last four editors of the magazine have been bank robbers; one supervisor always picks his secretary from their ranks and finds them "loyal, industrious, dependable and efficient." (Only don't frustrate them.) Over half are veterans of World War II or Korea, and of these over half had sergeant's rank or better, though there were no generals. Seventy-four percent thought they came from normal homes; the same percentage had never found alcohol a problem; only 13 percent had ever used narcotics. Their wives had divorced them twenty-three months (average) after they were jailed.

The editors had to notice that first offenders generally had the longer sentences; habitual criminals the lesser; and had to ponder on this brutal and cynical sadism of American judges. They also noted that bank robbers are punished five times as severely as bank embezzlers. Possibly in consequence, 42.5 percent reject "the American way of life," which they regard as "a materialistic rat race." Those who accept the American way of life thought that it offered the world's finest opportunity to a thief.

In their reading, bank robbers avoid adventure magazines and science fiction. Their writing is often heavy with academic jargon, such as "meaningful" and "recidivist." Semantics is the favorite subject of many, taking it as the science of proving that nothing that can be said is true. This is just what convicts want to hear, since their lives have been ruined on one little immutable fact. Anyone who thinks he is "far out" ought to read a penitentiary magazine; he will begin to see how far in he is.

The new kind of bank robber is a recognizable human being. He was raised in a world of John Dewey relativism, where nothing is absolutely good or absolutely bad, and there is an acceptable rationale for almost any misbehavior. Gone are the terrible old black-and-white hatreds and tragedies, to be replaced by a gray world in which cheating, embezzlement and armed robbery are all pretty much the same.

The old bank robbers knew they were bad, and wanted to be bad, or they saw themselves as a lone virtue in a bad society, which they would salvage. The old generation felt different from respectable people; the new generation thinks it is the same as all the others, who haven't yet been tempted or caught. The old generation admired somebody; the new admires nobody. The old generation may have been tragic; the new is simply unlucky. Progress as usual becomes an exchange of one set of evils for a new, and unexpected, set. And so we have about as many bank robberies as in the Dillinger era, when the old evils were in full flower, and a bad man was as bad as he knew how to be.

The old bank robbers probably had one advantage over the new ones: they were aware of the Ten Commandments. The violation of a Commandment ought to be accompanied by some degree of dread and guilt, unless one has never even heard of it. In that case the punishment will make one very bitter.

1961

THE CASE OF THE
OVEREXPOSED DYNASTY

*I*N THE MONTH of March, 1962, the house of Kennedy appeared as multiform as Hindu gods, and naturally drew comment from all those people of the press who, every day or every week, have to say something (italics omitted).

Look at it. One of them was President of the United States. That one's wife was wowing India and Pakistan, in all sorts of exotic settings, and was also on TV lecturing on the White House furniture, her demureness broken now and then by a dazzling smile. Her daughter was learning to ride a new pony named Macaroni, on what I believe was a misreading of "Yankee Doodle," and her son was mastering his first word. The President's nearer brother, the Attorney General, had just returned from a similar tour of world-wide trouble spots. His younger brother was declaring for the Senate seat from Massachusetts and had to admit that he had tried, unsuccessfully, to cheat in a college examination. The mother and father had both recovered from illnesses. All was right with the world, the hillside dew-pearl'd.

And what should be the pundits' analysis of this idyllic month? The first technological flaw they found in the total performance was "overexposure," a grim word indeed. The second word they used was even worse: "dynasty." There can be no doubt that an overexposed dynasty is in serious trouble. (If you believe that last sentence, *you* are in serious trouble.)

Let us take "overexposure" first. It is a show-business word of debatable value, perhaps a near-synonym for boredom. A synthetic noisemaker such as an entertainer may perhaps be ruined by letting people look too long into his shallow puddle. But surely the members of one's own family are much more "overexposed" to one and still one may remain interested in them: or one may not.

Any exposure at all is fatal for some people, such as criminals and cads, but other people benefit mankind the more, the more they expose themselves, and these are the historic names we all know. We have forgotten many who were overexposed in their time, the people of mere title and rank, but their contemporaries were awed by them and, even in the case of Nero, remembered them with adoration. I can see no occasion to suppose that those days are past. The adoration of the hollow tyrant is sometimes replaced by the admiration of the public figure who makes his appeal with swaggers, breast-barings, coquetries and sulks which lose their force on repetition. Such people are indeed the casualties of overexposure.

Real people with real convictions and real emotions are more unexpected and more interesting. When Jacqueline Kennedy said that she had no desire to be a public personage apart from her husband, she became something larger than a personage, a private person whom we do not understand but would rather like to know better. She has brought onto the stage a completed picture of herself, of which she shows us only as much as she wishes to show. This is not exactly the same thing as Milton Berle or Jack Paar, of whom we know all we want to know, or perhaps too much.

The word "overexposure" becomes ridiculous applied to a large and loyal family which is, in my opinion, decent, energetic, ambitious and cool-headed, rather than brilliant. One can identify oneself with them because one does not feel inferior to them. Yet, in part because of their familial solidarity, the Kennedys are in fact superior. But this fact is so invisible that they can afford to have one princely in-law and another who is a member of Sinatra's Rat Pack. Not even the Roosevelt boys ventured anything quite so sportive in public. A future president will have to have at least a Serene Highness for a sister, and a brother who does "sick" jokes for a living. The Kennedys are a wonderful release from the dullness of the bourgeois Protestant presidents (the reader can pick his own exceptions). If you are a Catholic, it might seem, you can do anything.

The Kennedy family reached the big time exactly at its prime, with both parents still alive to keep order in the ranks. The grandchildren are at their most charming; the dead brother and sister are now almost as remote as the heroes of 1914, a vanished superior race, semimythic. I am told that once during World War II, I had dinner with Jack Kennedy, but wrack my memory as I will, I cannot remember the event. So much for overexposure.

The second dread word is "dynasty." Since the trial of Senator McCarthy, when two Kennedys were first simultaneously in the headlines, there have been for some tastes "too many Kennedys." The fact that the Attorney General marches precisely in step with the President who appointed him, is given as a bad, not a good, thing. (But such a man is exactly what the President's mandate ordered him to find, if he could.) With Brother Edward showing political ambition, this peculiar opinion has increased, not by arithmetical but by geometrical progression. The political columnists take the position that every additional Kennedy compounds the Kennedy power, rather than adding one digit to an ordinary sum.

This is the most vulgar pretense at political thinking. Because of what stirs eternally in the human, especially the political, breast, the Kennedys must lose more than they gain, even if Edward succeeds in his reach for the Senate seat. The one friend the President will gain in the Senate with a brother there may easily be canceled out many times over by the half-friends he will lose.

A good testimony to the Kennedy family's understanding of mankind is that John and Robert have not so far supported their brother's ambition. One need not say that because John and Robert work very hard and are good at their jobs, their blood relative will also work very hard and be good at his job. Still the inference is very often justified in such cases (and Edward has not so far disproved it). The probability is that if two in a litter are effective, a third may very well be too.

To call an American family a dynasty is to corrupt its original meaning of a race of rulers. The American opinion of the world began with our violent revolt against the Hanoverian, or Guelph, dynasty, in order to make an American nation. As a people, we thus expressed our disbelief in dynasties, at a time when a royal family was genuinely considered a mystically superior race. Our decision that we did not need any such superior race to rule over us has since been borrowed by most other states.

In the new sense, however, dynasties have always been a benefit to societies talented enough to produce them. America has greatly benefited from the clans of Adams, Lee, Biddle, Harrison, Stevenson, Sherman, Roosevelt, Taft, Lodge, *et al.* and our early history was riddled with dynasties that were hardly noticed. Zachary Taylor, for one example, was a kinsman of James Madison, and father-in-law to Jefferson Davis. We still have available numbers of Roosevelts, Rockefellers, Stevensons, Lodges, Wadsworths, and we would surely not abhor a few Washingtons and Jeffersons, no matter how diluted.

The strength of an open society is that parents with rich mental and moral endowments, even though poor and "ill-born," produce children who can move into the highest seats of power. But it should be added that the original tradition can be passed on to the next generation and the next. And in families with a high morale it is passed on, in ways that the social sciences hardly understand. It may be done by the fleeting expression of a parent which the child interprets in its own way; or by the level of thought and language in the home, the assumption of an equal understanding in the children; or by an example of justice and sacrifice; or by respect for the dignity of the children; but probably most of it is done by the genes. In these transmissions of character, however, nothing can be faked. The child will ignore ten years of conscious character-building by the parent, and forever remember and cherish one moment of unguarded truth. Well-gened children born into such a home, even with a minimum of education, tend to acquire good manners, a feeling for the language, a natural humor, a way of carrying themselves, a sense of self-assurance and command, and are immediately recognized, later on, as valuable people. Unknowns from such invisible dynasties can move in on closed corporations with electrifying effects, and are constantly doing so.

Under a banner, " 'KENNEDY DYNASTY' HELD UNLIKELY," the columnist Roscoe Drummond explained that only one Kennedy has ever been elected to anything and that no F. D. Roosevelt son has ever won even a statewide election, though two have tried. From this he concluded sagely that "the dynasty tradition has had little appeal to American voters." This plausible generalization managed to overlook about half the area of the United States, starting with the Huey Long dynasty in Louisiana and blending into that whole vast and real set of kingdoms reported by tough detective story writers. Possibly Mr. Drummond meant only that in the big arenas, with honest elections, the man with the big name may have something going against, as well as for, him, and so much, said cautiously, is probably true. This may prove to be true of Edward Kennedy's campaign in Massachusetts but if he has his own unpredictable, individual talent, all bets are off. In America a dynast is on his own, though not quite so lonely as a man without money.

Continuity of power by a corrupt family, which must produce ever more corrupt descendants, is possible only in a corrupt society, of which of course we have some, typically in rural areas but notably in the South. Dynastic corruption in the big cities does not usually expose its members to public elections. A man who feels powerful, as one can so easily in the South by bullying Negroes, is not generally going to rear able sons, and there goes the dynasty. The sense of dynasty is strongest in the South, and seems usually a monstrosity of lathe and plaster, the Charleston or Montgomery or Houston hauteur that makes the same decadent joke as the Dowager Empress of China, Tzu Hsi, who virtually destroyed the Middle Kingdom.

The aim and virtue of the continuing social revolution are to destroy such dynasties. The evil is that valuable dynasties are also destroyed by those elements who seem always waiting to run with a dog pack if it is large enough and the stag has already been brought to bay. All societies have these elements; ours is not exempt. Fascism and Communism both flourish on this endemic strain in mankind. The dynasty's historical problem has been, in times of crisis, whether to lead the mob, or take the risk of being destroyed by the mob. The history of nations has been decided over and over again by the quality of the dynasties, in that awful choice, when the mob began running. On a petty level, the choice is currently presented by the John Birch Society; but it is always being presented. Of course the corrupt dynasties elect to lead the mob.

The dynasties in England generally have a high morale, have chosen well and have some continuity. An English writer has said that English politics and banking are riddled with relatives of the Dukes of Devonshire and Marlborough (that would be the Cavendishes and Churchills—and the dead Kennedy sister married a Cavendish). There must also be some Cecils hanging around somewhere. These people, even overlooking one first-named Winston, must have a continuing talent for the business.

The Rothschild family continues to produce people who behave well. The theater is especially rich in dynasties because it only requires qualities that are commonly passed on, such as physical appearance, manners, etc. Musical dynasties (Bach, Scarlatti, Strauss) are somehow much less usual. Painting dynasties were once a commonplace, but are no longer. Writing dynasties have almost entirely vanished. In general, the sons and daughters go into the business only if there is a fairly sure living in it, or the subsistence is independently guaranteed by Papa. At one end were the Holbeins and Lippi, at the other end the Tafts, Roosevelts and Kennedys. It is not asked of a dynasty that it produce fanatics generation after generation. These can only be self-made, and must be struck by lightning. But in some families the lightning does strike at generation after generation, and "the marvelous boy" reappears and reappears.

For this to happen, the social climate must be favorable (*vide* Pitts, Walpoles, Churchills, *et al.*). The success of a society, a state, considerably depends on its relationship with its talented and honorable dynasties. It does not want to be bullied by them, but neither should it yield to the natural underdog impulse to drag them down and avenge itself for their talent.

But perhaps there is something to the word "overexposure." The Holbeins and Lippi may have left too many masterpieces. For the unquestioned master of all time is Phidias, of whose work we have no proved examples at all but only a transcendent and immortal rumor. No exposure at all.

1962

$\mathcal{A}$ SHORT GUIDE TO GREAT WEALTH

$\mathcal{M}$OST PEOPLE harbor a peculiar idea that if only they had a great deal of money, they would be very remarkable people. Very rich men therefore represent a sort of ideal, since in fact they have a great deal of money. And so it might seem odd that no serious objective study of very rich men has ever been made, although the antics of their women and children have provided a whole literature. The notion persists that the character of the man is unimportant; the interest is solely in all that money and what it could do for the dreamer.

Into the unrich man's dream of vast riches, one is obliged to intrude several commonplaces. First, much that was reserved to the millionaire of 1900 is now shared by almost everybody in the affluent society. Secondly, some cynicism should be given to defining what exclusive privileges are left to the very rich. And thirdly, and perhaps for the first time, the envious might do well to consider the exactions that the very rich man must make on himself to get rich and stay rich, and the personality penalties he must willingly pay.

We can quickly dismiss the special powers of the multimillionaire. He can indeed say to himself, "I own everything as far as the eye can see," and so can a great many farmers. He can go far toward ruining somebody he doesn't like, but the very rich rarely spend even a nickel on revenge. He can move masses of people around, create and abolish jobs, but this is no fun, and is generally done by his managerial men. He can of course live well, with the catering of experts in the various branches of good living. He can command the allegiance of a coterie of sycophants, while he will never know whether anybody in the world really likes him, starting with his wife. He can get his name in the papers. He can buy a big boat whose wake will swamp the owners of small boats. He can buy works of art, so that he doesn't have to go to public museums to see them. The more we delve into the consumer advantages of the multimillionaire, the more trifling it all sounds.

And in fact such privileges are of absolutely no interest to the very rich man, though they may motivate the little rich man and his women and children. A fair amount of money, like social status, is available to anybody who wants it badly enough. But the big money is reserved to a special breed of man, who can now be considered.

It is true that he is dying out in the high-taxation nations or welfare states, such as the United States and Great Britain, where his best hope is diversified stock control. But in Goronwy Rees's book, *The Multimillionaires,* he finds four men who own everything they have outright in fee simple. These are Krupp of Germany, Onassis of Argentina, Greece or Monte Carlo, Boussac of France, and the last great American oil independent, Getty, who is still a minor figure in the total American oil picture. Still, adding two Englishmen, he found six men who owned six billion dollars' worth of this world's goods among them. The very rich are even more individualized than the un-rich, so that when an identical habit or cast of mind reappears again and again, one must be astonished and alerted.

Compare Getty and Onassis. One is tall, the other short. Getty's universities were Southern California, California at Berkeley and Oxford '14; Onassis was on his own at sixteen. Both were athletes. (Jack Dempsey claims that Getty once knocked him out.) Aristotle Onassis is a resounding name;

Getty's name sounds insignificant until one realizes it is that of America's greatest battlefield, if one adds a "sburg." Onassis is a suave boulevardier; Getty seems the model of the miserable rich man, holed up in his suite at the London Ritz with his cases of warm Coca-Cola. Onassis makes jokes about himself; Getty refers to himself in his letters and diaries, not as "I" but as J. Paul Getty. (I know this is preposterous; but it is the truth.) The fact is that both men take themselves with frightening seriousness. And this is the first of the clues that we find in the very rich man.

Both will freely tell anybody the second clue: they buy when everybody else is selling. This sounds easy, but such times are rare and when they come, few have the guts or the cash required. Both these men had both. Such men get ahead of everybody else by going in the opposite direction from everybody else.

Neither can strictly be regarded as citizens of any one nation on earth. For the past seven years Getty has been in London, Paris or the Near East; Onassis has been in Monaco or on his yacht. A lot of very rich men are likely to pay an occasional visit to Moscow. These are "one world citizens" in every practical sense; they use the maritime "flag of convenience." Both Getty and Onassis move in international society, Onassis at the vortex, Getty secretively on the outskirts. Both are at home in night clubs, though they "drink" scarcely at all. Both enjoy beautiful women and have had celebrated marital troubles, since both seem to enjoy trouble, a weakness of men who keep their composure in the midst of trouble. In fact, this habit can be related to the need that very rich men have to form, on any outlandish grounds, a romantic picture of themselves. They have to be good at arithmetic, but they are also fairly good at dreaming. They also tend to have, combined with an embittered disposition, a clownish streak. Getty, for example, used to break into an imitation of Charlie Chaplin's walk, on the street, perhaps in a touching attempt to show that he did not care what the bystanders thought. For it is true of the very rich man that he does not care what anybody thinks of him.

This impression is confirmed in Getty's biography, *The Richest American,* a peculiarly wistful book, and also by Rees's book. The very rich man seems to be a secretive, suspicious type, resigned to being forever misunderstood and taking himself more seriously than anybody one is likely to meet in this world. He has a peculiarly beaten manner, perhaps explained by his rigid habits of hard, prolonged, dreary work. As compared with his minor executives and managers, he is in excellent health and usually looks about ten years younger than he actually is.

For the benefit of girls who want a husband who is going places or parents who want such a son-in-law, it must be emphasized that in his youth the future multimillionaire is generally regarded as a jerk by his peers.

The very rich man must combine in one person two contrary attitudes toward money, of which almost anybody may have either one or the other, but not both. That is, he is extremely stingy, and he can also gamble whole-hog, after long study of the odds and the opportunity or "situation." It is vital to find the situation and it is even more vital to examine it very narrowly and it is most vital of all to gamble everything on one's final judgment. This sequence reveals another paradox in the very rich man's ingrained habit of mind: while he is necessarily involved in a very big picture, he concentrates on the most minute details. His theory is that very big things are only an accumulation of small things, big sums of small sums, and large acts only the climax of many small acts.

Even people in finance do not really know who the richest men in the world are, partly because their separate operations are not conspicuous, and partly because the very rich do not want to be known as such. Such very rich men as Abercrombie of Texas, David Ludwig of California, Jules Timmins of Canada and Edmond Rothschild of France, all of whom may be exceeded by men I have never heard of, are semi-invisible powers in the world. Poor Getty managed to remain unknown until *Fortune* magazine announced that he was the richest man in the world. The nature of wealth today is that there may be yet richer men hiding under the carpet.

Later on we might look at some less golden careers, to see where these lesser operators overlooked something or other in the formula of becoming very rich.

But the further secret of the very rich has not yet been given. This is a power of pure, prolonged concentration on a problem that is shared only by higher mathematicians and seems to an outsider close to lunacy. Of course, anyone thinks he knows how to concentrate, but real concentration requires an intellect and discipline that are not widely dowered on mankind. Anyone with this ability is going to discover something not apparent to ordinary men. If he is a businessman, it will be a "situation."

Often the something is so obvious that nobody had ever really noticed it. Clore of England, for example, vividly noticed that a shoe company (Sears) owned the properties on which its 950 stores stood. He bought control of the company rather extravagantly, sold the properties, leased them back, and so had $16,800,000 cash in hand to do something else with. The very rich man is typically merciless toward his money; he tells it to work night and day. He has a very sour attitude toward indolent values.

America is no longer the land of very rich men. The serious pursuit of money here now requires mastery of the latest decisions of the Bureau of Internal Revenue, the S.E.C., and such government agencies, and also contacts with applied science, especially electronics, and military procurement. A desirable "situation" will be of the order of a company with a big tax-deductible loss, or a new drug, or a cosmetics patent, or a government contract. In this terribly complex and competitive society, one solution is to swindle.

The swindlers have some of the qualities of genuine rich men. Their defects are that they are not really willing to gamble and, oddly, that they do not take themselves seriously enough. Alexander Leonard Guterma, who describes himself as "just a goddam genius," described himself again (when he was sentenced to four years and eleven months in jail) as "a mariner befogged in a sea of Federal regulations." The metaphor was most unfair to himself. He was perhaps born in Irkutsk, Siberia, learned his trade in the troubled waters of Shanghai, Tientsin, Tsingtao, Harbin and Manila and began shooting fish in a barrel in America in 1950.

There is no earthly point in trying to describe his intercorporate bookkeeping. (*Fortune* tried, December, 1959.) He used his gifts of secretiveness and concentration to satirize corporate accountancy into such an exquisite jest that all the U.S. Attorney General's men admit themselves unable to follow his trail, and say it might take ten years. He was not tried for his manipulations, but for not reporting them to the S.E.C. No list of stockholders of his basic holding company, Comficor, could be located. Loans and shares were pledged and discounted and passed back and forth in varying fractions among numbers of companies. As one stumbles along the trail, one can all but hear the fox laughing over his shoulder.

The satire here is that the government regulations that hamstring productive men are only a challenge to a Guterma. He played on a keyboard of diversification: Florida real estate, electronics, brokerage, detergents, United Dye and Chemical, hotels, lace, auto parts, a film studio and the Mutual Broadcasting System. This list is fairly typical of most diversified operations. Many of the companies rapidly became mere holding companies for accordion portfolios of nothings. An essential part of the operation was that he navigated the night life of New York, Las Vegas, Palm Beach and Havana, and was at the moment well liked.

Another man, Lowell Birrell, seems to have looted some of the same companies as Guterma. On Birrell, I can contribute the information that he was one of the most affable and poised habitués of the New York night-club world around 1940. I knew him only as MacSorley's Ale; I thought he was a salesman for it; but he is described now as a brilliant corporation lawyer. He had the collegiate manner of the campus politician, solemn but self-deprecating. He found a thoroughly nice, beautiful and gracious dancer and married her; she may be his wife of present record. With his Kewpie face, he always seemed to be just arriving, or just leaving, a night club; but somehow, with a word and a smile, he left the impression that he had been most hospitable. Though I don't believe he ever bought me a drink, I like Lowell Birrell. This bespeaks some talent.

Birrell's key company was Swan-Finch Oil, and he moved assets around somewhat in the manner of Guterma. More recently his problem, apart from hiding his money, is simply to keep the U.S. Government from extraditing him out of Brazil.

These two repeat some of the qualities of the very rich: secretiveness, internationalism, concentration, love of detail, the sense of being romantic figures, and the dabbling in social life. But they lacked the dead-seriousness, and perhaps the competence to do a real job. In a revealing way, these jokers as well as the very rich, are citizens of everywhere. They are in fact almost the only sincere, practicing devotees of One World, while they make extraordinary efforts to keep their local, provincial, and even collegiate identity. This is at least a third paradox, at which, it should be noted, the very rich are more proficient, in both directions, than the relative failures.

Failure can, however, come to a thoroughly honest and competent operator in this field, for the lack of grasping one lesson Getty learned from his father: to be able to distinguish between the possible and the impossible. Leopold Dias Silberstein, Berlin University class of 1924, joined the German Rothschilds, married Tilly Tiger and quit Germany for Shanghai when Hitler moved in. After Hitler's fall, he found a U.S. "situation" in a groggy Pennsylvania coal company and made it pay by mechanizing it. The resulting Penn-Texas Co. got into machine tools, airplane parts, power shovels, revolvers, shipping and port facilities, oil and gas wells, electronic equipment, and did a $100,-000,000 business. Not good but not bad. In 1957 Silberstein decided that he could have Fairbanks, Morse (pumps, diesel engines, rail equipment) and started buying its stock. He was wrong; he had mistaken the impossible for the possible, but he had committed several other errors not allowed to the very rich. Somehow he had not concentrated on the situation with sufficient purity. The reason may have been that he did not own, but only controlled, the companies he had stripped of cash for his unprofitable gamble. The stake was $20,000,000 that was not his own money. And for this he won an ignominious four seats on a board of nine members.

Getty, Onassis, Krupp or Boussac would have smiled thinly at such a setback. Since they would have spent only their own money and would have had a lot left to spend, the opposition would have remained, with reason, terrified. But this man could not afford one bad gamble. Penn-Texas presently accepted his resignation "with affection," as they said, and one must pray that one never receives such affection. For in 1959 Penn-Texas was so disaffected that it preferred a suit against Silberstein and his directors for $10,500,000.

This misadventure among the not-very-rich tells us one more secret about the very rich: they have no deadlines. They have grasped the factor of mere time, in both its productive and destructive aspects. (Loans pile up interest, and people die.) Anybody still in a hurry is not going to get very rich.

We can pass by the Texas oil millionaires (exception: Abercrombie) who, by no coincidence, violate every rule of the very rich man. God knows the Texans try to act like rich men, and they have the glorious advantage of the tax laws. As a result, they exude the aura of a hysterical lottery winner or of Marie Antoinette. An oil well is not an eternally advantageous leverage of nature; it is a simple, finite looting of nature's riches which must some day end. And the big money in oil is not its production, but its processing and distribution. Getty, for example, sorely needed the Tidewater and Skelly processing and distributing systems. The Texas climate of unearned wealth is debilitating. Texans are in some very large operations outside oil, but their approach is usually hasty and dilettante. Oddly, again, they do not take themselves seriously enough.

In America today, the easy road for an ambitious millionaire is into diversification and a tangled income tax picture. Abraham Malcolm Sonnabend, Harvard '18 and former U.S. Veteran Squash Racquets Champion, has a fine collection of nonessential industries plus two fine "situations" with big losses: Childs and Botany Mills. Louis Elwood Wolfson, Georgia '33 and an aggressive football end in his day, has diversified in the construction field. Both do a good deal of actual business in their bathing suits on Florida beaches. Wolfson has survived several failures to take over mighty companies. This would put him somewhere between Silberstein and the very rich who never fail. He used to take private-train parties to Georgia football games, and give stock in his companies to the Georgia graduating class. All that has stopped.

In England there is Charles Clore, whose empire combines both the Sonnabend and Wolfson types of industry. An English interviewer describes his "hard, sharp, appraising glance," the very look of the born satirist, who tries to conceal the disgust he feels at what he sees. He seems to like night life and the company of beautiful women, and is divorced, and controls about $300,000,000.

The rise of diversification in America and England is occasionally the result of advantages in doing several things, instead of just one, in one synchronous operation. But in fact most diversification is an adventure in bookkeeping, inspired by the tax laws. The skilled accountant takes advantage of the bookkeeping troubles of the old-fashioned producer. The people who love the product and the work disappear or are dropped into minor positions. The new regime sometimes saves the company; at least it uses its losses to fatten the profits of healthy companies, under the tax laws. Is this bad?

One trouble with diversification is that it intensifies the atmosphere of perpetual crisis. The very rich do not like this; the not-very-rich have to accept it. Diversification is the system of exploiting other people's crises, but some of the crisis is infectious, and can sweep like a disease through a whole diversified operation. Still, in America, a purging in these fires is almost indispensable for a young man who wants seriously to reach the $50,000,000 mark. It is really much more arduous to make only $5,000,000 by productive effort.

The little rich men looking for the shortcuts are a fairly familiar sight in all the Western capitals, and now in some Eastern ones too. My impression—and I have known perhaps a score of them—is that they share with the very rich the same secretive, appraising, slightly sour look. One can draw a caricature that would not apply entirely to any one minor rich man, but does roughly stand for the whole group. This is a man with a somewhat satirical, occasionally clownish manner, who tries to mystify you about his most ordinary affairs, has a flair for figures and bookkeeping, quarrels with his women, enjoys lawsuits, cultivates policemen and bartenders, and tends to navigate the smart night clubs as well as the "manly" saloons.

They are very friendly toward newspapermen and communications people generally, whom they are likely to meet only in saloons. They go to parties, and they are intelligently active at parties. For though they drink, they do not drink much. Some of them even put on a wonderful act of pretending to be drunk.

The idea that a smart man can profit from seeing a lot of miscellaneous well-to-do people at night when they are tipsy and he is not, may seem ridiculous. The male dancers who mostly entertain in night clubs (and rarely drink) have an inexplicable tendency to become millionaires: *vide* Nicolas Darvas, Tony DeMarco, Ray Bolger, Gilbert Kamie, Capella. Their only apparent advantage over other men, besides being able to move their feet, is that they are up late every night. It must be supposed that this latter is their secret.

There is another peculiarity about these minor rich men. They are very neat and fussy, and pick incessantly at very small details. I knew one who had a dressing table more completely equipped than any woman's; of course it was also for women. They all order in restaurants as if they were dictating a financial contract, and hold the waiter to the contract. I knew one who was suing a lady to get back a Christmas present he had regretted. His case in court would have been hurt very slightly if he had had to give a sample of his handwriting, and so he appeared with his right hand heavily bandaged. Next day the hand was bare. As any satirist knows, the best part of the joke lies in the details, in the small print.

In the welfare state the small millionaire is likely to remain this sort of specialist in the fine print. He will be the man who, to the smallest affairs, brings the concentration of a fight for his very life, and also, with a certain levity, the instinct of the practical joker who cannot, however, himself take a joke.

The Socialists and the aristocrats, with their contempt for the profit motive, may want to make the millionaire obsolete, but I would protest. His bookkeeping and his combinations are often an inspired benefit to society. But, more important, as we now realize that a healthy ecology needs its predators, its wolves, lions and hawks, so too the financial community needs the elimination of its weak, sick and sloppy members, before their errors become epidemic. The millionaire, stalking the forests of the night with his suspicious, appraising, sour look, is glad to do the job.

God, as if he needed Him, bless him!

1962